The Storytellers' Journey

The Storytellers' Journey

An American Revival

Joseph Daniel Sobol

University of Illinois Press

Urbana and Chicago

© 1999 by the Board of Trustees of the University of Illinois
Manufactured in the United States of America
1 2 3 4 5 C P 5 4 3 2 1

This book is printed on acid-free paper.

Library of Congress Cataloging-in-Publication Data
Sobol, Joseph Daniel.
The storytellers' journey: an American revival /
Joseph Daniel Sobol.
p. cm.
Includes bibliographical references (p.) and index.
ISBN 0-252-02436-2 (acid-free paper)
ISBN 0-252-06746-0 (pbk. : acid-free paper)
1. Storytelling—United States.
2. National Storytelling Festival. I. Title
GR72.3.S62   1999
808.5'43'0973—ddc21
98-19690
CIP

Contents

Illustrations follow page 88

Preface

I met my first professional storyteller when I was twenty-two, fresh out of college. It was 1977. I had just finished my workday, playing classical guitar in the courtyard of an old cannery resurrected as a complex of shops and boutiques, near Fisherman's Wharf in San Francisco. I was heading home for another long night of trying to be a writer. At the Cannery, my partner and I played recorder and guitar duets, music by Handel, Couperin, Loeillet—artifacts of the Age of Enlightenment, always the same, note for note, day after day, varied only by the intermittent clink of quarters in our donations box.

On this afternoon, we were walking along Fisherman's Wharf, heavier by several pounds of jingling change than we had been at noon. I strode with downcast eyes past the mime, the blues singer, the balloon sculptor, the puppeteer, the brass trio, the bluegrass quartet, and the psychedelic baked-goods vendor—all distressingly mundane to me by then. Some essential nutrient was missing from my life. My head was shaking a dim denying cadence, not this, not that, not this, not that—and then I saw the storyteller.

He stood on a patch of trampled grass and damp dirt at the end of the sidewalk. He wore blue jeans, a blue work shirt, a blue knit beret, and rainbow suspenders. He said his name was Brother Blue. He was a light-skinned African American, lean, tense, and hyperkinetic, with blue balloons floating up from his suspenders, bells on his wrists and ankles, and lace-winged plastic butterflies pinned to his shirt. In all this, he was hardly unusual on the wharf. It was the sound of the man that shocked me to attention.

He was telling the story of Hamlet, prince of Denmark, recast in a rhyming, chiming, rasping street jive that had come from the African American oral tradition with a detour through Harvard Square. Children sat on the ground in front of him, looking up, and behind them stood a ring of wary parents, looking down. He would drop to one knee and growl at the children, then leap up and croon in an impossibly tender, passionate tone, as if each syllable were charged with the fate of the world. He would drop down again and scratch up a handful of dirt and roll it between his fingers like dough, like food of the gods. He seemed to be madly in love with this planet Earth, with its mud and its wounds and its words. Whatever it was he was doing transfixed me. Several stories later I finally let my bored recorder player drag me off. I clearly recall feeling as if I had had some kind of conversion experience. But a conversion to what? If *this* was what I was meant to do with my life—what was it?

Two years later I ran into Brother Blue again. I was hitchhiking into Charleston, South Carolina, guitar in hand. A couple in a red convertible, top down, picked me up on the outskirts of town and called back into the wind, "So you've come for the festival?" "What festival?" "Spoleto USA. Starts today." I'd never heard of it. But before I knew it, I was in it, traveling around town with a troupe of musicians, a juggler, and a couple of storytellers: Floating Eaglefeather and Brother Blue. During that two weeks, watching Blue and Eaglefeather in different settings with different audiences and spending time with them offstage, I saw past the mountebank personas to glimpse the artists struggling constantly with issues of form, cultural advocacy, and, most important, communication—the business of building bridges of images that could span many hearts. The name they gave their craft, *storytelling,* they pronounced with a kind of reverence, as if it were a secret name of the Bride; and the stories they told were mostly passionate parables of the struggle for spiritual awareness. Brother Blue was a minister manqué, a street performer with a doctorate in theology. Floating Eaglefeather described himself as half-Jewish, half-Mayan Indian; his family name had been Rosenberg. He lived in a house in Charleston that was an ashram of the Ananda Marga Society, a Hindu meditation group, where he proudly wore his initiate's name, Shiva Das. His stories, borrowed from many different traditions, were always a plea for peace between the separate aspects of humankind and perhaps between the separate aspects of himself.

The following year, I was taking personal growth training at a large hotel in the Los Angeles area. In a group of about forty, we had confronted our limiting belief systems, written our epitaphs, died and resurrected in guided fantasy, and now, at the end of the third day, we were asked by the facilitators, "What would you do in this world if you had perfect freedom to do whatever you most wanted?"

The answer that sprang to my lips surprised me. I said, "I would *tell stories.*" "What kind of stories?" I was asked. I didn't know. I didn't think I knew any stories. In the language of the training, the facilitator asked me, "What stories would you tell if you knew any?"

"I would tell the story of the creation of the universe and its evolution up to its reunion with Infinite Being," I said. "That's fine," said the facilitator. "You can do that tomorrow. You'll have five minutes." "I'm supposed to tell the whole story of creation, evolution and reunion with Infinite Being in five minutes?" "You'll have all night to think about it. We might be able to give you seven."

So I did it. The next morning I gave a seven-minute improvised cosmogony, complete with sing-alongs. It was utterly unrepeatable—and indelible, at least to me. In a certain sense, my storytelling career was complete in that moment. I have only spent the years since trying to re-create it.

◄ ◄ ◄

In 1982, still living in Los Angeles, I attended a week-long summer workshop with Gioia Timpanelli at the Omega Institute in New York State. (Omega was founded in the 1970s by Pir Vilyat Khan of the American Sufi Order as a setting for workshops and retreats on themes of Eastern and Western spirituality, social and personal transformation, and the arts). Upon returning to Los Angeles, I immediately placed an ad in the local free weekly. "STORYTELLERS UNITE!" it began and went on to announce the formation of a storytellers' support group. I got a phone call the day the paper came out from a puzzled Kathleen Zundell, wanting to know who was forming a storytelling group, since she and a couple of comrades had just started one themselves.

I remember following her directions over the Hollywood Hills to another storyteller's house in the Valley one dark night soon after, emerging from the car with excitement and trepidation, and being met at the door by two lovely strangers and conducted to a chair in the living room, where we spent the next three hours in a tight circle with our heads bent forward, talking and listening. I remember our host saying that she had been an object of fascination at the local Jung Center; it seemed that her unconscious was almost entirely collective.

During that year, the storytelling support group became an important part of my life. First known as the West Side Storytellers and then more inclusively as Community Storytellers, we met monthly at the Santa Monica Public Library and between times at one another's homes, attracting groups of between a half-dozen and two dozen listeners, novice tellers, and emerging professionals. The form of the public meetings was an open story-swap: everyone was encouraged to tell one, with a suggested time limit of ten minutes to limit the damage from wandering tongues. Folktales learned from books predominated, visualized and retold rather than memorized, though there were also memorized interpretations of children's books and rhymed recitations of narrative verse. Once, a nervous beginner tried to break through his stage fright by reading out of a book, a violation of ethos that no one had the heart to call to task. Midway through his performance, a four-year-old girl, who had been to several meetings, spoke up so that she could be clearly heard around the circle. "Daddy," she said, "he's letting the book do it."

That was the year I found out about the National Storytelling Association (NSA), then known by the far more charming and challenging name of NAPPS—the National Association for the Preservation and Perpetuation of Storytelling—and joined. As NAPPS publications, such as the *Yarnspinner* newsletter and announcements for the National Storytelling Festival and Conference, came into my hands, I began to be swept up in the heady atmosphere of a national storytelling "community." That October I was in Jonesborough, Tennessee, on the Thursday before the festival began, helping to string lights and set up chairs in the empty tents. I remember walking down Main Street with Laura Simms, the festival's artistic director. We had just met. "You've been around here forever, of course," she said to me. I told her that I had never been to Jonesborough before, and she squinted at me, trying to reconcile the facts with the feeling we both had of being quite familiar to each other. That feeling, while walking through that little, restored nineteenth-century town, bathed in autumn light and brushed by falling leaves, has been expressed over and over again in my interviews: it was like coming home.

◄ ◄ ◄

In November of 1983, I made my first visit to Jonesborough in the role of ethnographer. For my introductory folklore class at Chapel Hill, I interviewed Jimmy Neil Smith, the founder of the storytelling festival, and his wife, Jean, who was then working as the executive director of the shoe-string operation known as NAPPS. It was headquartered in an mid-nine-teenth-century farmhouse, known as the Slemons House, leased from the town. The Slemons family and its descendants had faded from the scene, but the old house sat, rickety and peeling, in a meadow just south of Main Street, on the far side of Little Limestone Creek. There was no heat and no insulation—the wind blew, as in a Jack tale, right through the chinks in the walls. All the archival material from eleven festivals and from the three-year period in the late 1970s when Jimmy Neil had gotten a CETA grant to hire a five-person staff of novice field-workers and archivists was piled in boxes on the floor.

The festival was now entering a major period of expansion, but the staff had bottomed out at Jean, a secretary, and Jimmy, who was also mayor of Jonesborough and the owner of a pair of restaurants up the street. He divided his time between the restaurants and city hall, but he was never far from the Slemons House and was constantly stopping by with a hatful of ideas or to meet with a board member or a storyteller who was just passing through to pay respects. Jean later said that Jimmy ran the organization "in absentia" during those years. The house had something of the atmosphere of an eccentric southern family business, like a home-place museum for an early country radio star; but there was something more: a sense of being at the center of something curiously modest yet of incalculably broad human significance—like a small, out-of-the-way convent where a particularly homely icon had recently begun to weep.

Over the next six years, I made regular trips to the area for NAPPS-sponsored events: in October each year to the festival; in June of 1984 and 1985 to the National Storytelling Conference near Jonesborough; in the summer of 1986 to the National Storytelling Institute held at a retreat center near Gatlinburg, Tennessee. In a fragile, contingent, contemporary way, it was a pilgrimage place for me—a place to form, to maintain, and periodically to restore my identity as a storyteller.

The association grew and changed, and so did I—I graduated from North Carolina and moved into a career as a storyteller and folklorist. NAPPS, meanwhile, underwent the trials of growth detailed in this study. At a fork in the road, I entered another phase of reflection. I needed to step back from the storytelling revival to try and understand its sources, its motive forces, and its possible outcomes in this rapidly mutating culture.

Between 1990 and 1992, I spent several weeks in Jonesborough outside of festival time, working in NAPPS's basement archives, examining the documentary record as preserved in that germinal spot, talking with present and former NAPPS executives and employees, and absorbing the atmosphere and ethos of the organization in that phase of its growth. Beyond this, I draw on seventeen years of relationships within this web of enthusiasm and livelihood called the "storytelling community" and on nearly as many years of orienting my sense of that community as a national organism around Jonesborough. How a town of approximately two thousand has managed to capture that kind of centrality in a national movement, however small, is a story in itself, one that has implications for the future of community in a modern nation.

"The storytelling community" is a common usage, one that has great invocatory significance to those who consider themselves a part of it. But the nature of this particular community is problematic even to storytellers, let alone to those schooled in traditional folkloric categories. Since contemporary storytellers are usually seen as adapting folkloric sources to styles and contexts that are clearly "nontraditional," the actual traditional dynamics within the community have often been obscured. At the same time, the rhetoric of community and tradition that has constituted so much of the discourse of revival storytellers has the effect of blanketing our shallow communal roots in a humus of belief. Whether and how those roots endure and deepen or wither and lie fallow again remain a matter of suspense.

In modern folkloristic terms, *The Storytellers' Journey* is a study of "personal and occupational narratives." In that sense, it is of particular interest to students of folklore in the modern world, since it involves a community that has invented itself in the past twenty-five years, based on a kind of homesteading on the frontiers between traditional and contemporary, dominant and marginal cultural values. Its communal boundaries are neither geographic nor familial; rather, they have followed the occupational and informational organizing lines of postmodern society, even as we have sought to trace them back to a more holistic territory of experience.

This work is also, quite simply, an exploration of a movement within what has come to be called "postmodern performance art." The storytelling revival is part of a wider trend to give value to the oral performance of narrative that, though it references the history of oral tradition, is thoroughly grounded in present artistic necessities. Insofar as it deals with

NAPPS/NSA and the mythic subcurrents generated by its growth, this book falls into the burgeoning genre of "organizational folklore studies." In a less specialized language, it deals with the struggle to design responsive institutions and with the process of moving from charismatic sect to organizational routine, from a tribe to a nation to something more fluid and dynamic than either.

For this study, I have conducted and transcribed approximately eighty taped personal and telephone interviews between November of 1991 and June of 1992 with storytellers and storytelling supporters throughout the United States and Canada. These are people who have all made significant contributions to the storytelling revival on the national or local level and whose stories seem to reflect common facets of the revival experience. My method was straightforward. I would call people on the telephone and ask them a couple of basic questions: "How did you become a storyteller?" and, "What roles have NAPPS or other formal or informal associations played in your development as a storyteller?"

These are relatively open-ended interview questions and could be taken in a multitude of directions, according to each storyteller's experience and interests. Many felt compelled to return to childhood, others to seminal experiences in college or working years. What binds the accounts together is that they are stories of identification and affiliation. These categories are often tightly intertwined, since for so many, the moment of identification is linked to the discovery of possibilities for affiliation. Individual and community identities, in other words, are intimately joined.

The result is a portrait of a cultural movement at a pivotal moment in its mythic arc—trembling on the verge of its twentieth annual festival. In effect, a part of a generation had come of age, had passed into adult identities through the solitary and communal myths and rites of the storytelling revival. It was a natural moment to reminisce, to take stock, and to celebrate not only the innocent passion that had brought the movement this far but also the hard and bracing passages from innocence to experience. Now, after two years of writing and two more of moving aside to pick up other essential threads in my own life, I am content to let that story stand. It goes on, it seems to me, very much according to the pattern woven here.

◄ ◄ ◄

The great teacher of mythology, Joseph Campbell, who acted as a guide for the spiritual wanderers of the storytelling revival, constantly exhorted his students to "follow their bliss." Cultural revitalizations like the storytelling revival movement point us to a path that bliss often takes as it beckons to its followers. I have chosen to stop and retrace my steps, and the steps of those who cut the trail before I joined it, in the hope that this attempt at a survey map may be of use as we fare forward into the dark of day.

Acknowledgments

I must thank the storytellers and storytelling enthusiasts who have graced this study with the depth and inspiration of their experience and the passion and grace of their expression: to Jimmy Neil Smith, the executive director of NAPPS, who has fostered this work, as he has the entire panoply of the storytelling revival; to my friends in Jonesborough, Tennessee, and environs, particularly Jean Smith, Richard Blaustein, Jo Carson, Jane Woodside, Baxter Bledsoe, Toby Bledsoe, William Kennedy, Carolyn Moore; to the present and former staff at NAPPS, especially Sandra Moore Tucker, Kim Morrison, Lisa Fedele, Cindy Wallin, and Mary Weaver; to Carol Birch, Melissa Heckler, Andrew Leslie, Fran Stallings, and Kay Stone—my honorary dissertation committee; to Brother Blue, Margie Brown, Milbre Burch, Donald Davis, Pleasant DeSpain, Gay Ducey, Elizabeth Ellis, Heather Forest, Barbara Freeman, Jackson Gillman, Spalding Gray, Ellin Greene, Bill Harley, Ray Hicks, David Holt, Beth Horner, Larry Johnson, Gwenda Ledbetter, Norma Livo, Rafe Martin, Lee-Ellen Marvin, Jim May, Doc McConnell, Reid Miller, Robin Moore, Loren Niemi, Jay O'Callahan, Fred Park, Lee Pennington, Joy Pennington, Connie Regan-Blake, Gayle Ross, Lynn Rubright, Steve Sanfield, Peninnah Schram, Ron Short, Laura Simms, Mary Carter Smith, Ed Stivender, Gioia Timpanelli, Jackie Torrence, Ron Turner, Cathryn Wellner, Robin Williamson, Kathryn Windham, Diane Wolkstein, Elaine Wynne, and many others who have submitted patiently to my telephone probes and recorder-hugging visits, to all of you go my deepest gratitude and affection. It should be emphasized that while I have tried to give your insights and experiences appropriate presence in the fabric of this text, the responsibility for its theoretical and interpretive approach is mine alone.

Special thanks are due to a wide array of teachers, colleagues, friends, and family who have supported this work with their wisdom, guidance, caring, and, of course, their stories: to Professors Carol Simpson Stern, Leland Zahner-Roloff, Rives Collins, Paul Edwards, Frank Galati, and Dan McAdams, all of Northwestern University; to Dan Patterson and Terry Zug of the University of North Carolina; to my Northwestern graduate cohorts Richard Geer, Deryl Johnson, John Wat, and Derek Werner; to Judy Mc-Culloh, Jane Mohraz, and the staff at the University of Illinois Press; and especially to my wife, Mitzi Chambers Sobol, and my parents, Albert and Evelyn Sobol—whose loving support has made anything possible, even nine years of labor on this book.

Introduction

The storyteller is the figure in which the righteous
man encounters himself.
—Walter Benjamin, "The Storyteller"

Around Christmastime 1967, a young African American doctoral student
named Hugh Morgan Hill was invited to do a performance at a surprise
birthday party for the dean of Harvard's Divinity School, Sam Miller. In a
gathering that included the theologians Harvey Cox and Reinhold Nei-
buhr, the student, who has since become known to the world by his performing persona of Brother Blue, chanted and danced a wildly personal
version of *Beauty and the Beast.* When he had finished, the dean of the
Divinity School's eyes were moist. "On the simplest level," he said to Blue,
"it's the story of the Incarnation." Miller went to his windowsill, took
down a bird made of stained glass and another bird made of stone, and
handed them to Blue in return for the gift of the story. "Right then," Blue
says, "I knew that I was supposed to do more of those kind of things; and
I decided that I would spend my life exploring this."

The art of storytelling has about it the halo and the stigma of the ordinary. All of us who speak a language well enough to represent our experiences are entering into our storytelling birthright. The verbal, musical,
mnemonic, and kinesic "technologies" of traditional storytelling are, to
be sure, extensions of ourselves, in Marshall McLuhan's terms—but they
are inward extensions, technologies in which the body and mind are the
primary tools.

Millman Parry and Albert Lord, and all those who have drawn on their
work in cultural theory, make quite clear that in an oral society, in which
storytellers, seanachies, bards, or griots store and reproduce the culture's
accumulated knowledge, storytellers are specialists, technocrats of that

culture. They are accorded all the prerogatives and respect of a sacred functionary. In cultures in which the dominant technologies of information and representation are relocated in manuscript, print, or electronic devices, the sacred aura attached to storytellers shifts to the mythtellers of the locally dominant media. Once, these were scribes—scriptural authorities, philosophers, historians, poets. In the Elizabethan Age, the nimbus began to transfer to dramatists; in Victorian times, the heart of the age of print, to novelists. In the twentieth century, the storyteller's staff has splintered in the grip of filmmakers and film "stars," radio notables, television producers and soap opera celebrities, guitar-griots of album and arena, scientists and their popular interpreters, epic heroes of the gridiron or basketball court and their praise singers in the broadcast booth. As technologies multiply, each seems to perform a more culturally subdivided role. They are all touched by a ray of the archaic storyteller's light in that they provide a momentarily coherent narrative of the world, yet their narratives break down immediately outside the enclosed space of performance into a multitude of mutually incomprehensible stories: not whole culture but artificially inflated mass culture or reactionary subcultures.

With this ever-increasing technological extension and corresponding cultural fragmentation, storytelling has come to appear childish to many. The technology it embodies is primitive. It is apparently irrelevant to a hypervisualized electronic environment and might therefore be expected to be devoid of cultural magnetism. Yet within the past twenty years, a national—to some extent, even an international—community of performers has placed itself under the banner of a self-conscious storytelling revival. Although their actual practices cover a wide range of performance conventions—from a variety of ethnic traditional storytelling styles, to stand-up comedy, to theatrical impersonation, to autobiographical performance art, to oral interpretation—these contemporary performers share in the invocation of ancient traditions and roles as a common signifying framework. In the proliferation of storytelling festivals around the country, we find the image of the fireside folkteller projected onto a popular stage, framed by tents and spotlights, magnified by public relations machinery, amplified by the latest sound technology, all to satisfy mass hunger for a restored sense of rootedness. In all fifty states of the United States, in Canada, in many countries of Western Europe, and in Australia, professional storytellers have multiplied in public schools, libraries, and state-funded community arts programs. Support groups of amateurs and professionals have banded together to swap tales and potluck suppers and to create local, regional, and national networks for promoting one another's work.

Much as "The Folksinger" did in the early sixties, "The Storyteller" has developed a certain mythic resonance in popular culture and language—perhaps more in the way of a poetic conceit than in an anthropologically specific role. Yet it depends for its emotive force on the idea that somewhere, sometime, there is, or was, such a role—a role with expressive, didactic, oracular, and community-binding functions. Enough people have resubscribed to the idea over the last twenty years to have created little subcultural pockets of what performance theorist Richard Schechner calls "restored behaviors" (*Between Theater* 35–116). These pockets, taken collectively, constitute what is known as "the storytelling community" and "the storytelling revival."

The storytelling revival community has developed its own kind of psychic geography over the years—the mutable map of what the sociologist Howard Becker calls an "artworld." The self-proclaimed capitol of the storytelling world is the town of Jonesborough, Tennessee, where the first national festival devoted exclusively to the many facets of storytelling performance took place in 1973. The National Association for the Preservation and Perpetuation of Storytelling (known to intimates as NAPPS, though in 1994 it trimmed its name to the National Storytelling Association, or NSA), also headquartered in Jonesborough, emerged from the enthusiasm surrounding the first two national storytelling festivals and has developed into the closest thing that this artistic movement has to an institutional base.

NAPPS/NSA puts out a directory of professional storytellers, storytelling events, groups, and educational programs nationwide. The criterion for being listed in the storytellers' section is a willingness to advertise one's professional services, pay the required fee, and affiliate with the national community as represented by the organization. This excludes traditional and community storytellers who have not learned or chosen to translate their art into economic terms, as well as those performers who are uninterested in NAPPS for a variety of personal, professional, or political reasons. The 1994 edition listed nearly six hundred storytellers in forty-five states and the District of Columbia, as well as a handful in Canada, the Caribbean, England, Ireland, France, Australia, Israel, and several African countries (the 1997 directory showed about the same number). The 1994 directory also listed 304 local or regional storytelling organizations, groups, or guilds in the United States (the 1997 directory had only 227—

as much, perhaps, because of increased directory fees as because of actual plateauing or attrition of the movement).

Among those NAPPS-affiliated storytellers, between twenty and fifty regularly headline festivals around the country and are able to draw substantial audiences in well-publicized performances beyond their local or regional bases. These "national performers" might include, among others, Jackie Torrence, David Holt, Donald Davis, and the former members of the storytelling duo the Folktellers—Barbara Freeman and Connie Regan-Blake—all from North Carolina; Jay O'Callahan and Bill Harley of Massachusetts; Diane Wolkstein, Laura Simms, and Heather Forest from New York; and Diane Ferlatte and David Novak from California. Most of the tellers in the NSA directory, like most small performing arts entrepreneurs generally, make a full- or part-time living doing performances and residencies through local and regional networks of schools, libraries, and arts councils. Many have come to storytelling after some previous training and identification with other arts or arts-related crafts—such as music, theater, poetry, dance, or journalism. Many moved to storytelling from professions that dealt with cultural conservation and transmission, such as teaching or library work; and many came from helping professions with strong expressive components, such as social work, therapy, or ministry.

Beyond their professional affiliation, what unites these artists into a storytelling community is a shared sense that storytelling endows one with not just a job but a mission: it can revitalize individuals and the culture as a whole. This conviction reinforces the growing storytelling scene like steel rods in poured concrete.

As befits a movement that privileges the mythic and the marvelous, the storytelling revival is fueled by a distinctive mythos, within which Jonesborough plays a central part. While storytellers like Brother Blue were awakening to their vocations in isolated epiphanies all over the United States, the arc of the national movement could be plotted in synchrony with developments in the little Tennessee town. The founding of the first storytelling festival there in 1973 provided a touchstone for a widespread awakening of cultural missionary spirit. Over the next decade, this spirit used Jonesborough as an administrative and ritual center, as each region of the country developed its own coteries of storytelling activists and touring professional performers. All of these continue, to some extent, to look to the National Storytelling Association and the national festival for public and personal identity-formation, policy-making, and communal realization. Meanwhile, the town of Jonesborough used storytelling as a vehicle to form a new economic and cultural identity in a changing, tourism- and service-based regional economy. For Jonesborough, storytelling has become the flagship industry of its own civic revival.

The Background of the Storytelling Revival

The storytelling revival of the 1970s and 1980s is far from an isolated event. It is part of a longstanding pattern of folklore-based cultural revivals, and it is based firmly on its predecessors. These include—to name just a few—the fairy-tale vogue at the court of Louis XV, which produced the works of Charles Perrault, Mme. D'Aulnoy, and others; the Hasidic movement in eighteenth- and nineteenth-century Judaism, which gave important instrumental roles to such oral cultural expressions as storytelling, folk music, and folk dance, in contrast to the rabbinic fixation on the written word; the German romantic movement, fueled by the articulate enthusiasms of J. G. Herder, Achim Von Arnim, Clemens Brentano, and Jacob and Wilhelm Grimm (Kamenetsky 39–68, 181–214); and the romantic nationalist movements in Western European literature and music, which produced great collections of regional folklore in nearly every European country during the nineteenth century, as well as literary and musical works based on folk forms and themes from such major figures as Sir Walter Scott, Hans Christian Andersen, Joel Chandler Harris, Oscar Wilde, W. B. Yeats, Antonin Dvořák, Jean Sibelius, Béla Bartók, R. Vaughn Williams, and Aaron Copland.

In the United States, we have played host during the twentieth century to a continual recycling of folk material on the part of popular movements with diverse and often conflicting cultural and political goals— from the library-based storytelling movement of the early years of the century, with its explicit social service agenda of socializing immigrant children within a Western cultural norm (Alvey 15–18, 396–432), to the racist Anglo-Saxon nativist ideology surrounding the White Top Folk Festival in the 1930s (Whisnant, *All Things* 181–252), to the use of folk song in the communist labor movement of the thirties and forties (explored from opposing political viewpoints by R. Serge Denisoff and Robbie Lieberman). The folk music revival of the fifties, purged of its explicit dependence on old-left ideology, provided an alternative community of identification to the gray-flannel juggernaut of the Eisenhower years. Later it bred iconography for the civil rights movement and provided a medium of solidarity for the youth rebellion of the sixties (an evolution exhaustively charted by Robert Cantwell in *When We Were Good*). It was in the dwindling phase of this cycle of folk cultural revivalism that the storytelling movement took wing in Jonesborough and in communities throughout America.

"Revitalization Movements"

The most comprehensive and useful taxonomic framework for examining the dynamics of cultural revivals is in Anthony F. C. Wallace's 1956 article "Revitalization Movements." Wallace places revival movements as one genus of a broad and significant class of cultural transformations. "A revitalization movement," he writes, "is defined as a deliberate, organized, conscious effort by members of a society to construct a more satisfying culture" (265). Using the analogy of society as organism, he regards revitalization movements as homeostatic responses to cultural stress: "A society will work, by means of coordinated actions (including 'cultural' actions) by all or some of its parts, to preserve its own integrity by maintaining a minimally fluctuating, life-supporting matrix for its individual members, and will, under stress, take emergency measures to preserve the constancy of its matrix. Stress is defined as a condition in which some part, or the whole, of the social organism is threatened with more or less serious damage" (265).

Wallace uses the term *mazeway* to denote the image of self, society, nature, and culture as perceived by individuals and groups, and he suggests that this mazeway of perception is the medium out of which the social organism constructs its reality. To change the mazeway, in these terms, is to change social reality. He distinguishes several subclasses of revitalization movements:

> "Nativistic movements" . . . are revitalization movements characterized by strong emphasis on the elimination of alien persons, customs, values, and/or material from the mazeway. . . . "Revivalistic" movements emphasize the institution of customs, values, and even aspects of nature which are thought to have been in the mazeway of previous generations but are not now present. . . . "Vitalistic movements" emphasize the importation of alien elements into the mazeway. . . . "Millenarian movements" emphasize mazeway transformation in an apocalyptic world transformation engineered by the supernatural. "Messianic movements" emphasize the participation of a divine savior in human flesh in the mazeway transformation. . . . These and parallel terms do not denote

mutually exclusive categories, for a given revitalization movement may be nativistic, millenarian, messianic, and revivalistic all at once; and it may (in fact, usually does) display ambivalence with respect to nativistic, revivalistic, and importation themes. (267)

According to this classificatory scheme, the revitalization movement gathered under the term *storytelling revival* contains a mixture of revival-istic, vitalistic, and nativistic elements. Though most storytellers promote the revival of an art form presumed to have flourished in an ideally imag-ined past, many tellers are also eagerly importing traditions and reper-toires that were not part of their own particular backgrounds. Still others are performing nativistic exercises, selectively representing in their story-telling the traditions of their own ethnic ancestors yet often, quite natu-rally, wielding those traditions on behalf of explicitly contemporary po-litical and cultural programs.

Wallace suggests that coordinated efforts on the part of individuals and groups to bring the mazeway of self and society to a revitalized integrity are constant, organic features of human culture in times of stress. His par-ticular use of the mazeway concept also implies that the revitalization process can apply to individual transformations as well as to social move-ments. This was amply borne out in my interviews of movement partici-pants.

Wallace's account of the processual structure of revitalization move-ments is divided into a five-stage sequence:

1. steady state;
2. period of individual stress;
3. period of cultural distortion;
4. period of revitalization (in which mazeway reformulation, com-munication, organization, adaptation, cultural transformation, and routinization occur); and finally,
5. new steady state.

Wallace ascribes virtually all religious phenomena, whether innovated or routinized, to some early or late stage of the revitalization process. Signifi-cantly, his processual scheme parallels in many striking and specific ways the structural analysis of folktales and myths given by Vladimir Propp in his *Morphology of the Folktale* and by Joseph Campbell in *Hero with a Thou-sand Faces,* although Wallace cites neither of these theorists in his article. We will see how folktales and myths, as illuminated by these scholars and those they influenced, can be used as a virtual blueprint of the revitalization process. This formal congruence between mythic narratives and the process of personal and cultural revitalization is one key to understanding why traditional forms provide such powerful raw material for movements of cultural transformation.

Wallace's account of revitalization movements as homeostatic adjustments of society's mazeway goes a long way toward elucidating the persistent cycles of folk revival in Western cultural history. "Progress" and "growth" are dominant, highly mythologized constructs in the mazeway of Western societies. They have provided ideological underpinnings for much furious activity by power blocs in the political and social sphere. They have reflected and helped amplify the continually accelerating forces of technological and social change, and therefore stress, in the system. Cultural revival movements are an inevitable homeostatic backlash. They provide outlets for nonviolent resistance to dominant mythologies and to the powers they represent, weaving countermythologies of idyllic, neglected traditions and spinning visions of restored and transfigured futures.

Cultural revivals help us reorient ourselves to a mazeway full of alien information by revitalizing traditional oral and tactile media. Such movements are rarely strictly conservative. They generally contain a blend of conservative and radical elements—passionate attachments to a romanticized past intertwined with sharp critiques of present social relations and with implicit or explicit, narrow or sweeping, agendas for change. Revival movements adapt traditional media to the terms of the contemporary mazeway, and at the same time they struggle to adapt the contemporary mazeway to the terms of these traditional media. A parallel process takes place with the individuals involved, as personal mazeways are reconfigured to make a place for older forms of expression, and the expressive forms are adapted to fit the contemporary circumstances of participants' lives.

"The Anti-Environment": Conditions of Cultural Stress

In 1969, Harvey Cox wrote in *The Feast of Fools*, "We cannot really 'see' something if it fills in our whole visual environment. We need an 'anti-environment' against which to make out its profile. The background or field is an essential element in perception. Music on a concert stage we listen to. Music pumped into every closet and corridor by Muzak we may vaguely hear, but we do not really *listen* to. Conversely, an old automobile attracts our attention and becomes a work of 'art' when it is removed from the highways and set on a display pedestal at a fair" (44).

The "anti-environment" of the storytelling revival was the cultural turbulence of the sixties. Accelerating changes in the technological, social, and economic organization of mainstream America all seemed to be enforcing a rapid decline in conditions supportive of traditional storytelling and storylistening. Chief among those changes were the shift from rural to urban and suburban communities; the shift from extended to nuclear families; increased social mobility, leading to a decline in local, regional, and ethnic particularity; and the growing dominance of electronic media and the consequent decline in the cultural value of the spoken and written word.

The political and cultural mass movements of the sixties—the sexual revolution and the antiwar, civil rights, feminist, and hippie movements—can all be seen as homeostatic responses on the part of the social organism to critical levels of stress. The tenor of those movements, however, was overwhelmingly antagonistic. The issues raised were framed in such violently oppositional cultural narratives that they threatened to tear society apart. New cultural revival movements emerged in the years that followed as a kind of camouflage—artistic and religious sublimations that allowed psychic heat to diffuse itself in ritual and ceremony. One such sublimation was the storytelling movement.

In the seventies, after Woodstock and Altamont, the traumatic spate of political assassinations and massacres, the whimpering end to the Vietnam War, and the national catharsis of Watergate, the public atmosphere cooled. In small groups and private refuges, however, the culture was simmering away. There was an instinctive sense that radical changes in community and self were tragically frail without disciplines of awareness and communication. There was a surge of meditation practices, personal-growth and encounter groups, and intentional communities. Images of healing and connectedness began to unseat images of revolution and destruction in the iconography of a generation. The *counter*culture was turning to the difficult task of cultivating sustainable community. The antagonistic tone of the mass movements of the previous decade turned agonistic, confronting the demons of the personal psyche, often through the mechanisms of communal encounter, ritual, and celebration.

As Harvey Cox put it in *The Feast of Fools,* "I have become aware that there is an unnecessary gap between the world-changers and the life-cel-

9

ebrators" (viii). He wrote, "The epochal crisis of Western consciousness which we call the death of God is not just a passing fad. It is the result of a cumulative history that includes industrialization and the ascent of technology, pluralism, modern science, and cultural self-consciousness. Most importantly, however, the vivid cultural experience of God's absence, disappearance, or death occurred in a civilization where festivity in all its forms was in a state of steady decline" (27).

The difference between the confrontational drama of a street theater performance and the guided inner fantasy of a storytelling event is emblematic. Connie Regan-Blake's shift from being an organizer of the Tennessee chapter of NOW (National Organization for Women) in the early seventies to being a traveling storyteller and proselytizer for NAPPS encapsulates the shift from the revolutionary rhetoric of the sixties (We want it *NOW!*) to the evolutionary dreamtime of the seventies (Sleep on it: *NAPPS*). In going off to seek their fortune as storytellers, Connie and her partner, Barbara Freeman, went from confronting the giant with a club (bravely, but foolishly, since the giant was carrying a tree) to keeping him entranced with gently subversive dreams, even as the treasure they were seeking to recapture from him danced unopposed into their pockets. In leaving their jobs as children's librarians to "spend their lives at a festival," they were answering a Dionysian call that still resounded in the culture from the sixties. They were buoyed by a sense of plenty and protection that lingered from the postwar boom of their childhoods. But their careers, and those of many of their storytelling companions, have been dedicated to the service of festivity itself. Storytelling has been a vessel through which festival could incarnate in our culture, not explosively, as at Woodstock, but sustainably, as at Jonesborough.

Transforming the Envelope

Folklore collectors of the nineteenth and twentieth centuries worked diligently to preserve many of the world's tribal and regional folktale stocks in print, even as those stocks themselves drastically declined or disappeared from living tradition. This had the effect, from the end of the nineteenth century until the sixties, of making librarians the chief public custodians of that part of our cultural inheritance, a duty they performed in good faith. But as the dominant technology by which we store, process, and experience cultural information shifted from print to electronic media, this situation was bound to change.

In the field of folklore, the change was signaled in the shift of its dominant analytic model from *text* to *performance*. Audio and video recording devices made it possible for performance features to be recorded, with a much fuller reproduction of textual features than had ever been captured by dictation. The new technology, then, made certain ways of knowing possible and necessitated the creation of ideological frameworks to accommodate them. One of the new frameworks declared that it was inadequate to look at folklore as text—that we needed to look at the entire dynamic of performance in its cultural context to understand the form. This led certain key folklorists in the seventies, such as Dell Hymes, Dennis Tedlock, and Barre Toelken, to experiment with performance themselves to explore the dynamics of folklore from within (Elizabeth Fine summarized and consolidated these efforts in *The Folklore Text*). There was considerable academic resistance to this, but it was inevitable as our technological extensions altered the sensory envelope through which we experienced ourselves and our environment. Storytelling was undergoing a similar transformation, as conservators of culture were pressed beyond the performance prism of the book. There was a need to compete for the attention of the young, using the kinds of dynamics in which their environment had already soaked them: color, movement, music, vocal characterization, and sound—what McLuhan called the "reoralization of culture."

Hitlahavut: The Quality of Fervor

The concept of a storytelling revival can be useful, as Wallace wields it, as a category of sociological change; in its common use by enthusiasts of the movement, however, it quickly reveals an element of myth. In the eyes of its partisans, myth is not untruth—though the words are used interchangeably in the popular press—but a story, which, *in the telling,* acts to align the worlds of imagination and emotion with the world of social action and so shapes our human world. The death-and-resurrection narrative that is woven into the language of revival, for example, is powerfully generative. It was retold constantly in NAPPS publications and in the ritual form of its events. The mythic imagery and atmosphere of storytelling communities, particularly Jonesborough, in the 1970s and 1980s produced the revitalization movement's definitive quality of fervor.

A resident of Jonesborough who turned one of the restored antebellum houses into a bed-and-breakfast told me about her first exposure to storytelling at an early NAPPS festival. "It was like a religious experience," she said. She went on, "You know we get a lot of the institute people staying here over the summer. And we get a lot of people who are new to this storytelling stuff, and somebody's told them that they really ought to do this, and they're really, you know: 'I don't know about this. . . .' And I love to watch these people come back here over the course of the week, and they're just *glowing*. And they say, 'I've *never* had an experience anything *like* this, it's so *wonderful!*' It's like getting into some kind of cult or something."

This cultic atmosphere was generated partly by design and partly by a kind of unconscious collaboration of human agents with intangible forces—like those that previous romantic movements have named "the zeitgeist" and "the spirit of place." This fervor—which Martin Buber, writing of the Hasidic movement, called by its Hebrew name of *hitlahavut*— is an essential element in cultural revitalizations. "*Hitlahavut* can appear at all places and all times." writes Buber. "Each hour is its footstool and each deed its throne. Nothing can stand against it, nothing hold it down; nothing can defend itself against its might which raises everything corporeal to spirit" (*Hasidism and Modern Man* 75). It is a locus of psychological value so powerful that an encounter with it can reshape an art form, a community, or a life.

Archetype, Myth, and History

When I examine the storytelling revival, I find archetypal storyings at the center of its development, both in the collective products of its organized associations and guilds and in the public and private performances of individual storytellers. The performance repertoire has been dominated, at least until very recently, by world folktales and myths, the performances heavily inflected by Jungian, universalist, cross-cultural interpretations. Then again, the rhetorical framing of revival storytelling events is often suffused with an archetypal numinosity. There is the implicit and explicit narrative of cultural revival, in which the art of storytelling takes the role of a dying and reviving god. There is also a sacramental or priestly quality invested in the role of storyteller, which emerges in the experience of many revivalists and is revealed, sometimes magnified, sometimes obscured or trivialized, in the public and private discourse surrounding storytelling events.

Images and models invoked are legion. It may be the image of Christ the storyteller or of the founder of Hasidism, the Baal Shem Tov, telling spiritual parables in the marketplace; or the image of a tribal shaman restoring harmony through his spirit-journeying; or that of the village elder, uniting the roles of teacher, entertainer, and shaper of group identity; or an inchoate medley of related models—there is hardly a storyteller or storytelling enthusiast of the 1970s or 1980s who does not revel in the language and process of ritual, myth, and archetypal imagery.

Even the summary account early in this chapter partakes of a traditional mythic patterning. It poses an image of storytellers in their imagined or theoretical glory; traces a cultural theogony, a succession myth in which technological descendants usurp a sacred prerogative; and finally announces (albeit here in suitably qualified, intellectually balanced tones) a return of the vanquished to a new phase of power. Even a scholarly language cannot keep the old stories from reproducing themselves in us.

In employing the term *archetypal,* I follow James Hillman's approach and treat it not as a fixed repertoire of psychic structures but as a process. Hillman writes that an archetypal quality emerges whenever an image is precisely portrayed, amplified by listening to its metaphoric resonances, experienced in its psychological necessity, and finally, understood by experiencing "the unfathomable analogical richness of the image." Since any image can bloom in the light of this process, Hillman writes, the function of the word *archetypal* is not primarily descriptive but an indicator of value: "By attaching *archetypal* to an image, we ennoble or empower the image with the widest, richest, and deepest possible significance. *Archetypal,* as we use it, is a word of importance (in Whitehead's sense), a word that values" (*A Blue Fire* 26). I seek the archetypal values of the storytelling revival by allowing it to speak in the images of its own self-storying. At the same time I turn a lens onto the mythmaking enterprise itself to examine its uses and consequences in the world.

Documentary facts are plentiful on the revival scene. The National Storytelling Festival and the National Storytelling Association are quintessential media phenomena. They function as elaborate mechanisms for amplifying an oral, face-to-face communal art in the arenas of modern print and electronic consumer culture. Since their inception, the festival and the organization have been preoccupied with representing and interpreting their mission to the media and to their membership. In doing so, they have generated an ever-expanding archive of print, audio, and video documentation of the movement's evolution, in plainly marked historical sequence (most of which has been stored, but yet not catalogued, at the National Storytelling Resource Center, or NSRC, at NSA headquarters in

Jonesborough). What is most striking about much of this material is how persistently it is structured by traditional modes of narrativization and ritualization. When we turn to the personal, autobiographical tellings of the storytelling revivalists, the pattern is just as clear: the storytelling revival has provided a channel for the psychological urgency of myth and ritual to flow into this world.

There is certainly a sociological as well as a mythological dimension to the storytelling movement. The storytelling revival has been a mechanism for transforming the socioeconomic organization of the storytelling *profession* in this country. In the early 1970s, as Richard Alvey's study made clear, organized storytelling was almost exclusively the province of librarians, educators, and recreation directors, with a few figures working on the margins between those fields and the print and electronic media industries. Traditional storytelling—storytelling based in community, family, and ethnic traditions—had no presence whatsoever in American economic life. It was an unexploited, "natural" resource. As we will see in chapter 1, the resurgent mythological imagining of the storyteller as artist and cultural healer provided the impetus for storytellers to move out of those institutional settings and out of their family and community backgrounds to form a network of free-lance professional performers.

These new professionals are supported largely by those earlier institutions—libraries, schools, and recreation centers—but also by a national network of storytelling festivals, modeled on the National Storytelling Festival in Jonesborough. In the process, they have developed a web of connections among support personnel in established "art worlds"—publishers, media producers, arts councils, arts journalists, and public sector folklorists. All of these interlocking networks of storytellers and support people have come to constitute an "art world" of its own, in Becker's sense—a "storytelling world." In addition, community activists and civic boosters in a variety of towns and cities—paradigmatically in Jonesborough itself—have seized upon storytelling as a tool to identify themselves through distinctively local cultural productions. Storytelling festivals transform familiar settings into liminal frames in which threads of local and national, individual and communal identity can be unbound and rewoven.

Politically, the contemporary storytelling movement grew out of the sixties' cultural radicalism and the seventies' inward-turning politics of personal growth. It can certainly be viewed as a sublimation of politics in the realm of performance, a retreat to a constructed communal dreamworld in which intractable issues that were rending American society—such issues as war and peace, ecological destruction, and racial and ethnic strife—could be faced and overcome in imaginative transport, bypassing the physical realm of bullets and blood, in the hope of advancing the healing process to a point where more gruesome plot turns could be avoided. If the folk song revivals of this century were artistic wedges of the labor movement, the civil rights movement, and the peace movement, the storytelling revival has helped give form to various ethnic identity movements, the human potential movement, multiculturalism, environmentalism, the men's movement, and the goddess branch of feminism. The seminars, tapes, and books of Idries Shah, Robert Bly, Sam Keen, Michael Meade, Jean Houston, Merlin Stone, Claudia Pinkola Estes, Brooke Medicine Eagle, Alex Haley, Matthew Fox, Joseph Bruchac, and many of their colleagues and followers form intersecting circles of revitalistic activity, all of which feed on and nourish the fervor of the storytelling revival.

It is an occupational hazard for storytellers to be spellbound by the stuff of their stories, to spend their time climbing the beanstalk to the sky, and to ignore the earthbound pressures of history, society, and politics. It is an occupational hazard of the scholar to demythologize phenomena, to overlook and undervalue the powerful role of the archetypal process in moving and shaping an individual or a community. But the archetypal process, in James Hillman's terms, is a process of giving value to the imaginal life, and the need for a life of value is at the heart of the archetype of the storyteller.

The Storytellers' Journey, then, is a mythography, an examination of the uses of myth in an artistic movement whose basic program is the search for myth in a demythologizing time. It examines the stories we have told ourselves over the years to create, shape, and energize a vocational community. This involves a hard look at the complex interaction of personal ideals and economic forces—universalist impulses and their incarnation through the forms of commercial culture. Story is the form in which these intersecting forces come together so that they can be most fully perceived and metabolized by the imagination. Because stories are made out of images moving in a psychological field that is itself the image of the time-space continuum in which we have our physical being, they are the truest of all modes of discourse to our experience of being alive. Therefore I try to embody the ideas in this work in stories, mostly collected from participants in the storytelling revival and shaped by them and by the times and places of our lives.

Historical, sociological, and economic accounts are all significant here and answer partially our need to understand this movement. At the same time, it has been a movement of people who perceive themselves as being caught up in a mythic journey, permeated by the symbols and world-creating dramas that make their repertoires. Another lens is required so that we may get the creation story of an art world from the inside. That lens is mythology.

In *The Power of Myth,* Joseph Campbell divided myth into four functions:

> The first is the mystical sense . . . realizing what a wonder the universe is, and what a wonder you are, and experiencing awe before this mystery.
> The second is a cosmological dimension . . . showing you what the shape of the universe is, but showing it in such a way that the mystery again comes through. . . .
> The third function is the sociological one—supporting and validating a certain social order. . . .
> [The] fourth function of myth . . . is the pedagogical function, of how to live a human lifetime under any circumstances. Myths can teach you that. (31)

There is a crucial divide in contemporary thought between those who regard myth in a sacred and mystical sense and those who would treat it in a secular, critical mode. Many critics who employ the term limit its scope to Campbell's third function. From the depths of the popular press to the heights of academe, secularists invoke myth as a categorical signifier for illusion. Whether at the parrot-level of a Washington journalist or at the sublime level of a Sigmund Freud or a Roland Barthes, myth provides a fulcrum for instinctive or systematic critiques of mass cultural hypnosis. As scions of the Enlightenment, however many times removed by the addition of various posts, the secularist seeks and finds in myth the ingrained tendency of the human mind to resist the liberating operations of reason by turning archaic social relations and idealized cultural forms into escapist and potentially corrupting graven images.

Those who regard myth from a sacred perspective see in the imagery of myth an earlier form of language, a pictorial and narrative language, which can encode creative principles inaccessible to rationalistic systems. There are those, including many contemporary storytellers, who find a transcendent authenticity in nature, and in myth and oral tradition find a mirror of that transcendent nature in human culture. Others, influenced by a variety of contemplative religious traditions or by synthesists like Campbell and Jung, seek an inner experience of transcendence and find in the myths and symbols of world folklore a potent medium for communicating psychological truths that flow from such experiences.

The storytelling movement as a whole and many of its most influential proponents have been powerfully animated by this sacred approach to myth. Many have been motivated as well by more normative psychological approaches, such as Bruno Bettelheim's Freudian treatment of the therapeutic value of stories in *The Uses of Enchantment,* or by empirical observation of the benefits of storytelling in education. But again and again in my interviews, a certain emotional quality appears that has no normative equivalent, a quality of revelation, transcendent presence, *hitlahavut,* which I would identify as a stepping into the aura of the archetype.

These opposing postures, secular versus sacred, as stated here, are deliberately exaggerated into polarities. In "real life," they will be found to interpenetrate, to inform each other in a multitude of ironic, refractive perspectives. They are in fact depictions of positive and negative dimensions of myth. Myth, as Barthes points out, is a natural, gravitational tendency of speech. Myth is capable of giving meaning, higher purpose, and vividness to life by tapping into sources of energy beneath the conditioned surface of consciousness. It can provide us with vehicles for opening culture to vital pathways of growth, legitimating radical changes in social and personal relations through the sense of returning to an original, "natural" form. At the same time, those highly charged energies are susceptible to exploitation by all kinds of regressive, repressive, or hegemonic forces. The Dragon, too, is an archetypal form, which can often be activated under the banner of the Hero, its mythic antagonist—witness the pervasiveness of archetypal imagery in the rites of nationalists of every stripe, from the most innocent to the most bloodthirsty. I would rank Jonesborough and its national association of storytellers with the more innocent of romantic movements; yet over the years, charges of cultural imperialism and exploitation have been leveled at storytellers individually and as a group and at the NSA as an organization. It is by no means clear that these charges have been settled or that we are not due for another round. So we will pick our way over the field with care.

The battle over the uses and even the definition of myth in our culture is fought on the field of language. Which language is chosen and deployed, and with what intent, has consequences that reach deep into the social, economic, and political realms. But these are not the only realms in which the battle has had, and will have, its consequences. If there are spiritual realms, realms of *value,* in which the social, the economic, and the political move and have their being, then how the battle is fought becomes especially important—victory in this war is not to vanquish but to *connect.*

The Background of the Festival

In 1972, Jimmy Neil Smith, a schoolteacher and fledgling entrepreneur from Jonesborough, conceived the idea of a storytelling festival in his town. The story that surrounds that moment of conception has become an integral part of the folklore of the festival and is treated in detail in chapter 2. Suffice it to say here that Smith's primary interest at that time was not storytelling but civic revival. He was involved with the Jonesborough Civic Trust, organized to promote historic preservation in the town and the economic, political, and social transformations that would flow from that reconstituted civic identity.

Jonesborough was incorporated in the late 1770s as the county seat of the newly chartered Washington County. Then still part of North Carolina, the already presumptuous new county claimed territory "a little greater than the present State of Tennessee" (Fink, *Jonesborough* 8). It was the first town west of the Appalachians, and it retained its prominence as a center of Euro-American civilization for the region for most of the nineteenth century. The following account from a biography of a local dignitary named Thomas A. R. Nelson provides a glimpse of the town's character in its heyday during the 1840s:

> Jonesborough was situated in Washington County in rolling hills between the principal Appalachian watershed and Bays Mountain range. It boasted a male and a female academy with a total of about two hundred students. Presbyterians, Methodists and Baptists had church structures, and the former two operated Sunday School of about one hundred each. A Masonic Lodge was located at Jonesborough, and several merchants and professional men made the town their residence. There were some Democratic lawyers and another Whig lawyer besides Nelson. Six doctors practiced here, five of whom were Whigs. Two taverns competed along political party lines, one being operated by a Whig and the other by a Democrat. Many old log and frame houses, including churches,

were being torn down and replaced by brick ones. The former habits of wintering cows under porches and emptying refuse in the front streets had not been corrected, but some progress was being made. (Fink, *Jonesborough* 20–21)

Jonesborough went into eclipse in the late nineteenth century, after the main railroad junction was diverted ten miles northeast to Johnson City (until then a mere crossroad by the name of Johnson's Tank). A regional medical center, a VA hospital, a state university, and a succession of modern commercial shopping districts were established in and around Johnson City, while Jonesborough remained an agricultural supply center and courthouse town. Other than the slight accretion of twentieth-century commercial and infrastructural paraphernalia (Coca-Cola signs, powerlines, and the like) and some inevitable slow decay, its downtown and residential sections remained substantially intact and unchanged from its glory days. In 1969, the Jonesborough (then spelled Jonesboro) zoning board began to explore the possibility of basing civic redevelopment on the principles of historic preservation. A local resident who sat on that board told me, "The historic preservation movement started mainly because the planning board was trying to get a grant for water or sewer lines. And they had to meet certain specifications if they were going to get a grant. And they did sit down, and say, 'Hey, the main thing we've got to promote is probably our history.'" A variety of consultants from the Tennessee Historical Commission and around the country were brought in to study the feasibility of obtaining National Register status and federal historic redevelopment grants. As a result, in early 1970, the greater part of the town was designated a historic district, the first of its kind in Tennessee. The Jonesboro Civic Trust was formed, modeled after the National Trust in Great Britain. The late Paul Fink, a local historian and resident who was a guiding force in the preservation effort, described its mission: "to encourage and enlist public support in the preservation and restoration of historic sites and buildings, and to secure and administer gifts of properties and funds for this purpose" ("Rebirth" 237–38).

Historic Jonesboro Days, a Fourth of July weekend street fair, was initiated as a way of bringing regional and national attention to the work that was going on in the town. Fink wrote in 1973, "As part of its publicity campaign the Civic Trust, during the summers of 1971 and 1972, promoted 'Jonesborough Days,' celebrations that attracted thousands of visitors from all over the United States. It is planned to make this an annual event"

("Rebirth" 238). Local boosters began casting around for other kinds of events to bring tourists to town in the winter, spring, and fall. Jimmy Neil Smith was a young, energetic, and well-connected member of the Civic Trust circle at the time. Inspired by a Jerry Clower performance heard on his car radio, he brought the storytelling festival idea to his friends on the Civic Trust Board and offered to organize and promote an event himself with a target date of October 1973. The Civic Trust Board gave him a small grant to produce it. Somewhere in the course of that weekend, as I will show in chapter 2, the idea seemed to take on a life of its own.

The agendas of the storytelling revivalists and the civic revivalists in Jonesborough have been so consistently identified, through the unifying agency of NAPPS, that it has seemed to some, even inside the town, as if they were actually one. To visitors, it was as if Lake Woebegone had materialized in the hills of Tennessee, remote but accessible by road, complete with a miraculously preserved historic townscape and a populace eager to play host to fantasies of a time and place before the Fall. In fact, that sweet illusion, so palpable to those who arrived at the festival after, say, 1977, was achieved only through conscious choice, creative leadership, determined political maneuvering, some heavy-duty cosmetic engineering, and a confluence of social forces that Jonesborough had the simple grace to ride.

The first major restoration project undertaken by the Civic Trust—coinciding with the founding of the storytelling festival—was to pull down a two-story, eighteenth-century log cabin that was crumbling in the woods two miles from town and reconstruct it log by log in the center of Main Street, between the 1797 Federal-style Chester Inn and the 1840s Greek Revival Presbyterian church. The Christopher Taylor Cabin became the iconic registration site for the early festivals. During 1975 and 1976, by means of a $309,000 federal grant with matching in-kind contributions from the local power and telephone companies, all the utilities were buried under the streets of Jonesborough: powerlines, telephone poles, and streetlights were taken down and replaced by underground cables and gaslight-style lampposts. The concrete sidewalks were torn out and replaced by nineteenth-century-style bricks. One by one the large storefront signs from the forties, fifties, and sixties, which had obscured details of the older buildings, were removed. Buildings were sandblasted and repainted, foundations were secured, and later additions were torn off. By whatever means available, the town was renewed by being antiqued. Even the name of the town was restored: digging through old documents, "Jonesboro" historians determined that the original spelling had been "Jonesborough." The eroded spelling was seen to have coincided with the town's economic decline; so in 1983, a town ordinance was passed restoring "Jonesborough" to its full historic dignity (Fink, *Jonesborough* vi). The result now looks and feels like a town at once in and out of time: in because people still live and work there, unlike a Disneyland or a Williamsburg; but out because its every prospect has been shaped by an intense, multistoried dialogue with the ancestors.

The entire historic district also happens to be about the scale of a mid-sized shopping mall. Like Fisherman's Wharf or other historic districts around the country, it makes a compact environmental theater set for the festive comedy of artists, consumers, and citizens. The success of Jonesborough's civic transformation lay in its finding a fit, a synergy, between its new local industries and the transformation that was taking place in the American economy as a whole, as it shifted from the production and distribution of agricultural and manufactured goods to the production and distribution of information and images.

Modern tourism exports the image of a place while importing travelers and their money. It is a subtle, postindustrial form of exchange—the place stays put, its image goes out, in mediated forms. People come and go, leaving dollars behind and taking tokens of the imagination with them, which they might name: heritage, history, a sense of the past and of a simpler world. A life that was once hard, brutal, real, and gracious in poor, fugitive moments stolen from the imagination can now be altogether gracious, even in its brutality, because it is all imaginary, like a dream or a story. It's *once upon a time.*

In the 1960s and 1970s, a new conjunction of economic, social, cultural, and ecological concepts seemed to crystallize in this country. The key linking term was *resource*—a term from the economic sphere that was appropriated by activists with seriously competing agendas. In the creation of such categories as "natural resources," "cultural resources," and "historic resources," a variety of previously marginal natural and cultural phenomena were redefined as having economic value and thus as worth "preserving."

It was an inevitable but hazardous evolutionary change. Without a recognizable presence in the economic world, such things as wilderness areas, folk arts, or historic neighborhoods could be quickly eradicated by the dominant ideology of progress. But the moment the conjunction is made, the nature of the "resource" is irremediably changed by appropriation into a value system whose fundamental mythology is "the bottom line." By opening up the public policy realm to nature, culture, and history, these things are opened in new ways to the public marketplace, with the hope, at best, that values inherent in each might influence the other—that power might be exchanged for grace.

The crucial questions then become precisely what the exchange value of these newly declared resources might be and how it might be measured—since the calculus employed would likely determine the form in which "preservation" takes place and for whose benefit. There are the statistical yardsticks of the tourism industry: natural, cultural, and historic resources can be valued according to the number of dollars, jobs, construction starts, and so forth generated by tourists and by related services engaged in the resources' use. Or there is the aesthetic calculus, according to which resources are seen to carry irreducible aesthetic values in themselves, values that could and should be preserved and enjoyed but not degraded.

In the thirty-odd years since the environmental movement began its steady growth in public awareness, economic and aesthetic measures have been increasingly linked through a growing network of political, ideological, artistic, and business alliances. But in the meantime, various public agencies have had to mediate the perceived conflicts of interest. In the public policy realm in the 1960s and 1970s, federal legislation was passed, and federal agencies were established to perform this role. Most significant for Jonesborough and for storytellers were the National Historic Preservation Act, which established the National Register of Historic Places and the National Endowment for the Arts, with its Folk Arts Section. The Environmental Protection Agency was a cognate body in the ecological sphere. These agencies in turn helped create and fund similar bodies on state, county, and municipal levels. Taken together, federal, state, and local agencies formed integrated networks of professionals and involved citizens. Their programs of public and private action and their continuing dialogue on relevant issues both reflected and helped institutionalize a new public assumption of value in all things connected to history and heritage.

They also created intermediary mechanisms by which artifacts and art forms carrying these values could be insulated from "pure" market forces while being subtly or drastically refitted to flourish within the modified free market of modern society. So, for example, government grants and tax abatements were created to support the renovation of historic properties according to consensus standards. The properties would then be released back onto the real estate market, which thereby absorbed some of those consensus standards of historic preservation into its own schema of valuation. The sanctioned authority of a National Register designation became a marker of cultural and historic value, which became negotiable when incorporated in a touristic economy of sights and signs, sites and markers. It also provided support for the designated properties to be restored for reuse, in altered contexts, perhaps, but with their original characteristics marked out for renewed appreciation. The entire downtown redevelopment of Jonesborough was to be based on this official conduit of value.

Similarly, folk arts grants from the National Endowment for the Arts supported "documentation"—which is, in effect, the expert marking of marginal cultural expressions to encode their resource value. National heritage fellowships perform the same function for individual folk artists. In addition to financial support, the fellowships provide textual markers to the artists' names, so that, even if their indigenous, "natural" communities may be rapidly disintegrating, their expressions can be more sympathetically consumed by a new audience of informed cultural tourists. This process has given such artists as the North Carolina mountain storytellers Ray and Stanley Hicks a transformed, "official" status in and beyond their communities.

Dean MacCannell in his important 1976 study *The Tourist* gives a persuasive sociological account of how the tourist system operates in modern life. Briefly, he suggests that in a complex industrial and postindustrial society, in which people are systematically (or systemically) alienated from their workday experience, a cultural ideology has been generated in which "authentic" experience is located in exotic sites, objects, expressions, and time periods (read "natural, cultural, and historic resources"). Tourism becomes a systematic outlet, in which people are encouraged to make regulated pilgrimages from their workday lives to visit sites of "authentic" experience and return with tokens ("souvenirs") to help lift them through stretches of alienated labor.

Institutionalized tourism requires mediation. The dual insider-outsider status of guides, or "experts," allows them to designate sites and to mark for sightseers precisely what traces of authentic experience are resident therein, so that tourists can direct their attention to absorbing this sacramental substance. A site without a marker, MacCannell explains, is an incomplete attraction. Thus traditional storytellers from such "exotic" backgrounds as Appalachia, Native America, and even African America play roles in the revival movement akin to touristic sites—while storytellers from mainstream backgrounds who import or adapt traditional repertoires function in the manner of guides to exotic places in the cultural imagination.

MacCannell's analysis strongly suggests that touristic phenomena are not limited to the tourism industry per se but that the structure of tourism is endlessly replicated in the structure of modern consumption. "Our first apprehension of modern civilization," he wrote, "emerges in the mind of the tourist" (1). As local familiarity with the process of production grows more remote in our experience of everything from housing to clothing to food to art, these items are increasingly sold back to us in terms of "authenticity." If authentic authenticity is a sense of relatedness between a product and its place in individual and community life cycles, then it is this very form of authenticity that is abstracted from the product in the modern production process and added back in the advertising process, like vitamins to processed flour. The product-advertising dynamic parallels MacCannell's site-marker relationship. A usual by-product is alienation—or a cycle of hypnotic consumer conformity interrupted by energized outbreaks of counterculture. These outbreaks often seize on marginalized, "folk" forms to marshal renewed efforts at community-controlled production—authentic authenticity—which can then be reexoticized and reabsorbed into the tourist/consumer system with bewildering efficiency.

The modern festival is a popular form that mediates between "cultural resources" and the tourist/consumer system. Quite often locally recognized folk art forms are chosen for celebration in festival—festival as a kind of artistic game preserve where folk arts can flourish in free-range captivity. Festivals are open, localized, and volatile in nature. They can be constructed to celebrate virtually any community expression, and they can be sponsored by a wide range of sociopolitical interests and alliances. Generally, however, festivals retain an implied connection to their roots in religious feast days—a ritualized time period dedicated both to tradition and to renewal, the rule of custom and the liberation of indulgence. In many instances, they also retain their connection to the ancient belief in ritual efficacy: the efficacy of festival as a transformative agency in the medium of culture.

Magic is a key code word for the transformative power of festival, repeatedly invoked in the discourse of various festival promoters and enthusiasts (innumerable examples could be given from the productions of NAPPS). It can be seen as a simple rhetorical mystification, a shorthand for any aesthetic pleasure that defies the speakers' descriptive powers or analytic inclinations. But William Butler Yeats, whose work on behalf of an earlier folk revival changed the course of Ireland's political and cultural landscape, had an older and more specific usage for the term, which, as I will show, fits very well the communal trance sought by the storytelling festival-goer. Yeats wrote:

> I believe in the practice and philosophy of what we have agreed to call magic. . . . and I believe in three doctrines, which have, as I think been handed down from early times, and have been the foundation of all magical practices. These doctrines are: 1) That the borders of our minds are ever shifting, and that many minds can flow into one another, and create or reveal a single mind, a single energy; 2) That the borders of our memories are shifting, and that our memories are a part of one great memory, the memory of Nature herself; 3) That this great mind and great memory can be evoked by symbols. (*Essays* 28)

Robert Cantwell, in his writings in the *Journal of American Folklore* on the production of the Smithsonian Festival of American Folklife, seeks, as Yeats did, to relate the word to its roots in prescientific Renaissance humanism. He makes an eloquent case for magic as the form of ritual efficacy embodied in the modern cultural festival. "Magic," he writes, "I take to be that form of intellectual desire that influences the understanding and hence the operations of a symbolic system. . . ." Cantwell continues, "The best folk festivals, the most effective and memorable for all concerned, even from the point of view of cultural conservation, are those that somehow intimate the possibility of a desired or an ideal world, and do not limit themselves to such accounts of reality as social scientific method can generate" ("Response" 498–99).

Lacking a larger theme, a vision, or a medium of connectedness between peoples, local civic festivals can be contrived, routine, commercial affairs. But in creating the National Storytelling Festival, Smith stumbled on a transformative medium of connectedness. In the storytelling experience, as I will show in chapter 1, minds can flow into one another in palpable ways, and powerful symbols are constantly at work. The idealistic storytellers who flocked to Jonesborough and helped shape the festival provided the larger theme and vision—the force of desire for a better, more humane world that produced the sensation of "magic." Jimmy Neil

Smith and his town of Jonesborough provided the perfect setting, the physical grounding through which the currents of festive magic could flow. With its historic preservationists, its bed-and-breakfast keepers, its antique merchants, and its lovely, frail old buildings with numbered plaques on the doorposts keyed to guidebooks that could be bought in any store on Main Street, the town was the willing, waiting receptor of a nation's restless psychic excitement.

1

The Archetype of the Storyteller

Archetype: 1. The original or model from which copies are made; a prototype. . . . [2.b.] in *Compar. Anat.*
An assumed ideal pattern of the fundamental structure of each great division of organized beings, of
which the various species are considered modifica-
tions. . . .

                —*Oxford English Dictionary*

In the recent film *The Crying Game* by the Irish director Neil Jordan, a black
English soldier held hostage by the IRA, knowing that he will almost certainly be killed the next day, begs one of his captors, with whom he has
formed an emotional bond, "Tell me a story. Please. Tell me anything." But
Fergus, the IRA volunteer, is like the familiar character in Irish folklore
"The Man Who Had No Story." All he can think of to say in defense of his
emptiness is a quotation from St. Paul: "When I was a child, I spoke as a
child . . . but when I became a man, I put away childish things." "What
does that *mean?*" cries the soldier. But Fergus doesn't know what it means.
Without a story to give form to his beliefs, those beliefs quickly lose their
grip in the face of the soldier's simple plea for meaning. At the end of the
film, after experiencing an incredible series of adventures, he finds himself retelling the little Caribbean folktale that his captive had told him at
the beginning to distill his experience of the world and its creatures. Life
has finally yielded him a measure of wisdom and made him, to that extent, a storyteller.

  For months after the release of *The Crying Game,* one often heard the
director referred to as "a master storyteller" and the film described as "a
brilliant piece of storytelling." Even when a particular work exists in a highly
wrought technological frame, as a film so obviously does, critics tend to
invoke the image of the storyteller whenever the frame recedes from view
and we feel as if we are hearing the story through a human voice.

The invocation of an ideal pattern to that great division of *homo narrans* called the storyteller—a pattern that lends its original authority to particular individuals and species deriving from it—is common in criticism, as it is in popular writing and vernacular speech. To speak of an archetype of the storyteller, we need assume neither a Jungian accent nor a transcendental gaze. For those who patrol other intellectual boundaries, it could just as usefully be viewed as a mental-emotional construct or a rhetorical strategy. The archetype of the storyteller can be invoked in support of a great range of political, personal, artistic, critical, or commercial agendas, and it can always emerge with its essential nature unbounded, its potential power full.

The archetype of the storyteller during the revival period has been a generative dynamic, a mythic motif ritually invoked and amplified in storytelling events from coast to coast. To evoke it here, I will begin by examining a prescient essay by the German critic Walter Benjamin. Though written in 1936, "The Storyteller" richly foreshadows the aesthetics of later revivalists, even as it anticipates the images summoned by them to answer their own social critiques. I will then sample some prototypical encounters with the archetype of the storyteller during the seventies and eighties.

These encounters are culled from printed sources, my collection of storytellers' vocational narratives, and the folktale repertoires of performers on the revival circuit. From this last category, I have chosen three widely told tales that reflect powerfully on the role of the storyteller and the process of storytelling itself. Retellings of these meta-folktales became part of the revival community's ongoing process of definition and affirmation. I call them the three totemic tales of the storytelling revival: the tale of the restoried community, the tale of the restoried individual, and the tale of the restoried cosmos.

I will treat the archetype of the storyteller according to James Hillman's model, not as a transcendent category but as a dynamic process. I do not attempt to claim a mystical priority to the role of the storyteller, except, perhaps, by reflection in the rhetorical moves made by its partisans. I will simply examine some of the numinous imagery surrounding the word and the role, before and during the revival. As we listen for the metaphoric richness and emotional necessity of the imagery, the archetypal quality of the role emerges.

Why "archetypal" rather than something more neutral and "objective?" Because the artists who made up the core of the storytelling revival were motivated not primarily by an intellectual analysis or an artistic program but by moments of aesthetic arrest—"Aha!" experiences—which crowned long periods of searching. It was from such moments that the defining fervor of the revival grew—and eventually its artistic programs as well. It was an idealistic movement and remains so at its deepest well-springs. It consistently invokes a revival dialectic—basing itself on artistic and communal ideals located in an imagined past to heal a present brokenness and awaken an ideal future. The storyteller is the mediating image of restored wholeness, a prism of heightened presence through which these idylls of past and future can shine, clarifying the social matrix for at least the duration of the performance event.

In that sense, it is also a pragmatic movement. It seizes on a practice that seems to do an urgent artistic work: to transport the audience and performer and to connect them in a powerful and significant way. The movement seeks to invest that performance practice with the force of desire and, out of that conjunction of practice and desire, to make Renaissance magic: to turn the leaden spirit of the world to gold.

Within the archetype of the storyteller is an intrinsic sense of wholeness—what Jerome Bruner has called a "narrative mode of knowing" (xiii)—in which opposites coexist and paradox is contained and illuminated. Even such apparently simple traditional tales as the Br'er Rabbit stories carry this subversive and healing potential. In her book *Woman, Native, Other,* the feminist scholar Trinh T. Minh-ha can find no more powerful image of an alternative, feminine mode of knowing than that of the storyteller who weaves self and other into a web of identity: "An oracle and a bringer of joy, the storyteller is the living memory of her people. She composes on life but she does not lie, for composing is not imagining, fancying or inventing. When asked, 'What is oral tradition?' an African 'traditionalist' . . . would most likely be nonplussed. As A. Hampate Ba remarks, [s/he] might reply, after a lengthy silence, 'It is total knowledge'" (125–26).

Benjamin invoked "The Storyteller" in his 1936 essay, ostensibly in appreciation of the nineteenth-century Russian writer Nicolai Leskov. But what the essay most pointedly does is use the archetype of the storyteller to reveal the deep social alienation of the bourgeois intellectual of Benjamin's time. That time and place, Weimar Germany, shows certain social and economic parallels with post-Vietnam, post–oil embargo America. His analysis provides a primer on the kind of sensibility that, forty years later, broke out in the passion of the storytelling revival.

"Familiar though his name might be to us," Benjamin writes, "the storyteller in his living immediacy is by no means a present force. He has already become something remote from us and something that is getting even more distant." He continues, "The art of storytelling is coming to an end. Less and less frequently do we encounter people with the ability to tell a tale properly. More and more often there is embarrassment all around when the wish to hear a story is expressed. It is as if something that seemed inalienable to us, the securest among our possessions, were taken from us: the ability to exchange experiences" (83).

Benjamin's first flood of perceptive response to this loss so resonates with the Vietnam generation in whom the storytelling revival took hold that it deserves to be quoted at length:

One reason for this phenomenon is obvious: experience has fallen in value. And it looks as if it is continuing to fall into bottomlessness. Every glance at a newspaper demonstrates that it has reached a new low, that our picture, not only of the external world but of the moral world as well, overnight has undergone changes which were never thought possible. With the [First] World War a process began to become apparent which has not halted since then. Was it not noticeable at the end of the war that men returned from the battlefield grown silent—not richer, but poorer in communicable experience? What ten years later was poured out in the flood of war books was anything but experience which goes from mouth to mouth. And there was nothing remarkable about that. For never has experience been contradicted more thoroughly than strategic experience by tactical warfare, economic experience by inflation, bodily experience by mechanical warfare, moral experience by those in power. A generation that had gone to school on a horse-drawn streetcar now stood under the open sky in a countryside in which nothing remained unchanged but the clouds, and beneath those clouds, in a field of force of destructive torrents and explosions, was the tiny, fragile human body. (83–84)

What Benjamin is describing is a new level of alienation from subjective human experience fostered by the rapidly accelerating technologizing of culture. In the culture of warfare, this alienation reached a new intensity in each successive war, with poison gas and machine-guns giving way to carpet bombing and napalm, the A-bomb giving way to the H-bomb, the Holocaust giving way to strategic planning for winnable nuclear war. Each new development spread its fallout into the realm of language, with the "war to end wars" giving way to the abominations of the "final solution" and then to the chilling inanities of "pacification," "Vietnamization," and "civil defense." By the 1960s, the expanding culture of telecommunications made the horror of it, and the moral bankruptcy of its techno-speaking promoters, available for everyday consumption in the comfort of one's own home. In reaction, the youth culture initiated a furious carnivalesque rebellion. The search for alternative images of identity and authenticity led society through restless conflations of exotic arts, religions, sexual behaviors, grooming and costuming, politics, diet, and livelihoods. Eventually, for some, it led to the unifying, simplifying archetype of the storyteller.

One can only imagine Benjamin's response to the culture of television. No technological extension of culture more alienates people from their local traditions, by setting up a constant, cacophonous competitor on the very hearth to hawk the homogenizing cornucopia of consumerism. No cultural agency more effectively captures entire households and communities, shaming dialect variation, displacing customs of visitation, sundering generations through imposed obsolescence of experience, and silencing intergenerational talk, imaginative play, and storytelling. This was the symbolic dragon of modernity that the storytelling movement proclaimed itself ready to slay and did, within the closed frame of its own mythos.

With the eye of a folklorist no less than a literary historian and critic, Benjamin formulates his storytelling archetypes to show how the entire species is endangered by the productive forces of modernity. The terms of his portrait anticipate the structure of the storytelling revival movement to come:

> People imagine the storyteller as someone who has come from afar. But they enjoy no less listening to the man who has stayed at home, making an honest living, and who knows the local tales and traditions. If one wants to picture these two groups through their archaic representatives, one is embodied in the resident tiller of the soil, and the other in the trading seaman. Indeed, each sphere of life has, as it were, produced its own tribe of storytellers. . . . With these tribes, however, as stated above, it is only a matter of basic types. The actual extension of the realm of storytelling in its full historical breadth is inconceivable without the most intimate interpenetration of these two archaic types. Such an interpenetration was achieved particularly by the Middle Ages in their trade structure. The resident master craftsman and the travelling journeyman worked together in the same rooms; and every master had been a travel-

ling journeyman before he settled down in his home town or somewhere else. If peasants and seamen were past masters of storytelling, the artisan class was its university. In it was combined the lore of faraway places, such as a much-travelled man brings home, with the lore of the past, as it best reveals itself to natives of a place. (84–85)

Benjamin's account echoes through the contemporary world of story-telling festivals, local guilds, and traveling free-lance performers. Local and regional storytelling festivals are usually divided between a small number of touring "national" tellers, who come from afar and are advertised and compensated accordingly, and a motley crew of enthusiastic semiprofes-sionals and local or regional journeyfolk. Even at a "national" festival like the one at Jonesborough, where all the tellers are expected to have reached a certain official status, the roster can be divided between those who iden-tify themselves with a place and a particular set of local traditions and those cosmopolitan storytellers whose appeal is in their journeying through the breadth of world folklore, conscientiously gathering strands of spiritual, ethical, or political meaning to resonate with the needs of their cosmopol-itan audience. Ray Hicks, the North Carolina mountain farmer and Jack-tale teller, would be a supreme representative of this first type; Laura Simms, who was artistic director of the National Storytelling Festival from 1983 to 1985, epitomizes the second type. The festival circuit as a whole is the uni-versity of contemporary storytelling, much as the medieval guilds were in Benjamin's imagining of the Middle Ages. On this circuit, once again, the interpenetration of these twinned storytelling archetypes is maintained, as storytellers from Appalachia or the cornfields of Illinois become bearers of news from distant places and outwardly mobile professional librarians are impregnated with a passion for oral history.

Benjamin next notes the storyteller's ability to weave the immediate and long-range concerns of the audience into the web of the story: "An orientation toward practical interests is characteristic of many born storytellers. . . . All this points to the nature of every real story. It contains, openly or covertly, something useful. The usefulness may, in one case, consist in a moral; in another, in some practical advice; in a third, in a proverb or maxim. In every case the storyteller is a man who has counsel for his readers" (86). This leads him to a charge against his own culture that also rings through the discourse of later revivalists:

But if today "having counsel" is beginning to have an old-fashioned ring, this is because the communicability of experience is decreasing. In consequence, we have no counsel, either for ourselves or for others. After all, counsel is less an answer to a question than a proposal concerning the continuation of a story which is just unfolding. To seek this counsel one would first have to be able to tell the story. . . . Counsel woven into the fabric of real life is wisdom. The art of storytelling is reaching its end because the epic side of truth, wisdom, is dying out. (86–87)

Benjamin presages an important theme in the storytelling revival—that of storytelling as an essential mode for apprehending the human journey. Whether it be represented symbolically in fairy tales or naturalistically in personal narratives, the quest for meaning expressed in the revival of storytelling is equally a quest for communicable wisdom. It creates a format for small and large gestures of faith that our stories will continue and can be effectively shared. In that, it fulfills for the congregants gathered under its tents some (though by no means all) of the crucial functions of a church.

The archetype of the storyteller is, in its essence, the vision of one who seeks and finds meaning in life, who brings to the chaos of experience the order, connectedness, and redemptive grace of art. This definition could apply to narrative artists in any genre. What sets the storyteller apart are the qualities of relationship and immediacy. The archetypal image of the storyteller is one of relationship, teller-to-listener and teller-to-tribe. Benjamin contrasts this with the alienation represented by the novelist—which reached an extreme in the works of Franz Kafka, Benjamin's greatest influence: "To write a novel means to carry the incommensurable to extremes in the representation of human life. In the midst of life's fullness, and through the representation of this fullness, the novel gives evidence of the profound perplexity of the living" (87).

The resurgence of storytelling represented for its votaries an affirmation of the qualities of connectedness, counsel, and community, in the face of a social reality of profound perplexity. In that sense, it perhaps represented a radical withdrawal from life's intractable and alien "fullness" into an ideal, simplified world of traditional images and narrative forms. As a person afflicted with fever withdraws from the world into a darkened room to rest, dream, and heal, so the storytelling world of the seventies and eighties offered an asylum of simple immediacy in the midst of a media-vexed environment. Ron Evans's totemic tale "The Storyteller Knows Me" served this precise function—as a ritual rehearsal of a resilient oral tradition vanquishing a more complex, less satisfying contemporary reality.

Unlike less rigorous thinkers among the ranks of folk revivalists, Benjamin refutes the religion of nostalgia intellectually, even as one senses in him the emotional allure of its seductive backward glance: "This, however, is a process that has been going on for a long time. And nothing would be more fatuous than to want to see in it merely a 'symptom of decay,' let alone a 'modern' symptom. It is, rather, only a concomitant of the secular productive forces of history, a concomitant that has quite gradually removed narrative from the realm of living speech and at the same time is making it possible to see a new beauty in what is vanishing" (87).

In later chapters, I will consider some of the ways that "secular productive forces of history" also have their agency in contemporary expressions of the archetype of the storyteller. It would be as fatuous, though, to reduce the storytelling revival to an economically driven phenomenon as it would be to inflate it into a purely religious one. When most of the seminal figures of the storytelling revival began their work, there was little or no "storytelling world" to serve as an economic and emotional support network. As Rose Abernethy and Richard Alvey both show, storytelling had been institutionalized in libraries, schools, and recreation centers as a valuable adjunct to the socializing business of these centers. There had been important figures in the earlier years of the century who had advanced the cause of storytelling beyond those institutional boundaries. These included Marie Shedlock, Richard Wyche (founder of the National Story League), and Ruth Sawyer, whose *The Way of the Storyteller* painted a numinous image of the storyteller archetype that became an important source for later revivalists. But in the wake of those significant careers, storytelling tended to recede into the dedicated but unglamorous institutional care of custodians of the printed word.

Free-lance performers in the seventies seized on oral traditions as a potential source of resistance and transformation amid the dominant currents of culture. Their experience was that they were following a joyful but marginalized passion, very much at their own risk. "I see the importance of the storytelling movement coming from the fact that a very profound understanding and need for story and storytelling in the culture was the impulse for beginning the movement," said Simms in a December 22, 1991, interview. "And it wasn't—we would have been off our rockers, basically, if we had started out and just made a card and gone out looking for a job."

But as an economic support network did begin to coalesce around NAPPS in the late seventies and eighties, newcomers were able to use these trailblazers as business, as much as spiritual, mentors. Robin Moore, a Pennsylvania storyteller, expressed it plainly: "The first people that I could really identify with as professional storytellers were the early NAPPS gang. And what happened to me when I went down there was, I saw people who were doing what I wanted to do, and making a living at it. Although at the time it was probably a pretty subsistence-level living that they were making. I was a journalist at the time, and it seemed to me to be a real alternative to the kind of life that I was living."

"The Storyteller Knows Me": The Storyteller as Heightened Presence

The archetype of the storyteller is an image of heightened presence—but a presence built on a paradox, since it arises from the gift of conferring absence. The storyteller's presence embodies a concentration of physical, emotional, mental, and unconscious faculties, through which an audience is transported away from the physical plane. Through concentration on what she brings to the moment, the storyteller lifts the listening group out of the moment into a realm of imaginative play, to a place called "once upon a time." This in itself is a sort of everyday magic, like dreaming, which also can carry a healing gift. In her keynote article for the first issue of the *Storytelling Journal*, "The Lamplighter: The Storyteller in the Modern World," Simms pictured the storyteller as physician/heroine, restoring light and harmony to a condition of cultural chaos: "Several years ago I opened the door to a classroom and saw two boys fighting. The teacher was enraged and the children were either frozen at their desks or shoving each other. The air was thick with anger. 'Who are you?' the teacher asked. 'I'm the storyteller,' I replied, feeling like a doctor arriving in an emergency room. I slowly walked to the front of the room and said, 'I came to tell you a story.' Even the fighters took their seats. After a moment, the fidgeting settled and all eyes opened wide with expectation."

As they enter into the storytelling experience, she writes, "Gradually, the air in the room changed. All the anger dissolved as confused emotions went to work in sympathy. . . . I could feel the children's measured, even breathing as the story's events unfolded. . . . As . . . the rhythm of my voice echoed the inevitability of the events soon to follow, the bond between the children and myself was complete. We relaxed into the rhythm of the words. We relaxed into our mutual visualizations" (8).

The storyteller/physician brings harmony to a group because she carries the gift of self-forgetting. In her presence, we surrender the broken crusts of myth over which we are daily struggling—whether they are myths of power, gratification, acceptance, hunger, or survival. We let her lift us to an altitude from which we can see a whole mythic pattern un-fold—sudden reversals, miraculous escapes, supernatural helpers, happy or tragic endings. Our psyches need stories the way our bodies need bread, to give form to our experience and to rebuild our sense of possibility. We give this power to the storyteller's soothing voice when the teacher's rage has no more reach, because of what the archetype promises in a deep re-cess of our imaginations. Somewhere, we all know the storyteller.

This experience of the harmonizing power of storytelling that Simms describes from the inside is something that impacts witnesses as well. It can have the power to produce a kind of conversion experience, in which a storytelling vocation reveals itself. In a *Yarnspinner* newsletter from 1983, Marnie Crowell wrote, "I was at a Scottish festival in Maine when I saw a young woman with a circle of thirty people spellbound at her feet. I lis-tened and watched this storyteller weave her magic net of words, I saw that she was giving those people a very special gift. I resolved that I would like to learn that gift" (Crowell 2).

As she watched the storyteller "weave her magic net of words," Crow-ell and the other listeners moved into the heightened state of concentra-tion that Fran Stallings calls "the storylistening trance." The told story, ideally, exists only in the moment of telling. Yet in the telling, the mo-ment itself is expanded to encompass the imaginary time-space of the narrative. In this altered state, the particulars of the moment are left be-hind, and the group imagination lifts to dwell in the world of the tale, shaped and animated by the storyteller's voice, gestures, breathing, eye contact, and energetic presence. Stallings shows that this storylistening trance closely resembles a mild form of hypnosis, with symptoms includ-ing "flattening of facial expression, staring, absence of blinking, and al-most complete immobility" ("Web of Silence" 6). The role of the storytell-er takes on a charged aura through this state of imaginative transport. Ramon Royal Ross wrote of it: "What we experience as we listen to true telling is not the suspending of disbelief. Rather it is an altered state of mind which teller and listeners share. It is as if we were participants in a different reality" (12).

The storyteller is clearly the medium of the story, the facilitator of its altered reality; but since in an ideal storytelling event the actual story takes place as much in the group imagination and responses as in the storytell-er's words, the entire listening group is the true storytelling medium. This idea is a central tenet of the storytelling revivalist's creed. The shared investment through the oral process in the moment of performance is the source of much of the communal rapture and resulting rhetorical fervor in the storytelling world. Early issues of the *National Storytelling Journal,* which was the magazine of the storytelling community in its period of crystallization, contain many and varied soundings of this theme. Laura Simms set a standard in the very first issue when she wrote:

> The beginning of the story itself creates an imaginative landscape through which we will travel. It also draws the listener into direct relationship with the storyteller. This reciprocity ensures the listeners that they are participants rather than observers. It is a dance where instead of holding hands, minds link in a reverie of silent images. . . . Storytelling is a living art which takes place in the present between people. It is not a solo performance. The narrative urges listeners out of self consciousness into the story. As the imaginative response becomes more and more vivid, the listeners participate in heightened awareness of the event, as in a ritual. ("The Lamplighter" 9)

In a subsequent issue, Donald Davis, an influential North Carolina teller who grew up in a family with a rich oral tradition and later became chair of the NAPPS board of directors, described in his own terms what the folklorist Robert Georges would call the "emergent quality" of storytelling events: "In order to operate inside the oral medium, hearers are absolutely required, and the storyteller must be in dialogue with them. In such a dialogue, a teller's perceptive skills go to work and guide the tellings so that for this audience, in this time and place, the story being told is uniquely theirs. When storytellers are fully in the oral medium as coparticipants with their hearers, they edit, correct, lengthen, shorten, change, and add—all in the process of the storytelling event" ("Inside the Oral Medium" 7). In the same issue of the *Storytelling Journal,* George Shannon, a librarian-storyteller from Wisconsin, wrote, "Unlike painting, writing, and music where the audience 'enters into a direct relationship not with the artist but with the work,' the boundaries between art, artist, and audience in storytelling are porous. Each time a folktale is told it is written anew. The performance is the composition and all involved become co-composers. There is no pure audience in storytelling. As soon as the child begins to listen he helps shape the story" ("Shared Treasures" 4).

Innumerable examples of this kind can be cited from the journals, newsletters, and interviews of storytelling proponents during this period, to the extent that we can mark an artistic ideology, a performance aesthetic, which served to unite and define the emergent storytelling community. This performance aesthetic is based on the idea of an oral traditional relationship between teller and listeners. A truly oral traditional relationship is based in turn on the idea of community. Participants in an oral traditional storytelling milieu generally know one another and the stories as well before the particular performance event begins. The teller's personal identity is assumed to be a strong thread in the web of community. Unlike oral interpretive convention, in which the performance identity is given over to an assumed authorial voice, or theatrical convention, in which it is given over to a character, an oral traditional storyteller and listeners assume an I-thou relationship. Within the bonds of that relationship, the storyteller assumes or constructs both a stable performing self and a community that accepts this self-construction. The presentation and embellishment of self in the act of performance then becomes a theater of opportunity in which those assumptions can be played with in mutually pleasurable ways.

Ideally, storytelling offers a means of negotiating communal mores and individual sensibilities within a framework of shared tradition. This is a negotiation we constantly attempt, even when there is no real possibility of two-way dialogue—for example, when we talk back to our television sets. But the intimacy of the storytelling medium is conceived as a kind of returning to our communal senses.

A story that epitomizes that returning was brought to the storytelling circuit by the Canadian Chippewa storyteller Ron Evans at the 1982 National Storytelling Festival. It is the first of my three totemic tales of the storytelling revival—the tale of the restoried community. From Evans's anecdotal version, the story spread like wildfire around the festival circuit and was invoked over and over again as a miniature ritual enactment of the storytelling revival community itself.

A Western observer is visiting a small village in Africa, where electricity has just been connected, and he witnesses the arrival of the first community television set. "And *nothing* went on in that village for about two weeks, except the whole tribe glued in front of the TV set. And then they got sick of it, and never watched it anymore." The puzzled westerner asks the village headman why the TV has fallen out of favor. The headman replies, "Oh, we don't need it. We have the storyteller." Whereupon the westerner asks, "Well, don't you think the television set probably knows more stories than your storyteller?" The villager ponders the question for a moment and then looks at the westerner with an enormous smile. "Oh, yes," he says, "the television knows many stories. But the storyteller knows me."

The revival community of tellers and listeners saw themselves reflected in the ideal mirror of this tale as dwellers in a small, exotic village. They had been tempted for a spell by the seductions of media, worldliness, and esoteric knowledge, represented by the intruding television set; but they were brought back to their senses by the recollection of their true center of identity, represented by the storyteller. The storyteller's stories are fewer but deeper, because they are mediated, not by the false objectivity and mechanical novelty of television but by the moral and psychological relatedness of traditional form and by the warmth of the storyteller's presence.

The totemic tale itself provides a medium of transformation for its tellers and audiences. As identification shifts from the point of view of the Western visitor to the point of view of the villager, who has the victorious last word, so the shift is vicariously accomplished from the jaded objectivity of the modern cosmopolite to the restoried subjectivity of the revivalist.

The oral traditional model of storytelling performance came to ascendancy in revival discourse out of a conjunction of empirical experience and desire. Experience, whether consciously sought or serendipitously found, confirmed an ingrown longing for a form of expression that could evoke precisely this form of experience. It was akin to the experience achieved through the accoutrements of 1960s revitalization phenomena—psychedelic drugs, rock 'n' roll festivals, mass protest marches, Eastern religion, to name a few—only without certain unwelcome side effects, like schizophrenia, deafness, tear gas attack, or familial stigma. The experience was given many names—among the most common were "oneness," "connectedness," "community," "healing," and "magic."

Yet it should be noted that this ideology of performance—the rhetorical embrace of oral tradition as a foundation of revival practice—tends to mask an actual divide among contemporary storytelling performers, between those who are truly in a cocreative, oral traditional relationship with the audience and those whose performances are rooted in fixed, memorized, and recited texts. These oral interpretive performers come mainly from literary, theatrical, or library backgrounds and are often quite skilled. Many have prominent roles in revival performance events and in such storytelling revival organizations as NSA. To identify wholeheartedly with the revival ethos, they have had to adopt, or in some way come to terms with, an oral traditional performer-audience relationship. The Seattle-based teller Pleasant DeSpain confronted the problem early in his career:

> I came from my own background at the beginning; it was somewhat of a disaster. Where, for the first six months, I kept reverting back to the kinds of stories and poems that I had learned in Oral Interpretation experiences.
> And one night in a coffee house that I had been invited to, I had a hat sitting in the corner for donations, I had all of my material ready, and I got into the middle of the program and I just decided to—I had memorized a lot of things in the beginning—I just told a story that I knew very well, but I told it *spontaneously*. And got such a response, I realized, this is how one—I learned just through a lot of mistakes—this is how you communicate effectively through story.

Carol Birch is an example of a powerful teller who, in the course of moving from the library world to the world of revival storytelling, has had to wrestle with the theory and practice of oral traditional versus oral interpretive performance. What she has discovered is that her own subjectivity is her most powerful tool in preserving a dialogic relationship with listeners, even when she is performing a text-based piece. In this interview excerpt, she discusses how her practice evolved out of her early library school training:

> I think [I was] trained in recitation—not in storytelling. It's a form of storytelling, but it's not *telling*. Because, I always liked literary tales. And people always said, "You can be more free with folktales, but you have to tell literary tales word for word." And I did. . . . But what I did at the beginning, that has taken me now twenty-one years to articulate, and what I can see that is different between what I did and what my friends in that class did along the way, is, when I'm telling a story, I think people know that *I'm the Narrator*. They have somebody warm that they can come over and sit next to. And even though I was trained in a kind of recitation way, I never tried to be a disembodied voice. See, when we're trained in literature, you know about an omniscient narrator. And, especially women get up, and they try to be an omniscient narrator, and they *leave their best stuff sitting in a chair*—which is their personality. And I think that even though I was trained in this much stricter recitation style, I still had some of my fire and warmth up there visible.

Birch told me that her most significant moment of discovering the power of her own performing subjectivity came during her first performance at the National Storytelling Festival in Jonesborough in 1983. It was on the evening she had to follow the late, legendary, hyperbolic, guitar-picking teller Gamble Rogers onto a festival stage. She said that stepping into the atmosphere of delirious audience expectation that Gamble's performance had created inspired her to be herself in a way she never had before in more than a decade of library-based storytelling. She found herself spontaneously offering a series of short, humorous anecdotes about her personal life before launching into one of her repertory tales. The experience drew her further out of the "objective," book-centered world of library storytelling and deeper into the world of the revival, where creating the illusion, at least, that "the storyteller knows me" depends on the storyteller's ability to let the audience know her.

If oral tradition tends to dominate the aesthetic discourse of revival events and organizations, even when performance practices diverge, an explanation can be found in the mythos of the revival itself. In the revival dialectic, an imagined past and ideal future are summoned to the aid of the storyteller's passion for a restored present. This formula expresses the crying need for restored community that erupted simultaneously into a molten cultural landscape of intentional communities and encounter weekends. But the ideology of oral tradition also resonates with the new communicative contexts in which the revival performs itself—coffee-houses, festivals, support groups, the street, even television and radio—where the performance prism of the book has lost its official cultural status. In these settings, there is a need to reach for a freer, less fixed, more genuinely emergent relationship between performer, community, and cultural imagination.

"The Man Who Had No Story": Vocational Narratives of Contemporary Tellers

"The Man Who Had No Story," an Irish folktale that in an oblique way was the basis of the film *The Crying Game,* is the second of the three totemic tales of the storytelling revival—the tale of the restoried individual. There were 131 versions of the story in the archives of the Irish Folklore Commission at the time of Sean O'Sullivan's collection *Folktales of Ireland* (182–84, 274), but there have probably been at least that many variants on the storytelling revival circuit. Most have hewn closely to O'Sullivan's or other widely accessible versions. But they have begun to be localized as well: two versions heard at the 1992 National Storytelling Festival were transposed, one to Great Barrington, Massachusetts (Spelman), and the second to a suburban elementary school where a visiting storyteller is conducting a residency (Harley).

Wherever the story takes place, its outline is the same: a person journeying in an unfamiliar neighborhood, who at the outset has no notion of him- or herself as a storyteller, is unexpectedly challenged to tell a story. Terrified, he refuses and is summarily sent away. All at once, he finds himself in the midst of outlandish, supernatural adventures, which transform his sense of himself and of his world. When he returns, he pours out the story of his journey and is told that now he has a story to tell—that now he has become a storyteller.

"The Man Who Had No Story" is a parable of revitalization in the life of an individual. In its humorous, indirect way, it tells the archetypal story of a vocational awakening—the transformation of an ordinary spirit into one alight with its own unique inheritance. Each time the tale is told, it provides for audience and teller an unobtrusive affirmation of the storyteller's significance to culture in general, as well as an indirect confession of the particular teller's faith in her own gift.

The contemporary storyteller's journey from well-worn modern career track into the otherworld of an obscure performing art, especially at the outset of the storytelling revival, could be as fraught with wonder and terror as an Irish countryman's abduction into Faery. Like "The Man Who Had No Story," the vocational narratives included below and many similar tales collected in my interviews demonstrate the pattern of a revitalization movement expressing itself through individual biography. Anthony F. C. Wallace's steady state (phase one) is represented in the storytellers' accounts by early achievement according to fixed cultural standards. A period of individual stress (phase two) leads to a crisis point in which the future tellers renounce those professional expectations, whether pointing toward careers in the ministry, academia, libraries, or an established art form. This is followed in each case by a period of cultural distortion (phase three), in which the tellers live at odds with cultural norms while searching for a more satisfying vehicle of personal expression. An encounter with the archetype of the storyteller initiates a movement of personal revitalization (phase four), which in due course joins them together in the social movement called the storytelling revival and leads to a new steady state (phase five) of achievement within an expanded cultural model.

The storytelling revival is linked on all sides with other, deeper currents of revitalization in the culture. In each of these individual cases, for example, the encounter with storytelling is linked to a concurrent discovery of a new, more fluid, less dogmatic religious tradition. Brother Blue is content to call his simply "Storytelling"—though he makes it clear that this is a conflation for him of many strands of spiritual searching:

> Storytelling is a kind of religion. For me. But it doesn't have dogma. We're past the dogma. The exclusive thing. It includes. There are stories where everything is conflated. Time is conflated. You're in the Presence of God. So Storytelling is the religion past all dogma—it's the religion which *holds* religions. A storyteller will tell a story from the Buddhist tradition, from the Christian, from the Jewish, from Krishna, because *it's a religion.* It's the religion which holds all the religions. Say I'm talking to a Buddhist—well, I'll just go in that direction. Say I'm talking to somebody from India—Krishna, great. Native American, I'll go from there. 'Cause, man, a Storyteller, his mind, his heart is so capacious, man, he'll tell a story to a dog! He'll tell it to a little kid. Wherever the Loving Heart is there. The only thing is the Singing Heart, man, you listen to that Singing Heart.

Brother Blue

Brother Blue lives and speaks from amidst the turbulence of a mythologized existence. The bare facts of his life are not easy to discover from an interview, for they emerge already deeply embedded in the storying process—the weaving of experience into meaning. His adopted name, for example, is a tiny tone poem, a distillation of his proud yet ambivalent sense of ethnic heritage, his longing for a transcendent state of spontaneous communitas, and his fantastical drive for self-invention. In our interview he described the evolution of his name:

> When I was a little boy, the name Hugh was not a popular name among black, poor kids. You have to have names like Bubba, you know, or Bob . . . but Hugh is a funny name, and I didn't even like it. It wasn't me, you know. So they'd play with my name; they'd play games with your name, call you everything but Blue in a way. Well one day somebody said "Blue."
>   I said, "Well, I kind of like Blue!" It kind of shouts!
>   And I discovered I had a cousin, also named Hugh, and everybody called him Blue. And when I got to be a man, I went to visit this guy, this cousin of mine, in New York. And I liked this guy, I said, "He's so real." And everybody called him Blue; his name was Hugh, but they called him Blue. And I said, "Hey, I'm gonna be Blue! That's the name I want!"
>   So when I was in Pittsfield, Massachusetts, I happened to notice that whenever the sky was very *blue* . . . something would happen that was

like a miracle. So I got myself a blue beret. And I said, "This blue beret is the emblem of that blue day that comes to me."

So when I started going to jails, I'd wear my blue beret, and I'd wear blue, and I'd say, "Listen. You can call me Blue. That's my street name, my nitty-gritty name. I'm gonna bring you the blue sky past all the rain. Wherever you are, I'm going to give you the blue sky and that blue sky is smiling on you, and I'm wearing this blue sky on my head, you know."

And they said, "Man, he's a Good Brother. That's Brother Blue."

And I said, "That's me."

You know what? That *is* my name. My wife, everybody calls me Brother Blue, except—my mother's gone now—my mother. . . .

I say to people, "You ought to find *your* Soul Name, the name you had before you were Born, that you heard on a Horn, in Heaven. Get your name. Your name is the clothes you wear."

Blue neither denies nor hides his family name, but his stronger identification with the "street name" shows a self in a state of abandon to the transpersonal side of his being—his ruling passion to merge with the archetype.

Blue has told stories, in his idiosyncratic, improvisatory, chanted style, on the streets of cities around the country, particularly his hometown of Cambridge, Massachusetts, since the late sixties. There was no "storytelling movement" as such when he began. Blue, along with a few others like him who discovered storytelling on their own and wielded it as a unifying image of their own life path, was a storytelling movement unto himself. That was the guise in which I first encountered him in 1976, telling his stories on Fisherman's Wharf in San Francisco. With neither an introduction nor any kind of generic frame to place him in, I found him as wondrous and strange as some shining, singing bird from a Grimm brothers' tale.

About the evolution of his style, Brother Blue told me:

I'm the only itinerant storyteller I know that works the streets of the world. . . . See, when you're tellin' stories in Harvard Square and the places I go, there may be a magician out there, or a juggler, or a person swallowing fire. A lot of my style, I call it my street style, I call it Street Poetry—you have to lift it to a certain level. Because the people who are passing by, why should they stop, see? You have to do something, you have to tell it with your body, with music, with voice, and so forth, so that it's a whole genre, a whole style that came out of the street.

The street, like everything else in Blue's world, is a mythic site, an image that concentrates whole realms of experience. Blue came of age during the black freedom movement of the sixties, and his language has been influenced by the racial politics and consciousness of that time. "The street," then, draws its first set of meanings from African American urban folk dialect, where it signifies the struggle to survive in a concrete jungle. It is an image of wisdom wrested from an inherently hostile environment. But Blue is also storying his own richly idiosyncratic experience, as an African American religious intellectual apparently singled out for special privileges in a largely white educational milieu, who nonetheless remains strongly committed to the people and places in his background. The street, for him, is a place where these often conflicted streams of experience come together, a river of humanity from which he draws his stories and his style and into which he pours back his performances.

The archetype of the storyteller, too, is for Blue a transcendent, unifying image, through which he can incarnate all of his gifts, his graces, and his griefs. In our telephone interview of January 4, 1992, his response to the question, "How did you become a storyteller?" was a two-hour autobiographical narrative of prodigious drama, pathos, and eventual triumph. I never got a chance to ask my second standard question, about NAPPS and other associations—Blue was away after the first one, not to be headed. His wife, Ruth, was also on the phone and would occasionally interject, "Blue, would you let the man ask you a question?" He might hush for a moment, then, but jump in again over my first words—"And another thing. . . ."

Clearly the vocational drama of his emergence as a storyteller was a source of compelling personal mythology for him still. He began:

Well now, as I start telling you this, the things I have to say, and the way I say them will sound, to someone who's not used to this, sound extravagant, you know. But I think of storytelling as a sacred art. It's a calling. Like it's into the priesthood. The kind of storytelling that I'm calling "The Sacred Art of Storytelling." It's like being called into the priesthood, or to become a rabbi, or, something like that, you know, it's *total Self.* And the kind of storytelling that I pray to do, that I aspire to is . . . *life commitment,* that's what it is.

You wonder how I got into storytelling. Well, look. It's kind of mysterious. It's like, do you know any rabbis or priests or ministers, or any of that calling, a nun, or a pastor or something? It's a calling to the Heart, to the Soul. It's like asking Mother Teresa, "Why do you do what you do?" Something called to my heart from the time I was a little boy.

45

Blue told of his childhood experiences of oral performance—thunder-
ous sermons at the local black church, a saintly old Sunday schoolteacher named Mr. Washington who retold Bible stories so that even Blue's
mentally handicapped brother could understand, his father's eccentric
prayers around the dinner table, and his nightly bedtime stories. He also
spoke of his image of Jesus Christ as a storyteller, whose stories moved past
barriers of race, caste, and intellect and spoke directly "to the Heart." The
paradigm of the sacred storyteller was reinforced for him in the pervasive
religious performances of his youth and was magnified by his own dispo-
sition toward a life of performative service.

He decided to go into the ministry. Through his own natural gifts and
the help of the G.I. bill, he was able to go to Harvard and then to seminary
at Yale, apparently on his way to a successful career in a mainline Protestant church. Up to this point, his story conforms to phase one of Wallace's
revitalization schema: achievement according to preset cultural norms.
While at seminary, however, he had a crisis of faith:

> I was assistant to a pastor there, who was in a black area with very poor
> people, the poorest of the poor, really. And every now and then, he
> would have me do a sermon. . . .
> And so what happened, see, this was very important.
> The preacher was out of town one weekend, and somebody had to do a
> funeral sermon, and he said, "I want you to preach the funeral sermon."
> This is very important.
> So I got up, and—I was just a young guy—to preach this funeral ser-
> mon for some people I hardly knew; I didn't know them, really, at all.
> And I didn't know that much about life, you know. And this sermon
> was for someone who had lived a long time, had died, and all his fami-
> ly was there, people weeping. And I was to tell a sermon, or do some-
> thing there, to get them through this grief, this sadness, you know.
> And as I was telling stories and doing my thing, it just came out of me.
> I said something like, "I—There is a mystery here."
> "I can't say with absolute conviction all these consoling things," you
> know like—you know what's involved in theology, the idea that—one
> goes to Heaven, the whole theological thing; I suddenly realized that,
> um, I didn't have that, I just knew I had some stories, which were com-
> forting—but I wasn't *firm* in what these people were believing and want-
> ing to hear. Before this great thing called Death and the Mysteries of Life
> I had no—it was a Mystery, except I knew there was a Power . . . we were
> supposed to love one another. . . .
> But I got through the sermon. And I refused to take any fee, by the

way. And then also I realized that I didn't have that conviction that there's only one way to God, this is the only way to Salvation or Hell, all that stuff . . . the whole thing.

So the next day I got up in church and I said to the people, "Oh-h, I don't think I'm supposed to be a minister here."

I says, "I'm a Story——."

And then I said, "All I do is tell these stories."

"But I, before the Great Mysteries, am left, uh, I don't know what to say." I said, "I should not be a minister. I just have these stories. That's all. But I want to do it, I love to do it, and I love you people. But. . . ."

And so I told the preacher, "I probably shouldn't do this." I said, "I just have these stories to tell, and a certain way I want to live."

So when I left they said, oh, they called me to the Dean's office, said, "Oh, you could be one of the great preachers of the time, of all time, you have this gift, and you should—"

I said, "Look, I can't. It's called Integrity." I said, "I just have these stories."

And when I left there I felt, oh, my heart broke. Because I loved talking to people in their time of joy and need. I wanted to be that. I wanted to do that.

I didn't know at the time, "Look, I'm a Storyteller; it's a Sacred Art."

Blue emphasizes and reemphasizes the centrality of this crisis in his personal myth, even to the point of trying to inappropriately telegraph its resolution, then correcting himself ("I said, 'I'm a story——.'"). The crisis corresponds to phase two in Wallace's revitalization scheme. Dissatisfaction with the formulaic tenets offered by established religious institutions leads to his renunciation of expected goals and achievements. Blue continued with graduate school, but he had to deal with recurring bouts of inner conflict between the secular and sacred sides of his expressive life and the feeling that he never fit within traditional disciplinary boundaries. This period corresponds to phase three of Wallace's scheme, the "period of cultural distortion":

I came back to Harvard Graduate School and Yale Graduate School. I went through both divinity schools, I finished Yale School of Drama, all the time trying to find my calling: "What's my Reason for Being on Earth?" Like finding your Vocation, capital letters?

I got my master's at Yale Drama School. Playwriting came easy. I would just write; but writing these plays, I realized I was again trying to touch the heart, I mean I was trying to, in a way . . . it was like a Sacred art, except that—and I did some acting, directing, the writing—except that I

knew there was something between me . . . You see, in the theater you
have to have actors, director, costumes, what not. And that was okay, except I said, "This is okay, but my Soul is not realized." You follow me?
You see, it's the story of a guy working his way towards storytelling.

He found that when he told friends the plots and acted out the dialogue
himself from the plays that he was writing, it was a more satisfying aesthetic experience than when he submitted his work to the impersonal
industry of Western theater. But, he said, he "still hadn't put it together."
He went back to Harvard Divinity School to work on a Ph.D.: "And when
I came to Harvard Divinity School I was like on fire. I'd think to myself,
'Oh, how could I put together the theater—follow where I'm going?—the
theater, preaching?' I still hadn't thought of storytelling as a way of life."
   While at Harvard, he had his first experience of pure storytelling, which
he renders as an epiphany:

> Now the idea of storytelling still hadn't come to me yet. But strange
> thing, when I came to Harvard, they said, "We want you to do some-
> thing for Sam Miller." He was the dean of the Harvard Divinity School. A
> very wonderful man, he was a minister, who was also a poet, a storytell-
> er, an artist. . . . And they asked me to do something for him: a surprise
> birthday party, for Christmas.
>   I decided . . . I would tell a story for him. I thought to myself, "Gee,
> why don't I tell a story, which he'll like so much, it'll touch his beautiful
> heart." Now he was a storyteller and a poet.
>   Now this is a significant moment in my life, I think. I got up, among
> these theologians and all these scholars. I did a story for Sam Miller. It
> was from my heart. And it was the first time in my life that I had gotten
> up in a situation where, people I'd read about, Harvey Cox was there, all
> these people with big names, you know, Niebuhr, all these. And schol-
> ars. And I got up. And I told a story from my heart.
>   And I danced, and I sang. And he got up, when I got through; and his
> eyes were moist. He said, "Oh," he said, "On the simplest level . . . it's the
> story of the Incarnation." (I was doing a version of *Beauty and the Beast,*
> that's what I was doing. My own version. For him, for he was such a
> beautiful man.) And that . . . just took me home. . . .

For those encountering the archetype of the storyteller in themselves
for the first time in the act of performance, any story told becomes, in a
special sense, the story of the Incarnation. It is the story itself that incar-
nates in the body of the novice. Through voice and gestures, patterned
words and the images released by them, the storyteller weaves a mysteri-

ously single body out of the listening group. The resultant sense of height-ened presence and of heightened relationship with a group is a profound-ly revitalizing experience. It is "Total Self," and yet, at its highest, it is also a self-forgetting, an abandonment to the presence of the story—symbol-ized by the disappearance of Hugh Morgan Hill into Brother Blue. In ded-icating his life to exploring this form of practical magic, Blue enters a phase of self-transcendence that will lead him to a new personal and ar-tistic integration. Under the sign of the storyteller, in its fusion of imagi-nation, emotion, sensation, thought, and unconscious projection, he can reweave the torn threads of identity and desire in the ecstatic union of performance.

It is fitting that in Blue's own personal myth his reintegration began in the intellectual hothouse of the Harvard Divinity School of the late six-ties, with such figures as Harvey Cox, Reinhold Niebuhr, and Sam Miller in attendance as spiritual midwives. That school, which also produced Sam Keen (whose 1970 book, *To a Dancing God,* contained such theologi-cal provocations as the suggestion that "telling stories is functionally equivalent to a belief in God" [86]), laid an important part of the theoret-ical groundwork from which such performers as Ken Feit, Reuven Gold, Blue, and Ed Stivender drew support and inspiration. Perhaps it is most accurate to say that the theoretical writers were informing, while the sto-rytellers were performing, a current in the cultural psyche that played it-self out through many individuals, groups, and communities.

Laura Simms

Within the varied web of the storytelling revitalization movement, Simms is an eminent example of a vitalizer, in Wallace's special sense of the word as well as in the ordinary sense of having lent her own great personal vi-tality to the movement. Born of middle-class Jewish professionals in Brooklyn, New York, she has searched far and wide for living cultural models and meanings to import to her audiences and her students. She animates these models in the form of a panoramic repertoire of world folktales and linked personal anecdotes, charged by the intensity of her voice and gestures.

Simms is also a committed student of Tibetan Buddhism. Her sacred perspective, as shared openly in her teaching and communicated implic-itly in her performance, works to invest the role of the contemporary sto-ryteller with a metaphysical aura akin to that of a shaman or a guru. Like Blue, Simms also seems to conflate the spiritual path with her art. At the

1992 National Storytelling Festival, speaking to an audience of a thousand gathered to celebrate the twentieth annual event, Simms called storytelling "the most important spiritual movement in America today."

How does she arrive at this exalted view of a movement that, on the surface, resembles a number of revivalist artistic subcultures on the American scene? It seems that storytelling for her is the outward face of a revitalization movement in her own life, a movement of which her Buddhist disciplines form the core. In our December 22, 1991, interview, she described the relation between storytelling and reality in a way that reflects her esoteric training:

> I think for an initiated person, stories go way beyond psychological meaning into an experiential meaning in which opposites coexist. One has a very strong experience through the telling, which doesn't have that much to do with the content of the story; the content is one piece of it that explodes meaning for the listener. . . . The truth is, it is the way the mind works, it constantly—I mean that's the joke, is that we endlessly are creating stories, which are lies. And that's the work of the mind. And it is only through story that you can explode that. So the deeper level of story is definitely in the telling: in the mind to mind transmission of the story, which undoes conceptual thinking, and creates timelessness, in the moment.

As an "initiated person," she views her art and her meditation as part of the same outward and inward ministry of calling attention to the work of the mind in shaping the phenomenal world. Her telling of her own vocational awakening portrays a classic revitalization pattern, as it vividly conveys the spiritual anxiety and excitement of the time in which it arose. She skims over the early phases, her achievements in the mold of societal expectations, and her period of stress and renunciation:

> I had dropped out of graduate school—I was going to get an M.A./Ph.D. at University of Toronto in Medieval literature. I had put it aside for one year and had traveled throughout the Middle East and Europe, in the kind of vagabond way that one did when one was twenty, in the sixties—and now I was in graduate school, and whenever I tried to raise my hand, to ask a certain question, my professor just kind of demoted me, like this *girl* has a pretty foolish view. And I left and just decided that I didn't want to study other people's opinions of other people's opinions of literature.
>
> I was three days into graduate school. And I was scared, because everybody in my family was very professional. And I didn't know what to do.

And I was incredibly shy. And I was taking a walk with a woman who told me that she had been in the theater in Paris, and I was so impressed that anybody could just kind of *follow their heart.* So I dropped out of graduate school—twenty minutes later. And I surreptitiously came to New York.

She endured her period of cultural distortion, working as a waitress while taking courses in theater and children's imagination at the New School for Social Research, all under a cloud of familial stigma. Yet there was an ecstatic quality in her rebellious adherence to her own heart's path: "I remember leaving the New School that day, walking down the street sobbing. Because I understood that I was—I had dropped everything I knew and was going on some kind of quest." Simms auditioned for a play at LaMama and began to work in New York's burgeoning experimental theater scene:

And then I just followed every passion that I had. I took dance classes at Martha Graham, and I went to take jazz classes, jazz dance, and ballet. And I was so happy. Because I was just doing things I had always been too shy to do but loved my whole life, like dancing and singing. And then in the evenings I could read anthropology books.

And when I realized I had less and less money left in my savings— when I told my parents I had dropped out of school they just practically disowned me—so I was left really without any money. And I told the director I didn't think I could stay in the play, and she said, "Well, why don't you teach theater to children, you'd be great."

And I knew nothing about theater myself, really. But what I did know about was fairy tales, I grew up on them. So I just had this group of children, and I would bring in fairy tales, and incite them to write stories, and we would enact them.

A fateful chain of impulsive choices, opportunities, risks, and happenstance led her to an encounter with the archetype of the storyteller. She paints the scene in numinous tones, keenly aware that it initiated the next stage in her journey of personal revitalization:

And when we actually did our performance on April 15 in Central Park, it was a very sunny day. And this wonderful crowd of people gathered. These were the children of actors in New York, and they were great. And their show was much shorter than we had expected. So we decided to do it twice and have an intermission. And at the intermission they said, "Look. *You do something,* so we don't lose the audience."

And I did not know what to do, so I told a Russian fairy tale. I had heard this Russian fairy tale the day I dropped out of graduate school, and I went roaming through the library at University of Toronto. It turns out, I think, there was Alice Kane, giving a talk to librarians. And I don't remember anything else about the talk whatsoever; but that I actually sort of healed my anxiety by listening to this wonderful Russian fairy tale that my mother always told me.

So I just told this fairy tale. And I knew that the great experimental urge in theater at that time was to break down narrative so that you could experience formlessness and direct connection between audience and performer. And in the telling of the story, somehow I understood that this was it; that this was somehow akin to traditional theatrical ritual in culture. That the creating of this narrative form somehow created formlessness, and timelessness, and ritual space.

And I went back to LaMama, and I told people. Everybody thought I'd gone mad. Because everybody wanted to do away with form. And there I was in the most formal sense of form. And then, people that I had worked with in theater and with children thought that I had just lost my mind, because I wanted to do this seemingly ridiculous thing called stories. So I had no support system. Except my own passion for it. But I went on a quest. And it really started that day. Because somehow, I just decided that I would be a storyteller.

And the remarkable thing that happened that day that I think I've written about a lot, is that in the audience was the Baroness Dahlerup, who was an old woman at the time. And she's the one who had sat on Hans Christian Andersen's knee as a child. And she came up to me, and she said, "You are a storyteller." So she gave me the word. Because I had no word at that time. I was glad to have *something* to call myself. And she gave me a rose.

And everything in my life totally fell apart from there on. Year after year after year. Except for this incredible, consistent discovery that when I would tell stories—that space would exist between myself and the listener.

The most powerful encounters with the archetype of the storyteller are felt as a kind of overshadowing. Nothing Simms has seen, heard, or read has prepared her for the power she assumes as she stands within the aura created by the storytelling role in an interactive performance. In another sense, everything has helped prepare her; but all preparation remains potential prior to the activating experience of performance.

It is clear that the archetypal experience does not put an end to her cultural dysphoria. In some ways, it renders it still more acute. Her coworkers in the theater are unable to relate to her new enthusiasm; American culture of 1967 still has little place for a storytelling enthusiast outside of the library, the schoolroom, or the Sunday school. Yet there is now a sense that a corner has been turned and that whatever the chaos of her personal experience, from this moment on there will be a transpersonal connection to serve as a guiding and sustaining force.

In her storying of the event, Simms cherishes a number of apparent coincidences as destiny-markers, inwardly confirming her sense of initiation. One is the encounter with the storytelling librarian in Toronto on the day she dropped out of graduate school. The Russian fairy tale Alice Kane told that day serves as a vital link connecting a series of crucial phases of her life. Simms remembers hearing it as a child from her mother. The story is thus linked to her experience of receiving stories in the context of a direct, nurturing relationship. The story came to her again on the day she decided to drop out of graduate school. It "healed her anxiety" about leaving a setting where she would be studying "other people's opinions of other people's opinions of literature"—that is, stories bereft of that nurturing, relational context. In a crisis of public competence, the story comes to her aid again. It provides a vehicle through which she can integrate a nurturing past, a challenging present, and an intuited future.

Another apparent coincidence that takes on a magical aspect in the context of her narrative is the appearance after her performance of the Baroness Dahlerup. The baroness not only is royalty—like many a magical helper in fairy tales—but also represents a direct link to a lineage of storytellers extending back to the "immortal" Hans Christian Andersen. She gives Simms a name for her new path and a rose for a token, in the manner of a dharma-teacher confirming satori. In the structure of a wonder tale, this is the beginning of the return journey. Though there still may be trials, temptations, and hazards along the way, the possession of the redeeming token or treasure makes a successful outcome seem predestined.

Rafe Martin

One of the oldest arguments in folklore scholarship is the one between the historical-geographic method, which seeks to trace folktale motifs across cultures and times from a single hypothetical original (as represented by the works of Antti Aarne and Stith Thompson), and the theory of polygenesis, which asserts that motifs arise independently in widely separate times and places, according to deep-seated patterns in the human psyche (as in Campbell and Jung). If the contemporary awakening of the archetype of the storyteller can be taken as a motif in the life-stories of individuals, then my interviews clearly validate both sides. Later examples show the seminal influence of the National Storytelling Festival and of certain key storytellers who ventured forth from that spot to make converts to the art. Rafe Martin's story of his own vocational awakening, however, is intriguing when juxtaposed with Simms's. It demonstrates the independent emergence of the storytelling archetype for two people who traveled strikingly similar paths, though they never encountered each other until much later, when the pattern had already been confirmed.

Martin and Simms became acquainted in the eighties, when both were already accomplished professional storytellers. But in the sixties, they were both undergraduates at Harper College in Hamilton, New York. Both graduated with high or highest honors in English, and both went to graduate school at the University of Toronto—high achievers according to cultural norms. Both experienced mounting dissatisfaction with their paths and dropped out of the university, Simms after three days, Martin three hours short of attaining his degree. Both became students of Buddhism, Simms of the Tibetan school, Martin of Zen. Both had significant encounters with the archetype of the storyteller, and both found vocations as professional tellers. Yet they never met until Simms visited Martin's hometown of Rochester for a performance in the mid-eighties. When they began comparing notes, they discovered after the fact, as Martin says, "that it was like brother and sister, [we] went down many, many of the same roads."

Each came to the archetype of the storyteller out of an urgent quest for meaning, propelled by personal need and fueled by the zeitgeist. While Simms traces her movement from experimental theater into storytelling, Martin's journey shows the parallel movement from a literary-critical background. Both reveal the needs that were left unmet in their traditional university disciplines or the established literary and theatrical art worlds—needs eventually answered, at least in part, through the developing storytelling world.

Martin strongly feels the importance of storytelling to a spiritually functioning community. But he makes a clear distinction between his spiritual path, Zen Buddhism, and storytelling, which is his livelihood and his expression: "Something I thought was very interesting, that you expressed how many people have looked at NAPPS as a pilgrimage place. A spiritual connection. And that there's something almost spiritual about the NAPPS festival—going, and being there, among lots of different tellers. And I guess what I felt, that for me it wasn't that kind of connection, but a way of *expressing* connections that I had established, basically, through years and years of sitting practice. And training in a particular tradition."

Here is how these levels of self-discovery connect in Martin's vocational narrative. The pattern of personal and cultural revitalization will be familiar enough that the reader can trace its steps without interruption:

Twenty-five years ago, I graduated from college. And what I was majoring in was literary criticism. English literature and literary criticism. And a mythic approach—my major focus was *Moby Dick,* which had been my lifelong companion since sixth grade, which I'd read every year since sixth grade; and William Blake. And I went to the University of Toronto to work with Northrup Frye—still probably the world's foremost mythopoeic literary critic. So I went to the University of Toronto because of Frye; and also worked a bit with Marshall McLuhan while I was there. It was an interesting time. And there were a lot of draft dodgers—the war was on, '66 to '69 was when I was there.

And though I was doing quite well in graduate school, I wasn't happy. There were a lot of reasons not to be happy between '66 and '69. But part of it, in fact, was the sense that I didn't feel. . . . The closest we were coming to the power of what stories, literature itself, was about, was in Frye's work. But that was purely academic. And I felt that there was a power to stories, which had moved me my whole life, which was *why* I was in English literature, and literary criticism. . . . But . . . we didn't have a language to communicate about it. And we were jumping over some territory that I felt intuitively was absolutely crucial.

And one question that became real important for me was, *"Where are all these characters we're talking about?"* We talk about Hamlet—but there's just squiggles on paper in front of me. So the whole play, *Hamlet,* all the characters, all the meanings, are really taking place *in us.* They're not on the page. There's another dimension to the story, where its life is in fact *alive,* in the imagination.

And eventually, after—I think I had one two-hour in-class paper owing to get my master's—and I walked out. It was kind of like *The Loneliness of the Long Distance Runner,* if you remember that movie, in the 1960s. About this long-distance runner who is British, in prison. And he gets his freedom by running; he becomes this track star for the prison. And he's in this big race, and the warden and everybody's yelling, "Go on, go on, go on!" And he stops, like, two feet in front of the finish line. He won't cross it. He lets everybody else run across it. It's his only way of saying what he thought of the whole system. I won't say it was that intense. But I just kind of drifted out.

And then the next few years were quite confusing—where I was basically just *reading fairy tales*. And Rose and I were kind of living—eventually we moved back to Binghamton, to Harper, where a lot of our friends from around the country had dropped out, from different universities, and were living semicommunally, and had a house, and raised vegetables, and I did a lot of reading.

And in Toronto I'd begun, I'd read *The Three Pillars of Zen,* which I thought was an extraordinary book. Mythic, as well as quite direct. And we began to become very interested in the path of the Buddhist tradition. And Campbell's work actually had led me in that same direction. A lot of the very crucial stories in *Hero with a Thousand Faces* are stories of the Buddha's leaving home, and his enlightenment, and things like that. That had a very big effect on me, it just, like, stunned me. It somehow felt that these stories were extraordinarily direct, in speaking right to what I was experiencing in my life.

So eventually, we met some other people who were *sitting* at that time. Actually it was a guy from Timothy Leary's group at Millbrook, a very sweet character. He said, "Gee, you should really read *The Three Pillars of Zen.*" It was a very mythic period in our lives; we were just encountering lots of different people.

And so that's when we began sitting. And then when our son was born—let's see, he was about eight weeks old—we came up to Rochester to go to a workshop at the Zen Center here. And decided to stay. And we moved here, and just began practicing the traditional and formal practices of Japanese Zen. And in the process, began seeing myth and story functioning within a traditional community. Because what we were kind of re-creating, being here in a community of people—that is, not living at the Zen Center, but all in Rochester who had moved here from different parts of the country in order to practice—was restoring a kind of ceremonial, religious, sacred traditional vision. Where you are part of a community, in which a certain vision is in place. And so I began to discover how the stories were *not* just things on a page but functioned in the life of a community. And passed on information from generation to generation.

So eventually I was asked to—there's a little ceremony, or a little festival, every spring, called Vesak, which is in all the Buddhist countries; and it celebrates the Buddha's enlightenment, and birth, and the entrance into Nirvana, and it's basically a children's event. And I was asked to create a character that might, you know, be fun for kids; and do something with the tradition.

And the year before that, somebody had kind of goofingly created this character called "The Sleeping Sage." Which is like this hermit in the Himalayas, the kids have to scream at to wake up—he keeps falling asleep. And he tells them a story and then goes back to sleep for a year.

And so I said, "Okay, well I'll do that." And I discovered—I began reading the Jataka stories. So this must have been almost, geez, about eighteen years ago. And I thought, gee, some of those are really neat stories. I'd first seen some of them in *Hero with a Thousand Faces,* by Campbell. And I did a couple of those. And the kids loved it, and the parents loved it, and *I* loved it. I had a gray beard, and a Tibetan hat, and wearing kind of hermit-in-the-Himalayas kind of clothing; and it was just wild, there were lots of animal masks around, and costumes, and—it was fun! So I began doing that each year.

And in the meanwhile, I began to discover—I was reading aloud, Rose and I were reading aloud to Jacob, and then our daughter was born in '74—the real functioning of stories, which I'd missed in graduate school, was that they simply *lived*—that they be *put in human voice.* That they were not to be on a page. But they were to *live.*

And all the analysis that I was learning, and all the mythopoeic approaches, came down to, simply, if you paid attention and gave life to the story, all those things were going to *appear.* It was natural. You didn't have to make a big intellectual deal about it. If you were hearing the story. And every night we were reading aloud, fairy tales and traditional tales, to Jacob, and then lots of the great children's literature, and my favorite stuff in poetry. And it was *voice,* more and more and more, saying that this is the life of the story—something that I had not found in my work as a literary critic.

Martin's crisis highlights the question of where to locate the archetype of the storyteller. His process of reintegration highlights the positive answer that emerged for him and for other storytelling revivalists. For him, the living human voice contains the experience of the archetype, and the voice is most human and alive when it is listened to—not overheard but actively apprehended in the context of an immediate, personal relationship. The storyteller archetype is a guiding constellation in the personal and cultural imagination that constantly urges us toward relationship and community. It does so by giving voice to the personal and cultural past, the creative moment, and the hoped-for future, within the crucible of presence that is story performance.

Carol Birch and Doug Lipman

Similar accounts could be multiplied from the evidence of my interviews. I will conclude this selection with two more vocational narratives, chosen because they are framed by the political tension of the early years of the storytelling revival but also because they carry their archetypal encounters into the two most typical settings for storytelling revival activity: libraries and grade schools.

These elements, the political and the institutional, are deliberately and significantly counterposed. Schools and libraries were relatively neutral institutions—in need of creative infusion and paradigm change but providing an arena for young artists fresh from the turmoil of political, social, and spiritual identity crisis. Schools and libraries were and still are "societies of the weak" (in Victor Turner's anthropologically relative phrase), occupied and staffed primarily by women and the young. In the personal stories of revivalists, they served as places of what Erik Erikson calls "psychosocial moratorium" (McAdams, *Stories* 92–94, 313n). They represent settings in which transformational tensions could be diverted from the major institutional concentrations of power and alternative powers could be nurtured.

Carol Birch recalled:

I was in library school in 19 ... when were the Cambodian bombings? Maybe it was '71. 'Cause I got married the day after I graduated college. I went to Princeton and worked in a public library. And then I didn't get into library school right away; and then I got into library school, and it was shut down for the Cambodian bombing. You remember how all that stuff was—it sort of controlled our lives?

I was going to library school, and it was my last semester. And I decided I was going to take a course on storytelling *instead of* a course on how to organize government documents.

I was going to take the course on storytelling because I lived on a road called the Great Road in Princeton, and just off the Great Road, there was a new reformatory where my girlfriend was a nurse; and it was like brand new, it was just going to open when I graduated. It was for little boys from six to eight years old. And it was during all that upheaval. And I thought, as I was getting more and more involved in the upheaval, it was better trying to make a difference in the world by helping little boys than it was to help rich people at the Princeton Public Library reference desk find the name of a company where they could buy moccasins.

So I decided I would take a children's lit course and a storytelling course. And I came home, literally, from the second class, and I said to my husband, "The most wonderful thing has happened to me today: I have found out who I am!"

He said, "Who are you?"

I said, "I'm a storyteller."

He said, "What does that mean?"
I said, "I have no idea!"
"I just *know* that that's what I *am*."
It's a nice little epiphany story. I think that's the way it is inside for a lot of people—that once they have a *label* for it, there's just some sort of resonance, they just start vibrating inside like strings on a guitar or something.

Other librarian-storytellers in my interviews have had similar epiphanies but in eras not shadowed by this kind of pervasive social unrest. Augusta Baker, Anne Pellowski, and Ellin Greene, for example, came of age in the thirties or the fifties. Each was magnetized to storytelling by an encounter with a strong mentor and by the personal power and institutional security that the craft and career could offer. But storytellers in the seventies had an entirely different social ethos to frame and color their experiences and to redefine their career directions. The prevailing winds of spiritual and social dissent contributed to the movement's Early Christian aura of spontaneous communitas, which in turn helped stimulate the community-building reflexes detailed in chapter 5. But they also, paradoxically, helped stir the individualistic entrepreneurism of the free-lance performer.

In Birch's personal narrative, the phases of Wallace's revitalization scheme can be seen but in transposed order. Her revitalizing encounter with the archetype of the storyteller (phase four) took place near the end of an early phase of obedience to societal norms (marriage and professional accomplishment, phase one); soon afterward, she went through her crisis of renunciation (phase two), in which normative social ties fell away (a dissolving marriage and withdrawal from a conventional librarian career) and her period of cultural distortion (phase three). Attempting to live out her dream of free-lance storytelling in California, she endured poverty, loneliness, and self-doubt; yet it was leavened, in her account, by the security that came of knowing "who she was"—a gift of her early archetypal encounter.

Doug Lipman, a conscientious objector to the Vietnam War, was working off his alternative service in a variety of institutions for behaviorally disordered children when he began investigating the healing potential of folk arts. By declaring himself a C.O., he had already broken from the structure of institutional obedience and accomplishment that had ruled his youth. Slipped loose from the social machine, he drifted into a series of service jobs in remedial institutions for more severely broken cogs. There he had to search for a set of tools that might help him rebuild the machine from the bottom or modify it to run on cleaner fuel:

I came to the Boston area in '69, to take a conscientious objector job during the Vietnam War. And that job was working on the children's ward of a mental hospital. I had never worked with children at all. And so suddenly I was faced with children with pretty severe levels of emotional disturbance. And I just frantically kept trying everything I knew, to try to make a connection.

But there was a volunteer who came in once a week and sang folk songs. Kingston Trio kind of folk songs. And during her hour there, even though she wasn't especially skilled with children—and her songs weren't even especially appropriate for children sometimes—something magical happened on the ward. And children who just walked around reading labels on fire extinguishers on the walls were suddenly doing that on *that* end of the ward.

And so, since I had gone to college during the first folk revival—as Martin Mull calls it, "the folk scare"—one of the things I'd done in college to have an excuse not to study was to teach myself to play a guitar. And so I pulled it out with these children, and it really worked, it really made a connection with them.

My next job was with slightly less disturbed children in a private school. And it also meant that I was on the faculty of a college—this was a lab school. Which meant that I got to go through the college library and take out records. So I was working on the folk music records.

It was the fall of 1970. And around November somewhere, I got up to "*H.*" In the folk music shelf, there was this record called "Ray Hicks, of Beech Mountain, North Carolina, Tells Four Traditional Jack Tales." And I'd never heard of Ray Hicks. And I'd never heard of Jack tales. I knew Beech Mountain, because of all the good folk music there, and I knew Folk Legacy Records. And I said, "Well, if it's on Folk Legacy, it's probably of interest to me. So, I'll try it."

And, having one of the stereotypical associations with storytelling, I thought, well, this'll be a bedtime story. And so I put the record on around bedtime. Now, of course, with Ray's accent, I had to read the notes to follow the story. And somewhere in the middle of the second story on side one, I fell asleep. So it worked, as a bedtime story.

Now, this school, children were bussed there from all over—some of them traveled an hour to get there, and because of the bussing schedule, some of them got there a full hour before the teachers did. And mostly, the assistant principal supervised them on the playground. But on rainy days, he brought them in and told them stories, that he had made up. I remember there was something about whales—that's all I remember. His name was Ted Sileski.

Now it happened—as the gods will have it—that the morning after I fell asleep to Ray's record, it rained. And Ted Sileski was out sick. So I got to school, and they said, "We've got a roomful of kids—Ted isn't here—we don't know what to do."

And I said, "Well. I heard a story last night. I'll try and tell it."

And so, I stood up in front of them and started to tell "Jack and the Three Steers."

And . . . these are kids that I had taught math, science, arts and crafts, and music to. And they had fought me every inch of the way in all of them. And I'd finally gotten them to sort of not rebel against music, *if* I passed out crayons and paper, *before* I started singing, and then they would kind of let me sing to them. If they had something else to do.

And so I stood up in front of, not just one class of eight, like I was used to, but the whole school, of fifty. And said:

"*Well, Jack and his mother were having a hard time. And Jack had to go off in the world, and make his own fortune.*"

And I got that far, and I looked around, And a-a-all these hard-ass kids, their eyes were rolled back and their jaws were slack. And, you know, being no more resistant to a conditioned response than anybody else, I said, "*I like this! Now we're talking!!*"

And that moment to me is the moment that all of the people in that first generation of the storytelling revival—all the people who discovered it independently—every one of us found that moment somewhere. We found that there was a *hunger*. And we lucked on it, one way or the other. And just finally tried the right thing. And I tried zillions of things, you know. Making leather wallets with these kids *did not do it*—if it had, I might be an arts and crafts teacher. But telling a story did.

Lipman's story, like Martin's, highlights the deep need for the role of the storyteller on the part of the community with which he was involved. Martin's intentional Zen community, Blue's or Birch's university communities, or even Simms's elite children's theater class may have been typical of the liminal spaces in which the storytelling revival was bred and nurtured; Lipman's school more resembles the gritty institutional communities where the typical storytelling professional eventually earned the bulk of his living in free-lance performances, residencies, and workshops. It is an enforced community of children and staff who come together from widely scattered neighborhoods, with little in common but their socially constructed and opposed problems—for the children, socialization, and for the staff, control. As in the classroom that Simms wrote about in her "Lamplighter" article, Lipman found that his storytelling had an instantaneous effect of inducing a harmonious state of relaxed, focused attention in an environment starved for those qualities. It was all the more stunning to him because of his lack of studied preparation. His own innate qualities of heart, mind, and voice, a memory fresh from the night before, and a willingness to put it all on the line in the service of the moment were all that were apparently required for the archetype of the storyteller to manifest its power through him.

"The Story Was Sufficient": The Third Totem Tale of the Storytelling Revival

In concluding this brief sampling of vocational narratives from contemporary storytelling revivalists, I would pose two primary, related values that the archetype of the storyteller offered to women and men coming of age in the seventies and eighties: self-realization and service. These are values that have been taught through initiatory rites of cultures the world over. The ebbing potency of such rites in our own society led to a surge of exotic imports and revivalistic enthusiasms to fill the experiential void. For those with a receptive personality, stepping into the archetypal storyteller's role in the heightened presence of performance was a transcendent shock that created its own initiatory field. It allowed the devotee to identify with an image of self that both magnified the ego and effaced it by merging it with an inexhaustibly resonant lineage. At the same time, it quickened the spirit by directing it toward a clear and present avenue of service to the cultural environment. Different personalities, even in this small sampling, emphasize these values in different proportions: Blue and Birch place greater emphasis on self-realization, Martin and Lipman on service, Simms on the balance between the two, as expressed in the I-thou relationship of storytelling performance.

There is a potential energy, a numina, within the archetype of the storyteller that allows us to return to it again and again in times of great cultural stress, not for direct, intellectual answers to our dilemmas but for release from our dilemmas—for a journey to the once-upon-a-time place where opposites coexist. We go to the storyteller, as the great North Carolina mountain Jack-tale teller Ray Hicks says, "to ease the heart." That sense of release—or of the self-fulfilling desire for release through storytelling—can be eloquently summed up, as usual, in a story.

The third totem tale of the storytelling revival is a Hasidic story, originally passed down through the followers of the nineteenth-century zaddik Israel of Rizhyn. It was put in its compelling contemporary form, shorn of the thorny particularity of sectarian folklore and rife for universalization, in Elie Wiesel's holocaust novel *The Gates of the Forest* in 1966. A few years later, it made its first appearance as an emblem of an embryonic storytelling revivalism in Sam Keen's *To a Dancing God.*

Like our other two totemic tales, this one could be heard recounted at most any storytelling festival during the early eighties, as an invocation of the essence of what the storytelling revival meant to its devotees. If "The Storyteller Knows Me" is the tale of the restoried community and "The Man Who Had No Story" is the tale of the restoried individual, here is the tale of the restoried cosmos:

> When the great Rabbi Israel Baal Shem-Tov saw misfortune threatening the Jews it was his custom to go into a certain part of the forest to meditate. There he would light a fire, say a special prayer, and the miracle would be accomplished, and the misfortune averted.
>
> Later, when his disciple, the celebrated Magid of Mezritch, had occasion, for the same reason, to intercede with heaven, he would go to the same place in the forest and say: "Master of the Universe, listen! I do not know how to light the fire, but I am still able to say the prayer." And again the miracle would be accomplished.
>
> Still later, Rabbi Moshe-Leib of Sasov, in order to save his people once more, would go into the forest and say: "I do not know how to light the fire, I do not know the prayer, but I know the place and this must be sufficient." It was sufficient, and the miracle was accomplished.
>
> Then it fell to Rabbi Israel of Rizhyn to overcome misfortune. Sitting in his armchair, his head in his hands, he spoke to God: "I am unable to light the fire and I do not know the prayer; I cannot even find the place in the forest. All I can do is to retell the story, and this must be sufficient." And it was sufficient.
>
> God made man because he loves stories. (Wiesel 6–10)

At once convicted and consoled by this legend, storytelling revivalists knew that we, too, had forgotten much on the journey of the generations: we had forgotten the place in the forest, the fire, the prayers, and the rituals that could reconnect the stability of home and community to the wildness of Creation. Yet, touched again by the archetypal sway of the storyteller's voice, we knew that we could at least remember the simple story and find, perhaps, the rest within it: the place, the prayer, the fire, and even atonement in our own hearts' core for the dark and weary ways we had wandered without them.

2

The Motif of Serendipity

The word *serendipity* was coined by the eighteenth-century belletrist Sir Horace Walpole. He was inspired, serendipitously enough, by a fairy tale, "The Three Princes of Serendip." The heroes of this story, he said, "were always making discoveries, by accidents and sagacity, of things they were not in quest of" (*Oxford English Dictionary*). The hero of every fairy tale is touched in some way by this quality of serendipity. The help or guidance he requires on his quest rarely materializes from any expected quarter but comes from some chance encounter with a tattered beggar or a wounded animal. This stray being, when met with a guileless heart, suddenly swells with an uncanny awareness of the moment's dilemma and a capacity to bestow the blessing that leads to a resolution.

So it is with any folk revival movement, in the lives of its individual devotees and for whole cultural groups and subgroups. The art form generally appears, like the hungry beggar or wounded animal, from an oblique angle to the immediate social or individual dilemma—a cultural naïf and waif. Yet in the serendipitous encounter, a power is revealed to address the dilemma—not directly but obliquely, as Scheherazade addressed the king's rage by holding him in the story trance for a thousand-and-one nights. Every storyteller, folksinger, dulcimer player, or potter becomes like Jack, the folktale's youngest son, who gains because in his foolishness he is not ashamed to treasure a fallen leaf for a magic boat or to accept the gift that is always rejected by his goal-driven brothers.

In this chapter, I will explore the motif of serendipity as it weaves itself into the vocational narratives of contemporary storytelling revivalists.

Then I will examine the narratives of the founders of the National Storytelling Festival, which reveal that serendipity is a carefully framed and emphasized element in the birth and growth of the festival and works in counterpoint to other, more active character traits, such as cleverness, shrewdness, or boldness. Serendipity acts in these narratives as a kind of psychological counterweight to the urgency of economic, social, and emotional need. The constant intrusions of serendipity play the same structuring role that magical encounters and supernatural assistance play in wonder tales. It is the "evidence of things unseen" that Paul defines as faith. The myth of serendipity is the narrative encoding of the search for pattern, by which our personal needs and desires become part of a teleological scheme, an intelligence of the world.

Storytelling, particularly oral storytelling, is an ideal medium for the myth of serendipity to express itself. Serendipity becomes part of the design of every good folktale because it mimics the action of human destiny as we are psychologically able to perceive it. Conscious effort seems to produce its own built-in resistance. We are often best able to experience our defining moments if they seem to have come unsought, snared in the web of subconscious desire, in a moment of relaxation of struggle. Yet those moments are also made possible by the intensity of effort that has gone before them. In the dream-logic of folktales, the failures of the older brothers are an inseparable part of the triumph of the youngest. In the Zen tradition, one may knit one's brows over the koan, the impossible riddle, for decades before the flash of illumination comes in a moment of surrender. Afterward, when we preserve and transmit the experience, as we must, through storytelling, it is the serendipitous character of the moment that will be cherished and enshrined, through the reverence of our ritualized repetitions.

Serendipity is necessary to good storytelling in a purely technical sense, yet at the same time this artistic process forms a golden mirror for a psychological need. Serendipity keeps us awake and alert as listeners, knowing, even expecting that crucial plot turns will appear from unexpected directions. It is the cultivation of this alertness as story-listeners that spills over into our daily life in the form of wisdom, openness, and faith. The congruence between our experience of storytelling and our powers of receiving and shaping life experiences has caused such psychologists as Bruno Bettelheim, James Hillman, and Robert Coles to declare exposure to stories an important indicator of emotional health. This psychological imprimatur of "the uses of enchantment," in Bettelheim's now standard phrase, has become one of the pillars of storytelling revival activity.

Joseph Campbell calls the serendipitous encounter "the call to adventure," and he describes it thus: "A blunder—apparently the merest chance—reveals an unsuspected world, and the individual is drawn into a relationship with forces that are not rightly understood. . . . But whether great or small, and no matter what the stage or grade of life, the call rings up the curtain, always, on a mystery of transfiguration—a rite, or moment, of spiritual passage which, when complete, amounts to a dying and a birth" (*Hero* 51).

Anthony F. C. Wallace refers to this transfiguring moment in his discussion of revitalization movements, when he explores the process he calls "mazeway reformulation":

> Whether the movement is religious or secular, the reformulation of the mazeway generally seems to depend on a restructuring of elements and subsystems which have already attained currency in the society and may even be in use, and which are known to the person who is to become the prophet or leader. The occasion of their combination in a form which constitutes an internally consistent structure, and of their acceptance by the prophet as a guide to action, is abrupt and dramatic, usually occurring as a moment of insight, a brief period of realization of relationships and opportunities. These moments are often called inspiration or revelation. (270)

Folk arts, of course, are always present in society in ever-changing yet remarkably consistent and universal forms—recessive yet constantly available as symbols of continuity and of fresh personal and social integration. Wallace adds that mazeway reformulation also "seems normally to occur in its initial form in the mind of a single person rather than to grow directly out of group deliberations" (270). This emphasis on a single charismatic leader holding sway over a group of enthusiastic followers seems more applicable to purely religious revival cults than to a relatively anarchic cultural movement like the storytelling revival. But Wallace's general account highlights the sudden reorganization of personality around an unexpected, visionary encounter, which then initiates a revitalization movement around newly instituted rites, customs, or devotional forms—all of which perfectly fit this particular folk revival and its pervasive motif of serendipity.

The motif appears repeatedly in the vocational narratives quoted in the introduction and chapter 1. For Brother Blue, serendipity comes when he performs his version of *Beauty and the Beast* for Sam Miller at Harvard. Miller, like the *senex* guide figure of the wonder tales, announces at the tale's conclusion that this innocent child's diversion is the nondogmatic spiritual vehicle Blue has been seeking. In a moment that perfectly echoes the design of the wonder tales themselves, Miller then seals this annunciation with a magical token, a gift of two bird figurines from his windowsill—an image of freedom lifted from the threshold of vision. "Right then," Blue concludes, "I knew that I was supposed to do more of those kind of things, and I decided that I would spend my life exploring this." How does he know? This dawning of inner certainty is a key to the mythic passion of a revival movement. It is born in a moment, from the meeting of desire and serendipity.

For Laura Simms, serendipity appears in her Central Park moment. As she faces an unexpected demand, what wells up inside her is a folktale heard, by chance, as she wandered through a library on the day she dropped out of graduate school. The folktale, in turn, connects her, like Cinderella's dove, to her mother's nurturing in childhood, but it also gives her a magic word to bear her toward her destined life. Serendipity arrives for Rafe Martin when he is asked to perform as "the Sleeping Sage" for the children's festival in his Zen community. In this zone of liminality where identities freely mutate and merge, Martin is able to meet the guide in the psychologically condensed manner of a twentieth-century personality— he literally meets the *senex* in himself. Stepping into the costume of the guide, he discovers a compelling mask through which he can perform the guide function for others.

Serendipity is woven into Carol Birch's vocational story as an ironic trope, a rhythmic juxtaposition of outward pressure and inward discovery. Doug Lipman highlights the outward pressure of the time in his story as well, but he also takes time to vividly reconstruct the motif of serendipity. As befits the culture of secondary orality that birthed the revival, Lipman first meets the *senex* figure on a phonograph album. As it always does in a Jack tale, the meeting with the wise old man produces an immediate testing. Like the Man Who Had No Story, Lipman suddenly now has a story to tell, and in telling it, he discovers the mutual hunger that will guide his life from now on.

Jackie Torrence's vocational narrative is a primer on the revival storyteller's uses of serendipity. Torrence is probably the most popular performer of pure storytelling that the revival has produced—"pure" in the specific sense that although she has some casual acquaintance with theatrical and literary conventions, she has no special background in these fields; she uses no musical instrument to bolster her performances, nor does she tailor her tellings to any predetermined psychological or spiritual interpretation. Her public persona remains what it was when she began at the High Point, North Carolina, Public Library as "The Story Lady." Though she has published a few albums, cassette tapes, videos, and even two books of her storytelling and has appeared on radio and television, these forays into popular media have not been crucial to her career. Her essential medium is the storytelling circle at the libraries, schools, festivals, and concert halls of the revival circuit. She sits on a bench on a bare stage and speaks. Her chief tool is a deep, expressive voice, gifted with crisp comic and dramatic timing and highlighted by arching brows and dancing hands.

Torrence was working in a semiprofessional capacity as a reference librarian when her storytelling career began. The serendipitous aspect of that initiation has become a part of her official biography, having been endlessly repeated and reprinted in newspaper publicity and festival program notes over the past two decades. Over the telephone, she told it to me simply:

> It must have been about 1972, in the library. And my boss asked me to fill in for a storyteller who was late. It was by accident. I often tell people it was by accident, but my mother used tell me, "No, don't ever say that. God had His intentions. You know, it might have been accidental to you—if that was the way that God had of getting you into that."
>
> So I found storytelling that day, by accident. And, lo and behold, it was . . . just a good feeling. It was satisfying. And I thought, "Well, maybe I'll do that again."

In a 1987 interview with high school student reporters for a Foxfire-style journal, *Bronze Reminiscence,* in Atlanta, Georgia, Torrence gave a more elaborate account, with the richness of incident that marks her full-fledged storytelling style. At every turn, the measure of her skill is in the way she is able to highlight the serendipitous elements in each situation to create an alternating current of crisis and release:

> I became a storyteller in a most unusual way. I worked in High Point, North Carolina, as a librarian. . . . And one day in January, 1972, my boss said to me, "There's nobody upstairs to tell stories."
>
> And I said, "Uuuh. But there's a bunch of kids up there."
>
> "Somebody's got to do it," he said, "How about you?"

I said, "No-o-o. I'm a reference librarian. I don't want to tell stories."
He said, "I'll tell you what. I'll give you five minutes."
"I'm gone."
Well there were books upstairs, and there were two children's librarians at work, but neither one of them were storytellers. They found nice books for me to use—Dr. Seuss's *Cat in the Hat* and such as that. I don't like to read those books to my own child because I have never thought Dr. Seuss's books were for children. . . . I thought, "Why don't I just tell a story to all of these beautiful little preschoolers sitting here waiting for me."

So I began. "I shall tell you about 'Little Red Riding Hood.'" The prettiest child of all said, "We don't wanna hear that."

And then I thought, "Uh, oh." And then I said, "What about 'The Three Bears?'"

"We heard that last week." And all the classics went down the drain. They didn't want to hear any of those stories.

I said to myself, "What will I do?" And then I remembered a story that the librarian of our school, my school, Monroe Street School, had read many years ago. . . . It had been twenty years since I'd heard the story, but I did remember that the bear ate up the town. So I started telling about the bear that ate up the old man, the old woman, the little girl and the little boy. And the kids were saying, "Yeah, that's a good story." And I thought, "How can I bring this story to a close?" Finally I figured out how to get to the end. I couldn't remember the story, but I kept telling it, and finally it started coming back to me. I ended it and the kids said to me, "Tell that one again." They *loved* it.

For three days I told that same tale, and each time the bear ate up something different. He ate trains, and wagons, and trucks. I became the official storyteller. And that started an interesting chain of events. Children started bringing their parents. Parents started bring other parents and other children. And in a room that held fifty people, we had one hundred and fifty people. Sometimes two hundred people packed in that room at any given story hour. . . . When we couldn't get all the people in the one room we had, my boss said, "Well, why don't you start going out to the schools."

I would come to work at eight o'clock and go immediately to the schools. I wouldn't see the library again till nearly three o'clock. Since I got off work at four, I hardly spent any time at the library. People started saying, "How can she do that?" I would work an hour at work, and the rest of the time I'd be out in the schools. My calendar was filled for weeks and weeks and weeks at a time. Then adults started inviting me to dinner parties on my day off and on Sundays. They would pay me for it.

Well, when my boss found out that I was getting extra money on my day off, he said, "If you do this again, I'm going to fire you." Well, he found out. So ended my job as a librarian, and thus began my career as a professional storyteller. (Glass)

Torrence's account of her first storytelling experience is strikingly similar to those of Simms and Lipman. Confronted unexpectedly with an expectant story audience, she is forced to rack her memory for some adequate resource. In her case, it was a telling of "Sody Salleratus" from Richard Chase's *Grandfather Tales,* heard perhaps twenty years earlier. The serendipitous recollection and the courage to follow its impulse rather than settle for one of the safer alternatives offered by the nonstorytelling librarians—this is her crisis and her opportunity, her trial and her triumph, which open her to a serendipitous career.

In my own interview with Torrence, her narrative shows the ways in which the myth of serendipity acts as a counterweight to the pressures of social, economic, and psychological need. Torrence made explicit much that was only implied in her performance for the high school reporters, as she described how difficult it had been for her to arrive at a career as a storyteller:

I had been one of those people who was just sort of preoccupied with finding out what job it was that God had given me to do. . . . I mean it was like a treasure hunt or something. And I prayed for it constantly. And there were just so many things that I found to do; but nothing really stayed. When I'd fall in love with something, something would happen and it would just show that, you know, "Well, you can't do that."

So when I found storytelling, it was miraculous, you know. But I didn't even consider it the thing that God had given me. It was something exciting and new. And interesting. And I worked in it. And had the best time. And it was two or three years going before I even thought that, maybe I could do something with this. . . .

But you know what? While all of this was going on—here at long last I had found something that was giving me satisfaction, was making me feel good going into work each morning, was making a different person out of me—when I looked around, people were getting angry with me. . . . They were unhappy because, here was a happy person. You know, they complained every day about disliking their job, disliking the place they were in, disliking who they were, and all of that. And here I'm just having a ball. And one thing led to the other, and before I knew it I had been fired.

And I was without work for almost six or seven months, trying to find a new job. . . . Because I wasn't even aware that there was a "storyteller." I was still, you know, telling stories at parties—in adult parties and children's parties. But I'm still looking for "a job." Because my husband was unhappy with the fact that I was a storyteller. He said, "Nobody calls themself a storyteller. That is not a legitimate thing to do. Nobody hires you as a storyteller."

A clerk at the unemployment office, hearing that she was a teller, wrote her a slip for a job at Wachovia Bank. "And between her desk and the door," she said, "I tore it up so that she could see me do it. I didn't even have the heart to say, 'Woman, you are stupid.'" Torrence's precarious economic experiences force her to develop her active qualities of courage, boldness, and persistence, to stay true to the path revealed by serendipity.

Lipman's experience, too, suggests the ways in which the mythic aspects of serendipity can work in concert with market economic forces. In 1976, he called an administrator about a job in the Boston-area public schools as a folksinger—"which is what I thought I was." The folk music boom was still on, however, and the schools were glutted with folksingers. The administrator said, "But I've heard you. And you do storytelling in with your songs. Why don't you call the woman over in Literary Resources. They're hungry for a storyteller. . . . They're dying for a storyteller over in Literary Resources."

"And on the phone," Lipman told me, "I made one of those instant marketing decisions. 'You're going to get songs with stories?' No! 'You're going to get stories with songs!' He went on:

And that's the day that I called myself a storyteller, as a performer. In other words, I discovered—I think this happened to a lot of people in the revival—I discovered the hunger for stories. But the name and the categories I responded to as an outside, externally defined thing. And I think a lot of us did that.

"Yeah, I tell stories. Oh, okay, you want a storyteller? Yeah, that's right, I am one, aren't I? Okay! Here I am!"

Fields of spiritual hunger can be as lucrative as oil fields, which also grow in darkness from the simmering weight of the dead. It is a cheerful and maddening trait of the market system that spiritual hungers, promptly upon their discovery, are apt to be crisscrossed with entrepreneurial claims. Religion in our society is perhaps the most visible of these perversely zoned fields of spiritual enterprise. But the arts are equally pervasive and lucrative, dwelling as they do among the vast, dim plains of imagination that form the borderlands between spiritual and material worlds. Should it shock us that those who stepped into the archetypal aura of the story-teller in the sixties, seventies, and eighties, those who found their lives transformed by the serendipity of the encounter, should then seek to es-tablish the fact in the realm of commerce? As the Irish poet James Ste-phens wrote during an earlier folk revival, "Beauty, also, is usefulness. The arts as well as the crafts, the graces equally with the utilities must stand up in the market place and be judged by the gombeen men" (38).

"The Station Wagon Creation Story"

In 1972, Jimmy Neil Smith was teaching English and journalism at a high school in Johnson City. He was also one of the three-member planning committee that inaugurated Historic Jonesborough Days, the three-day commercial heritage festival over the Fourth of July. He was the faculty adviser for his high school's newspaper, a tabloid-sized production he proudly proclaims was one of the best in the state of Tennessee. One af-ternoon he was driving a group of his students to the print shop in the neighboring town of Elizabethton when something on the radio caught their ears:

> [S]ome of my journalism students and I were traveling to Elizabethton to print the school newspaper. And we were listening to the radio. And on the radio was Jerry Clower. And he was telling a story about coon-hunt-ing in Mississippi. And we were laughing, and talking, and slapping our knees and nudging each other, and enjoying the telling of the tale. And at that moment, I turned to the students and said, "Wouldn't it be nice if we could bring Clower to Jonesborough—No—bring storytellers *like* Clower to Jonesborough, to tell tales?"
> And I don't remember, really, any further discussion at that point. The idea was essentially dropped.

It is a fairly innocuous story in itself. It would hardly seem worth men-tioning were it not for the fact that it has been mentioned so often over the years in public relations efforts for the festival. It has become a kind of secular origin legend—the "Station Wagon Creation Story." Its telling always highlights the chance element in the incident—the creative hap-penstance of the story coming over the car radio. For the purposes of mythography, it is worth a closer look to see what has turned this simple anecdote into a mythic staple.

First, there is the teller-protagonist himself. Smith vows regularly that he is "not a storyteller." This claim has become part of his public autobiography. But as the founder and driving force behind a public event, particularly one that centers on storytelling, he is required to have some story to tell. Public relations, which is simply popular storytelling in its mechanical extensions, demands that he produce some kind of narrative crystal of his founding inspiration. The reporters who interview him each year around festival time, like the festival-goers themselves, are looking above all for a story to structure and dramatize their perceptions of the event. Were Smith to insist, like the Man Who Had No Story, "Oh, no, I have no story—this is just what I do in autumn, like birds fly south," they would quit him in disgust, and the interests of the festival as a media event would be poorly served. So he has produced this polished memory—sturdily recyclable and by now standard.

The anecdote shows the protagonist in three fitting and instrumental roles: he is one member of an appreciative audience; he is driver of the car and leader of the group; and he is observer of the group's reactions. As audience, he is the passive receiver of the storyteller's gift. As teacher and driver, he is responsible for the group's safety and the cultural efficacy of their work. As observer, he is able to take note of what the storyteller's performance does to their group energy and to speculate on how that performance might fit into the larger scheme of local cultural and economic development, of which even the Davy Crockett High School newspaper is an exploratory device.

Carolyn Moore, a shrewd observer of the Jonesborough scene, told me in an interview about Smith in those days:

> Jimmy was writing for the *Herald-Tribune*. He was doing local—by local I mean Washington County–Jonesborough—good, correct history, but what we also might use as gimmicks for the tourists. . . . Jimmy was trying all sorts of things. Because . . . he was a child of East Tennessee. And a lot of East Tennesseans are—I'm speaking out of a point of prejudice here, so be careful with what I say. But East Tennessee has traditionally been Republican. And been very resistant to change. And probably the people who made the most noise about change have been the Democrats. And Jimmy came from a Democratic family. So Jimmy was interested in bringing about a change, but a change that would improve—and by improve it, I'm saying, get dollars and cents.

Smith was clearly on the lookout for ideas for another seasonal activity in the town, one that could bring in tourist revenue and increase awareness of the local historic preservation movement. This is the motivating framework that tends to remain unstated in the mediated account, even as social and historical detail are generally elided in the process of traditional legend-formation. What we are left with, as in a Child ballad, is a kernel of action. For purposes of later storying, at least, inspiration is always most effectively received through serendipity.

In terms of the mythology of the storytelling revival, it is significant that the messenger, the bringer of inspiration, should have been a car radio. The radio is the serendipitous soundtrack of our twentieth-century lives. Always in the background of our daily activities, it floats a meandering stream of cultural stimulation into our ears, while our eyes attempt to stay glued to the road of the here and now. It can act on us like Proust's madeleine—some sudden burst of song may plunge us into an inward reverie from which we emerge with a deepened emotion, a transformed perspective.

The radio is perpetually mysterious, even numinous. To the natural mind, for all its scientific indoctrination, there will always be something supernatural-seeming in this welter of human and angelic voices, sounding brass, and tinkling cymbal erupting from a banded box. Mythologically, the radio is of the realm of Hermes, he of the winged sandals, who flies great distances invisibly to deliver a message of destiny. In the early days of radio, popular magazine iconography showed families gathered around the stately, altarlike edifice of the console, gazing up at the glowing dial with glazed, worshipful countenances. Signature voices emerged from those consoles to became "stars," images of distant, serene, unchanging light. Radio stars were of a different order of magnitude, perhaps, from those planetary beings whose nitrate images flickered from the sister medium, film—less incandescent but more familiar. Radio personalities were like miraculously amplified neighbors and family; film stars were our dream lovers and ravishers, our Venus and Mars. Even today that distinction endures, encoded perhaps in the geometry and scale of the mediums. An increasingly dominant radio genre is the "national call-in talk show," a national front porch of the air, where the hosts are our crotchety uncles, aunts, or brothers-in-law writ extra bold.

The radio truly inaugurated the world of secondary orality, McLuhan's phrase for the electronically mediated sensory environment, which has now become inextricably woven into our communal dreamscape. It is appropriate, then, that in narrativizing the origin of the National Storytelling Festival, Smith refers not to any direct experience of family or community "back-porch" storytelling but to a disembodied yet familiar country voice happening out of a car radio. "The Storyteller Knows Me" may have become a narrative byword for the tellers and the audience. But for the founder, the inspiration for basing a far-flung revival of storytelling in his hometown came from noticing how his students responded to the voice of an ingratiating stranger, electronically projected.

It is also significant that the voice was Jerry Clower's. Clower is a former fertilizer salesman from Yazoo City, Mississippi, who began a second career for himself in the early seventies with an album of down-home storytelling. Through the widespread hunger for stories, mentioned in so many of my interviews, and the hunger for identifiably human voices to tell them, Clower's first recording became a radio hit.

Clower described the phenomenon, still fairly fresh, in his performance at the first National Storytelling Festival in October 1973. His story is full of serendipity, as we might expect, but also of reflections on the peculiarly powerful conjunction of storytelling and radio and on the odd cultural, political, and economic alliances that have forged both the storytelling revival and the postmodern world. An Alabama acquaintance offered to put up all the money for Clower to record his first album, *Clower Power*. This partner, who was farm director for a radio station, mailed copies of the record to other stations with agricultural programs. They sold eight thousand copies through the mail, but when the record was aired on WSM in Nashville immediately following the Grand Ole Opry, Clower said, "We got so many orders for the bloomin' album, we couldn't fill it. Now if these orders had been for fertilizer—I could have eased everybody's pain. But I wasn't in the record bidness; I didn't know nothin' about it. And I told my partner, I said, 'Now let's just sit tight. If this record's got any possibilities, somebody in the *record* bidness'll want it.'" Sure enough, calls began coming in the next day. After stringing along the city slickers for a suitable interval, Clower signed with the company whose emissary courted him the fairest: "That feller flew to Yazoo City, Mississippi; y'all ought to have seen him. He came skippin' offa that airplane. Had them Hollywood boots on; pistol-legged britches; black leather vest; had a *Afro-American hairdo*—and he was a white feller. But after he patted his inside vest pocket and told me how much cash money he had brought with him—my attitude got a lot more tolerant about them hairdos. In fact, I thought he had the purtiest head o' hair of anybody I ever saw" (Clower, *Storytelling Has Been Very Good to Me* . . .).

Clower drew a moral to his story:

And folks, here I am, just travelin' down the highway, supervisin' thirty-three salesmen that sells a hundred million dollars worth of fertilizer annually. A guy dares me to make a record, I make the record, MCA buys it from me; eighteen months from the day we make the record, they put my name in the walkway of stars in front of the Country Music Hall of Fame, and the bloomin' record's sold a million dollars worth. Now, this is somethin' that impresses me, *because,* when I made my first album, I was told, unless I put a little risque, vulgar stuff on my record, "it'd never get to be known nationally."

Well, friends, there ain't never been a talkin' record, in the history of music, in the top ten in Billboard, *ever!* until *Clower Power* got in there, and it's in there now, and that's the first one. And they ain't a risque word on it. And I want to tell you somethin'. This country has done got tired of people with no talent, that think that the only way they can entertain a audience is get up and tell 'em something vulgar and off-color. And I done proved that to be a out-right lie! And during the ole Storytelling Festival, if somebody thinks he's got to tell something that the smallest girl-child in the audience is not supposed to hear, you run him back to where he come from! Tell him he ain't welcome here! (Clower, *Storytelling Has Been Very Good to Me* . . .)

Clower's performance on Saturday night was the official main event of that first National Storytelling Festival, but according to Smith and others, it was not the model for later festivals. That model emerged only gradually, through a dynamic alternation of serendipitous discovery and traditionalizing repetition.

Clower had made his own name, not through the National Storytelling Festival but through his recordings and performances on the Grand Ole Opry. Apart from his performances at that first festival and the reunion festival in 1992, he has never affiliated with the festival or other storytellers. Like Garrison Keillor with *A Prairie Home Companion,* he has fed the same hunger for storytelling voices that has fueled the revival movement but from within his own privileged performance domain. Politically, too, Clower was more at home in the Nixonian, Moral Majority ambiance of the Grand Ole Opry than with Smith's slightly shaggy, liberal democratic regime that would lure a flock of smiley but wild-haired margineers to Jonesborough. Yet his prohibition against art that "the smallest girl-child in the audience is not supposed to hear" has remained a stumbling block in the festival's ongoing struggle to define and expand its artistic limits.

"Let's Be Presumptuous!": The Naming of the Festival

In the months following his station wagon brainstorm, Smith says that the idea of a storytelling festival kept recurring to him. Finally he brought it to the Civic Trust and got its approval to sponsor an event featuring storytelling for the fall of 1973. He received funding from the Civic Trust, as well as some grant support from the Tennessee Arts Commission. Now the question was what to call the event.

This is another matter around which a particular piece of festival folklore persists. The story is still maintained, in festival programs and news releases as well as in the casual mythologizing that feeds the more formal expressions, that the festival was originally intended to be called something far less dignified than "The National Storytelling Festival." Here is how the two motifs, the station wagon creation and the naming, were twinned, condensed, and traditionalized in the festival souvenir program of 1988 to 1990:

> It was very nearly named the Buggaboo Springs Storytelling Festival back in early 1973 when the civic leaders of Jonesborough contemplated their first storytelling festival. "Is there any other such event anywhere in the country," they queried.
> "None that I know of," answered the high school journalism teacher who had conceived the idea.
> "Then let's call it the *National* Storytelling Festival."
> The school teacher, who later became town mayor, was Jimmy Neil Smith, and his inspiration, quite simply, had been a well-told tale heard over a squawking car radio. It was a story told by Grand Ole Opry regular Jerry Clower about coon hunting in Mississippi. Nothing particularly awe-inspiring. But enough to fire Smith's imagination. When he proposed the idea of a storytelling festival to the Jonesborough Civic Trust, they quickly acquiesced. The rest, of course, is history.

Naming, of course, is one of the fundamental rituals of identity. The question of how a tiny "Podunk" town like Jonesborough had the brass to inaugurate an event with the imperial pretensions of a National Storytelling Festival and then, by will and public relations skill, to make it seem legitimate is one that rewards investigation on every level, from the touristic to the journalistic, to the artistic, to the anthropological. It is a riddle—a coiled, self-revealing, and self-concealing irony—and the attempt to unravel it creates a significant part of the magnetism of the event. Smith, in our interview, told a fuller version:

> Actually the name that I would probably have chosen, if I had chosen a name myself, without naming it anything quite so bold and presumptuous as the *National* Storytelling Festival, the *National* Association—I would have probably called it the Buggaboo Springs Storytelling Festival. There is a Buggaboo Springs real close to Jonesborough. And it's an old spring; there's a legend about it—I never knew the legend. But my ex-wife lived on Buggaboo Springs Road, near Buggaboo Springs. So I was very familiar with it—I did my early courting on Buggaboo Springs Road. I knew that that was a catchy, charming name. I don't think I would have ever named it Podunk Hollow, because that is not a name characteristic of this region. I was using that as an example. So when I said to people, "Well, I started to name it Podunk Hollow or Buggaboo Springs," I was using that in jest, to indicate that I had *no notion,* initially, that I would ever call it the *National* Storytelling Festival; [I] would have seriously considered naming it Buggaboo Springs.
>
> So then I began to feel terribly presumptuous about it. So I went to people. I went to Jean; I went to Carolyn Moore; and I went to other people as well. But it was Carolyn Moore's answer that sparked a solution here.
>
> I went to Carolyn and said (I called her Mrs. Moore, and still do) I said, "Mrs. Moore, what do you think we ought to call this storytelling event that we're planning? Do you think it's too presumptuous to call it the National Storytelling Festival?"
>
> And I guess it kind of embarrassed her. And she looked down, and thought a minute, and then she looked up and asked me, "Well, is there anything like it anywhere else in the country?"
>
> And I said, "No, as far as I know, this is the first festival devoted *exclusively* to the art of storytelling anywhere in the country."
>
> And her eyes kind of sparkled, and she said, "Let's be presumptuous."

"BE BOLD—BE BOLD," runs the inscription over the gate to Mr. Fox's house in the well-known folktale. Boldness is a necessary trait if the hero or heroine is to receive the knowledge that will lead to her royal estate or protect her in the midst of its perils. This is the punch line of Smith's story, as delivered through the oracular voice of Mrs. Moore, who here as elsewhere plays an instrumental mythic role in festival lore.

"BE BOLD—BE BOLD, BUT NOT TOO BOLD, LEST THAT YOUR HEART'S BLOOD SHOULD RUN COLD," run subsequent inscriptions in the tale, as the heroine passes through portals that lead her toward the dark side of her infatuation with worldly success. These injunctions, too, are built into the structure of Smith's story. "Podunk Holler" and "Buggaboo Springs" are designations that would have enshrined his Appalachian, small-town sense of self-deprecation. The clear implication of the story is that these names would have doomed the festival to perpetual small-time status. Yet in framing these as his "first," "natural" impulses, he is setting up a humorous safety valve against the charge of self-aggrandizement that might be leveled from within and beyond his own cultural milieu. For fellow townspeople, he is maintaining a comfortable stance as one of the good ole boys, keeping visitors entranced while dipping one hand casually into their pockets for the sake of the local revenue base. For the visitors, he is playing on their stereotypical images of the Appalachian South as a place of simple, colorful rubes.

At the same time, he and they are all aware that the event they are actually attending, and inquiring about through their journalistic surrogates, goes under the far grander rubric of the National Storytelling Festival. Storytelling itself, in its apparent simplicity, suggests itself as a kind of Podunk Holler or Buggaboo Springs of the arts, where a soul can come to find release from the maddening complexities and alienations of sophisticated but soulless urban art. Through our enjoyment of this modest piece of ironic storytelling, Smith is appealing to the rube in us all. He is shrewdly enlisting our membership in what turns out at the climax of the story to be a national empire of rubes, postrubes, and neorubes. The moral of the story is that a rube can be presumptuous, and thus achieve empire, but not without serendipitous timing—"Is there anything like it anywhere else in the country?"—or without taking counsel from the elders and wise women of the village.

The Folktellers' Call to Adventure

Barbara Freeman and Connie Regan-Blake, who for twenty years made up the seminal storytelling duo called the Folktellers, are first cousins, originally from Nashville, Tennessee, and Birmingham, Alabama, respectively. They have played a major role in the storytelling festival movement, as leaders of NAPPS (both Freeman and Regan-Blake served on the first

NAPPS board of directors, and Regan-Blake was chair of the board and director of the festival for many years in the seventies and eighties) and as the first emissaries from the emerging storytelling scene to enter the already established world of folk music festivals.

At the time of the first National Storytelling Festival in 1973, Barbara Freeman was a children's librarian at the Chattanooga Public Library. Connie Regan (now Regan-Blake) also worked there in an outreach program, driving a bookmobile to sites around the city and telling stories to children in the character of "Ms. Daisy." At the same time, Connie was also on the steering committee for the Tennessee chapter of the National Organization for Women and would travel around in the evenings speaking to adults about the burgeoning feminist movement. By October of 1973, the cousins had already been to one folk music festival, the Folk Festival of the Smokies in Cosby, Tennessee. There, listening to the old-time music floating across the sward and walking among the tables of revival crafts—candles, pottery, dulcimers, sandals, all the nativistic iconography from sixty years of Appalachian folk revivalism fanned into new urgency by the back-to-the-land fervor of the late sixties—they both had a vivid but inchoate sense of calling. Freeman described it thus:

> And as we were walking along the grounds, and listening to the music in the background, you know, Doc Watson-type people up on stage, we just turned to each other and said, "Wouldn't it be great to ... make candles, or something to where we could you know, kind of ... you know, *live*—" (now this while we were still librarians) "—wouldn't it be great to make candles, or turn wood, or do something, to where we could ... sell crafts at a festival like this and be able to just, you know, *spend your life at a festival!*" One weekend after the other.

Regan-Blake's recollection, in a separate interview on January 21, 1992, was complementary, reinforced doubtlessly in years since by repeating it to friends and strangers in groups small or large:

> In '72, some people that we knew through the library told us about a folk festival that was going on . . . it was called the Folk Festival of the Smokies. And it was *wonderful*. . . . and I was blown away.
>   And I really *distinctly* remember walking around—'cause they had crafts, and all people with booths set up—and thinking to myself, "What is it, what could I do to be able to travel, and hear this music all the time, and be a part of this kind of lifestyle?" I just *really loved it,* instantly. . . .

And it's amazing to me to look back on that. Because it's a very visceral memory for me. You know, I really remember everything that was going on as I was thinking that. And we really did love our jobs, it wasn't at all any kind of *dis*-pleasure with it. And I don't know for me if it was so much the nine-to-five. I don't know if that was in my mind, of, ooooh, not wanting to have to get up every day and go in to work; it was almost more to be around *this* kind of atmosphere all the time. There was just such a *sense* that I had never experienced before.

When the National Storytelling Festival came their way, then, Freeman and Regan were primed for just such a vehicle. Their story of their journey to the first festival is transcribed below, edited together to show the dovetailing of their memories, though the interviews were recorded separately.

Regan-Blake:
Actually it was the same people that told us about the folk festival, I believe, that told us about the Storytelling Festival. And I wrote to Jimmy Neil and told him I was a storyteller, and I was very interested in coming up. And got a *nice* letter back from him.

Freeman:
And it sounded like a really nifty thing, so, once again, we go up in my pickup truck. . . .

Regan-Blake:
So we took off, and in true Folktellers' style, what was to *become* Folktellers' style, stopped at a revival along the way, and heard some gospel music, and met some folks and chatted, and ended up taking probably four or five hours, what should have been a two-and-a-half or three-hour trip at the most.

Freeman:
The first night was in a high school, and there were over a thousand people, easily. And the whole festival was based on Jimmy Neil having heard Jerry Clower on the radio. . . .

Regan-Blake:
And we actually did not hear very much of Jerry Clower; we got there towards the end of his thing. The place was *packed,* so I remember we sat up in the balcony. And we had not even thought about what we would do afterwards. I think we had brought our sleeping bags; but we were in Barbara's pickup truck and it did not have a camper on it or anything at the time.

Freeman:
And then we—we had no place to stay, or anything. We always went by the cuffs of the sleeve, you know. It was just like, [dumbo voice]: "OH, LET'S GO TO THE FESTIVAL!"
"WELL, NOW WHAT DO WE DO?"
So we went up to Jimmy Neil—I thought that was his name, Mr. Neil. Mr. Jim E. Neil. And we asked him, was there a hotel in the area, or what the deal was, 'cause we'd never been. And he said, "Oh, you need a place to stay—follow that lady!" And we see this lady turn around with this black cloak. And she looked like something out of the thee-ay-ter, you know, just wonderfully dramatic, and very graceful and tall, and just a striking woman.
And we go running up behind her, and we say, "Jimmy Neil said to follow you, that you might know a place to stay tonight."
"FOLLOW ME!" she said.

Regan-Blake:
She said, "FOLLOW ME!"
And she went out and got in her Jeep;

Freeman:
And we get in our truck. And we think, "Gaw, we don't even know where we're going, you know, or anything."

Regan-Blake:
It was great, because she was in this flowing kind of an outfit, and then to get into a Jeep; and then all these thousands of cars were leaving the place, and I'm amazed that we were able to keep behind her.

Freeman:
So we followed her. And she drove us to—do you remember where the Blue Iris used to be, the big brick house by the graveyard? That was her second house. And her daughter, Cassandra, was living there. So she gets out of her car and says, "How do you do, I'm Carolyn Moore."
And we say, "Well, I'm Barbara," you know, "and Connie."
And she says, "Well, come on in!" And she walks into the kitchen and she says, "Darling, I've got to be going, but these two people will be staying here tonight." And she furls around with her cloak, and leaves.
And we're standing there in the middle of this kitchen, in this strange house. . . .

Regan-Blake:
Of course we didn't know it at the time, but that was the very same house on the hill by the cemetery where we held the ghost storytell-

ings for many years during the festival. And those ghost storytellings were to become *so* important to the festival, and to the whole storytelling movement. So for me, it was kind of prophetic that our first night in Jonesborough we spent *in the house* that was to be the site of that ghost storytelling.

The Folktellers' story shows with wonderful clarity how storytellers' biographical accounts reproduce the traditional patterns of folktales. Here the two of them combine in the part of wonder tale heroines. With the innocent openness native to the type, they hear of the magical boon and immediately set out. Always receptive to serendipitous blessing, they stop at an unscheduled revival meeting along the way. Because of this, they miss most of the supposed main event of the festival—which, as we will see, turns out not to be the main event at all. The main event for them will be their own self-discovery as storytellers.

But first, of course, they find themselves in a perilous situation—young women alone in a strange town, with nowhere to stay. They are rescued by Smith, in the role of the good king, and by the wise and mysterious older woman, dressed in her swirling black cape and riding her contemporary equivalent of a stallion. She leaves them in an old house in the keeping of her daughter. The house turns out to be an omen in itself, the future site of the most popular event of the National Storytelling Festival—and of many similar festivals around the country—where the Folktellers will eventually hold a regal position.

As in the wonder tales, the heroines' openness to serendipity, though it may appear wayward, turns out to connect them more immediately to the people and places that will form their destiny. The Folktellers' tandem personal myth allows them to communicate the sense of grace that infuses their vocational choices, with humor, humility, and innocence—just as for millennia the wonder tales have reminded us of our royal estate of soul, in the midst of the darkness and waywardness of exile.

The Search for a Festival Form

Smith had the intuitive sense that a storytelling festival needed to find its own peculiar form if it were to survive and thrive. It would find that form through attracting its own committed group of performers, who themselves would find their voices and performance styles in the emerging storytelling festival context. Smith reflected:

What was interesting to me was that I had only the Historic Jonesborough Days planning experience behind me. I had no knowledge, no specific knowledge of storytelling. And I certainly had no knowledge, no specific role model of a storytelling festival. So essentially I began to create the model. Without having an instruction manual. . . .

I intuitively knew that there was more to it than a concert by a well-known storyteller. It was very important for me, I think, to look at Clower as the first-ever storyteller for the National Storytelling Festival. He told the first story. And it was important for us to use him in the first performance, because, for us, he was the spark that ignited the concept, for the National Storytelling Festival. But at the same time, we knew that there was more opportunity for storytelling than just a concert Saturday night. So I began to look at the importance of having a very grass-roots element of the first festival. In which we pulled an old farm wagon into Courthouse Square and planned an afternoon of storytelling activities on Sunday.

Regan-Blake remembered it thus:

I think one of the things was, Jerry Clower wanted to fly in, go to his dressing room, go out on stage, get his paycheck, and leave. And it was that sense of hangin' out that Jimmy Neil really liked. And I think we all felt—we had not seen the whole concert that he had given the night before, because like I say, we had come late—but the *feeling* and the *sense* of what happened on that Sunday afternoon was just so different. It was like on a level you could comprehend; the other thing was almost more like TV. I mean, it was gone when it was gone.

And I think, too—you'd have to ask him to be sure, but *I* would think that he also—you know, the other thing was indoors, at night, in a gym, a huge area, you know. *This* was in the town that he *loved,* and he could look around and see his buildings—it was a gorgeous, sunny, autumn afternoon, on Sunday. And I think that was his . . . element, you know, and I think right then he thought this is what he wanted, was not some gymnasium twenty miles, or five miles away, at night; but I would think he was taken by the atmosphere, the setting. Because he loved Jonesborough so much, and to have people then, sitting there taking in Jonesborough as well as taking in stories, was probably real appealing to him. (telephone interview, January 21, 1992)

Indeed, the siting of the festival within the historic district of the town of Jonesborough was to become an essential part of the festival mythos. The town would soon go full-steam into its restoration phase. It was already apparent that the restored town would make an ideal setting for the restored performance context of revival storytelling. Its cobblestone streets, brick sidewalks, gaslight-style lampposts, and antique hanging signs were a splendid physical analogy to the antique, primitive, or folk-flavored performances that made up the bulk of the festival repertoire for many years.

Although the boundaries of the repertoire and the backgrounds of the performers may have begun to shift in the early eighties toward the literary, theatrical, or cosmopolitan, still, the unifying ideology of historic preservation in the forms and materials of the site seemed to give physical expression to the notion of traditional roots, roots that could unite these diverse personalities and styles into a coherent artistic movement. As already noted, the town provided an ideal environmental theater for the social drama of storytellers and storytelling pilgrims. It would make an authentically festive, carnivalesque setting—a parade of tellers and enthusiasts in ethnic and period regalia, strolling a narrow main street bedecked with cornucopia baskets, pumpkins, hanging quilts, and straw men dressed up in overalls and bandannas. All of this would generate the very thing the historic preservation movement promised—a brisk import of affluent, non-polluting business traffic, to serve as an engine for economic prosperity.

The siting of the storytelling festival was thus part of a local political and economic agenda that soon saw Smith elected alderman and then mayor of Jonesborough, even as he was devoting a good deal of his time to a fledgling organization called NAPPS. Yet there was another level on which the siting of the festival in this small, out-of-the-way village was mythically just right for the emerging storytelling movement. It seemed mystically fit that the de-centered center of this national revival should be a pinprick of a place, whose atmosphere was the more envelopingly real for all of its self-conscious artifice. The festival adventure must begin with a journey, not to New York, Paris, London, or any comparable center of modernist faith but to a small-town simulation of an ideal past, far from the main roads, where local Davids face the Goliath of progress armed only with cobblestones and antique bricks in a sling of homespun yarns.

"Telling Tales with the Masters"

Most of the tellers who performed in that first Sunday afternoon session have not remained a part of the movement. Less storytellers than "after-dinner speakers" whom Smith had found through Clower's Nashville agent, they went straight back to the banquet circuit, never to return. But a few of those who appeared on the courthouse square on that first festival Sunday afternoon went on to play key roles in the storytelling revival, both at Jonesborough and around the country. Ray Hicks, a farmer and teller of Appalachian wonder tales from nearby Watauga County, North Carolina, was a featured teller that Sunday. Freeman and Regan came out of the crowd to tell stories in the open-mike section of the program. And a hospital custodian from Rogersville, Tennessee, named Ernest ("Doc") McConnell (whose nickname came from his hobby of performing humorous pastiche medicine shows at street festivals and county fairs) was there in the small crowd, listening and looking on.

Jimmy Neil Smith had arranged for the sound crew to include an open-reel tape recorder, and both Saturday evening and Sunday afternoon sessions were preserved on tape. The whole affair was, in some respects, more like a generic small-town street fair than the festival that was to evolve out of it. Clower shared the bill on Saturday with another big-name veteran of country radio, Bill Monroe and the Bluegrass Boys. On Sunday the square was ringed with crafts displays and demonstrations and carnival booths with traditional games like apple-bobbing. The farm wagon/stage in front of the Mail Pouch Building (named after an old advertising sign for Mail Pouch Tobacco painted on one wall) featured sets of old-time fiddle and banjo music, a clog-dancing team, and a guitar-strumming folksinger from Nashville with nary a story in her bag.

The afternoon also featured the open-mike session, dubbed with Smith's usual gift for hyperbole, "Telling Tales with the Masters." Out of the crowd struggled a variety of local folks to tell jokes, brief versions of tall tales, or bits of local lore; then, in the midst of it, up leaped Connie Regan to tell "The Brave Little Indian" to the wandering preschoolers in the crowd. She was followed by her cousin, with an already thoroughly professional rendition of "Two Chinese Brothers," a literary folktale that turns on one of the brothers' having an impossibly long name. Nineteen years later, when I reminded Freeman of the story, she exclaimed, "Rikki-Tikki-Timbo No-Sah-Rimbo Cherri-Berri-Ruchipit-Pimbo!" never missing a beat. "I don't think I've told it since," she said. Then she shrugged, "It's like typing, you know."

Smith told me, "We only had sixty people in the audience Sunday afternoon; but we knew, almost intuitively, that it was what was happening Sunday afternoon that would be the format for the future festivals. I think it was the honesty of the event. The genuine nature of the event. It was very real, it was very honest, it was very genuine. And seeing people from all walks of life, little-known people, from all walks of life, telling stories, was the most powerful experience that I had had ... in my life."

In 1974, Connie Regan drove up to Jonesborough to visit Carolyn Moore, with whom she had kept in touch. There Moore stepped right back into her role of fairy godmother. As Regan-Blake remembers the story:

So I pulled into the driveway, and before I even got out of the car she came r-r-running out—she was very dramatic—and she said, "Oh, Connie! Get in the Jeep!" So I got out of my car, got in the Jeep. And she said, "*You* are *just* who I've been looking for!"

And she knew I was comin' and all. So I was not sure what she meant. And so she took off, and we went into to town and went up to a building. And she said, "Come in with me!" It was very mysterious.

She opened the door. And there stood Jimmy Neil. And she said, "Jimmy Neil! Here she is." And she left.

And Jimmy Neil knew instantly what she meant. 'Cause he had been looking for a children's storyteller for this second storytelling festival.

And during that year's interim he had realized that the part that he liked about the festival was not so much Jerry Clower on the Saturday night and three thousand people, but what happened on Sunday afternoon. So he wanted to re-create more that feeling. . . .

So he asked me if I would be the children's storyteller. And we ended up, that night—this was in the afternoon sometime, I would guess like two or three o'clock in the afternoon—we stayed together and talked until probably until one-thirty or two in the morning. It was amazing. I think that's really when our friendship was sealed. You know, instantly, like that. I had met him the year before, but just so briefly. And this—we just talked about so many different things. I remember I showed him how to clog. And he showed me all around—you know, the Widow Brown's was not even built. We were in a room that was the *old,* old parsonage, before it was redone as "the Widow Brown's," that's where his little office was. That's where the mythical one-drawer filing cabinet that *was NAPPS* was. And actually we were even in a pre-room of that—it was a room right next door to that.

And also that same night, as we talked, and I told him stories, and told him all about the storytelling, and about the music, 'cause I had started to get into the folk music and stuff then . . . and it was also that very same night that he went to his file cabinet and pulled out a *story,* and said, "You ought to read this." And it was "Two White Horses."

And I knew in reading it that it was a story I wanted to tell. And I really, in that moment, knew that storytelling was for adults. I really kind of already knew that, as far as that I knew that adults were interested in listening to children's stories. But *this* was a story that was meant for adults. As opposed to a children's story that adults would enjoy too. (telephone interview, January 21, 1992)

We can see in this memory the special kind of genius attending the principals at the beginning of a revitalization moment. It is not an individual genius but a migrating genius of receptivity, temperament, and timing that brings individuals and groups together in combinations that reach toward a cultural critical mass. It is the genius of serendipity. In a sense, it is also the genius of youth, the same spirit that guides any biographical narrative to its fulfillment from the thrilling and perilous stage where patterns are cast away and new beginnings are invoked. It is the moment in the wonder tale where the hero or heroine sets out on the road to an unknown redemption. The genius of the moment is to recognize the wise old woman, to feed the beggar, or to stop and engage with the prince, even if he appears in the shape of a frog sunk in a well—or, as in this version, a fledgling businessman in a cramped office, with a one-drawer filing cabinet full of dreams.

"Two White Horses" did become Regan-Blake's personal signature story, which she told for the first time at the second National Storytelling Festival and has told constantly ever since. A literary tale adapted from folkloric sources by the Tennessee writer Elizabeth Seeman, it concerns a woman who is buried alive and awakened by grave robbers. She drags herself home and has to convince her husband that she is not a ghost. He would have left her outside to freeze, but the whinnying of their two white horses makes him realize that they recognize her, and so she must be alive. It is a story of literal revitalization, in which the two white horses stand as vivid symbols of instinctive wisdom, which will not let what is truly precious die. In a symbolic way for Regan-Blake, it is a totemic tale of her own storytelling revival.

More than a personal landmark, Regan's encounter with Smith marked a decisive moment in the formation of an art world. The storytelling world grew, as many such worlds do, through relationships and an intensity of interactive commitment that turns a job, a pastime, an idea, or a technique into what was once commonly called a "school" but now is more often dubbed a "movement." The symbiotic relationship between Regan-Blake and Smith was to guide and influence NAPPS for much of its first twelve years, until her retirement from the board of directors in 1986. Their complementary efforts in the areas of performance and promotion formed magnetic poles, around which the constellations of artists, organizational forms, and ritual expressions that made up the festival and NAPPS arrayed themselves.

Jerry Clower at the first National Storytelling Festival, 1973.
(Photo by David Cortner)

Ray Hicks at the first National Storytelling Festival, 1973.
(Photo by David Cortner)

Ghost stories at the cemetery, Jonesborough, pre-1982.
(Photo courtesy of NSA Archives)

Ray Hicks tells tales on the Swappin' Grounds.
(Photo courtesy of NSA Archives)

Doc McConnell's Medicine Show in the 1970s. *Left to right:*
Doc, his brother Steamer, and daughter Hannah.
(Photo courtesy of NSA Archives)

Tenth Annual National Storytelling Festival
October 1982   Jonesborough, Tennessee

Bottom row, seated:
Hannah McConnell, Elizabeth Ellis, Ron Evans, Laura Simms, Connie Regan,
Jay O'Callahan, Pete Boyer, Doc McConnell, Chuck Larkin, Ed Stivender.
Second row:
Henry Hatch, Jackie Torrence, Linda Morley, Gwen Ledbetter, Diane
Wolkstein, Maggie Pierce, Nancy Schimmel, Kathryn Windham, Linda Goss,
David Holt, Heather Forest, Lee Pennington, Gamble Rogers.
Third row, on porch:
Ed Bell, Julia Ruth Richardson, Brother Blue, Cora Bardwell, Bernard Bragg,
Fred Park, John Basinger, Pleasant DeSpain, Harriet Allen, Doug Elliot,
Barbara Freeman, Donald Davis, Michael Parent.
(Photo courtesy of NSA Archives)

The Lakota storyteller and fancy dancer Kevin Locke performs in
one of the large National Storytelling Festival tents, 1994.
(Photo by Tom Raymond)

3

From Serendipity to Ceremony

At the climax of the folktale, the youngest son is crowned with riches, a kingdom, and a princess to wed. What begins in serendipity ends in ceremony. Folktales are discretely silent about what happens afterward. So it goes, too, with the folk revival story. What happens when the outsider artist or art form becomes celebrated, venerated, the toast of the town? What happens when the return of the prodigal has been accomplished, when the happy discovery that sparked such shocks of recognition has become a formula to be ritually repeated, and when a "dying tradition" has become retraditionalized as the hub of a widespread social and economic enterprise?

In this chapter, I will look at the traditionalizing process as it secretes its ritual fluids around a serendipitous act, transforming the wayward social irritant into a ceremonial pearl. It is the process that the sociologist Max Weber called "the routinization of charisma." The historians Eric Hobsbawm and Terence Ranger call it "the invention of tradition." In their book of that name, they give copious examples of cultural revitalization movements that began in the enthusiasms of a few and evolved into ritualized performances that could absorb and affect large groups. Hobsbawm writes:

> Inventing traditions . . . is essentially a process of formalization and ritualization, characterized by reference to the past, if only by imposing repetition. There is probably no time and place with which historians are concerned that has not seen the "invention" of tradition in this sense.

However, we should expect it to occur more frequently where a rapid transformation of society weakens or destroys the social patterns for which "old" traditions had been designed. . . . Such changes have been particularly significant in the past 200 years, and it is therefore reasonable to expect these instant formalizations of new traditions to cluster during this period. This implies, incidentally, against both nineteenth-century liberalism and more recent "modernization" theory that such formalizations are not confined to so-called "traditional" societies, but also have their place, in one form or another, in "modern" ones. (4–5)

In Anthony F. C. Wallace's scheme, this phase is crucial to the period of revitalization; it is the phase in which the movement either establishes its effect in the greater society or fades away in solipsistic dreams. To institute cultural change, Wallace writes, communication of the founding vision must proceed among networks of students, supporters, and followers. There must be organizational efforts that allow action programs to move from the visionary to the cultural, political, and economic spheres. If there are radical qualities to the social critique implied by the founding visions, they are often buffered by ritual adaptations that help express the vision according to commonly accessible performative conventions and hierarchies of value. The end result is a new steady state in which culture and vision achieve a mutual, homeostatic accommodation.

For the storytelling revival movement, the National Storytelling Festival and NAPPS were primary vessels of this process of communication, organization, and adaptation. They present significant but not incompatible variations on the revitalization pattern Wallace describes. The visionary founder of the storytelling institutions, Jimmy Neil Smith, was avowedly not a practitioner of the art but a promoter and businessman, whose enterprises intersected the storytelling movement at an acute angle. It would be as if the prophet of the Ghost Dance or the Peyote Cult, to take two of Wallace's examples, were not Paiute or Comanche but white businessmen from a nearby mining town or dude ranch, seeking a boost to the local tourist trade. Yet Smith managed to gather around him a host of talented women and men who were not only bona fide performers but also could proselytize with their performances in the name of the art, the festival, and the organization.

In a certain sense, this bifocaled founding vision is not as odd as the Ghost Dance or Peyote analogy might suggest. As much as their revival fervor might have elided the fact, many storytellers were looking not just for a religion but a profession, not just a congregation but a network of professional contacts, colleagues, and support personnel. This is a thoroughly consistent expression of the revitalization urge in a contemporary American context. Here, to create a more satisfying cultural set means, in good part, to create opportunities for more meaningful work—not just a way of life but also a way of making a living. The storyteller Elizabeth Ellis used traditional Buddhist terminology when she told me, "The concept of right livelihood seemed very important to me, and I think to other people who became storytellers early on." Correspondingly, their movement summoned not just prophets, of which there were plenty, but also promoters, of which Smith was the most gifted, persistent, and compellingly situated.

The second National Storytelling Festival was held entirely in the Jonesborough historic district. Without a big-name drawing card, it was held in parlors, on front porches, in church basements, and in the park by the newly rebuilt and resituated Christopher Taylor Cabin. Doc McConnell was invited to perform his medicine show. He said that the event was so small and low in visibility that some of the townspeople accused the organizers of having a "secret storytelling festival":

> We were so small at our first festivals that—Jimmy Neil Smith had asked for sponsorship from a local historical group, and local business people and civic leaders were accusing him of having a "secret storytelling" in Jonesborough. That we were operating "underground." And probably it seemed that way. Because we were having these storytelling sessions in the basement of the Presbyterian Church or some other remote location around, and we could have all the people that came to one, which was probably less than a hundred people, and nobody could tell there was anything special going on. And they would ask, "Where did you have your festival, we didn't see anything happening!"
> So we made a joke out of that, by calling it a "secret society" or an "underground storytelling festival." (taped reminiscences)

Smith's strategy seemed to be to find people who were neither well known nor highly paid but who were passionate about storytelling or could become so. These would indeed form a kind of secret society, a small group charged with a sacred mission. Kathryn Windham and Lee Pennington were invited on the strength of their books of Alabama ghost stories and Kentucky legends, respectively. Their reactions to their invitations were similar. Windham said:

> Funny thing. I was at the office one day, and I got a call from this man who said his name was Jimmy Smith and he lived in Jonesborough, Ten-

nessee. And he wanted me to come tell stories at the National Storytelling Festival. And I thought the whole thing was a joke. I never heard of the National Storytelling Festival. Certainly not of Jimmy Smith or Jonesborough. And everybody in the office thought it was a big joke. And then here came a ticket. An airplane ticket for me to fly up there. So I said, "Well, why not, let's see what they're doing." And I went up there and told stories at the second festival.

I never knew I was a storyteller. When he called, I said, "I don't think you want me, I think you want my daughter, who has a master's in drama and theater, and does that kind of thing."

And he said, "No, I'm sure it's you I want." I certainly don't know why. He swears to this day he does not know how he heard of me.

Likewise, Pennington:

My first hearing of the Jonesborough festival came in the form of an invitation to come perform there. I suspect, if I'm connecting things right, I suspect it had to do with my connection with the Kentucky writer Jesse Stuart. On an awful lot of occasions folks would get in touch with Jesse to do some kind of a program, and Jesse would say, "No I can't do that, but you ought to call Lee Pennington."

And I remember early on being very curious as to what a storyteller was. Because I didn't relate to that word at all. I just didn't even know what that word meant—in relation to myself. I understood storytellers and what not, but I never did think of myself, even though I had given by that time hundreds of programs all over the United States, I still didn't connect myself as a story-*teller*. I thought I was a writer, a poet, and the things that I told were connected with that rather than the oral tradition of storytelling. So it was somewhat of a surprise to me when I was invited to a storytelling festival.

Still, Windham and Pennington came, and, as the story goes, the festival was enough to fire their imaginations. Pennington remembered, "I know that Jimmy Neil and I hit it off real nicely, right off the bat. We had a lot of aside-conversation concerning the direction of the festival, and the direction of NAPPS itself. It was just a marvelous kind of exciting time. To see all that kind of thing taking place."

During that weekend, a breakfast meeting was held at Smith's restaurant, the Parson's Table, to discuss forming an organization for the promotion of storytelling in the United States. Connie Regan and Barbara Freeman attended, along with Windham, Pennington, McConnell, and Ardi St. Clair (now Lawrence), an editor for the *Tennessee Conservationist* magazine who had written the first published article on the storytelling festival. Lawrence recalled that at some point in the meeting everyone looked at one another and said, "Well—I guess we're the board of directors."

McConnell said, "I can't remember much about it, other than we said, 'Let's have this organization.' And I remember Kathryn Windham said, 'Here's my five dollars. And I want to be the first member.' And she became the first member of the association. She just whipped the money on us right there, she was so enthused about it" (telephone interview).

Pennington recalled, "We were all bright-eyed as to what things might be called, and how we might attract, through an organization, attract or have a place where people could congregate on an annual basis. And I remember we even talked about establishing Jonesborough as the 'Storytelling Center of the United States'; we even talked about maybe getting road signs put up, so that people coming through would see 'Jonesborough, the Storytelling Capitol of America' and start posing questions about it."

Naming, once again, is a fundamental ritual of identity, a basic element in the movement from serendipity to ceremony. In the case of an association, the name invokes a mission, defines ambition, and sets a resonant frequency. The name is the map of the organization's psychic geography, its logos. In this case, no one seems to remember who actually came up with the name, but it carries Smith's characteristic stamp. The name that he and his friends devised announced a vision of their little town as the center of a national movement. It associated storytelling with the economic and psychological forces of historic preservation. It proclaimed the past its resource and the future its preserve. And it offered up the festival and the town itself as the symbolic hometown for a community of spiritual wanderers.

The construction of the name was loaded with concealed energy: the cozy acronym, NAPPS, so redolent of embroidered quilts and bedtime stories, sprung open to unfurl the full Victorian Gothic crusade banner. Especially when the movement was small, the twin names had the function of an initiatory task and token for neophytes, who, after they learned the long form, never used it again except to initiate others. With normal variations, the introductory ritual would run something like this:

Neophyte: So, where do I find out more about this storytelling stuff?
Initiate: Well, now that you mention it, there is an organization down

in Tennessee that's sort of a clearing house for storytelling. They run a big festival in the fall, and they have workshops and publications. It's called NAPPS.
Neophyte: Huh? (This is the propitious moment.)
Initiate: That stands for the *National Association for the Preservation and Perpetuation of Storytelling*. N-A-P-P-S. NAPPS.
Neophyte: Ah!

The initiation had now been performed. If the neophytes cared enough to remember the content of the ritual, they could use its key word, *NAPPS,* to identify themselves as members of the tribe. They could also initiate others, at which point the form of the ritual, encoded in the twin logos, would spontaneously perform itself again.

By 1975, many the key elements of the storytelling festival form were falling into place, generally through serendipitous innovation, followed by increasing ritualization. These elements were picked up by other storytelling festivals that were already springing up around the country—sometimes faithfully imitated, sometimes refined and altered to fit the personalities of key organizers and their local communities. I will explore some of these local variations in chapter 5. Here, I will enumerate the elements, in order of appearance.

The Ghost Storytelling in the Cemetery

In 1975, the first scheduled ghost story session took place in the old cemetery on the hill behind Cassandra Moore's house. McConnell described its origin:

> One week we decided that I would take the children to the cemetery, and tell ghost stories to them; while the adults would stay downtown and listen to adults tell stories. And I would be a babysitter. So I got a team of mules, and a farm wagon, and a driver, and we're going to take the kids on a hayride and tell ghost stories in the cemetery. It turned out that it had such an appeal to the audience, that just about everybody who was supposed to be going to some other session wanted to follow the wagon to the graveyard to hear the ghost stories.
>
> The next year we put on two wagons; and those two wagons wouldn't haul all the people, all the children. So from then on we dispensed with the wagons, and we all just walked up to the local old Jonesborough cemetery. And we were so small that we could actually have a storytelling right there in the cemetery itself. But as our crowds grew more and

more, we finally moved out of the cemetery into the lawn, and finally into a vacant lot next door, and into a man's turnip patch next door to the cemetery up there.

And that continued to grow and has become one of the leading attractions to all storytellings throughout America, as I've visited them. And it seems like folks have fashioned their storytelling festivals and their ghost storytellings after the telling that we had in Jonesborough. (taped reminiscences)

Ghost story sessions have indeed become the most popular attractions at virtually every storytelling festival around the country that features them, but those who have told their ghost stories in graveyards have seen phenomena that are truly frightening. When Pennington started the ghost storytelling at Long Run Cemetery during the 1983 Corn Island Festival, his audience went from a couple of hundred a year to four thousand people at that single night's event. The crowd was so thick that none of the featured storytellers could get in. Pennington, who had laryngitis, had to wander through the crowd with a notepad that read "CAN YOU TELL A STORY?" He recalled:

We got five volunteers out of the audience and went up on the stage—it was nothing more than up against a tombstone—it was a pretty good-sized tombstone, made a nice little backdrop. And we sent a patrol car down the wrong side of the road with blue lights on, stopping cars, asking if there were a storyteller in the car. And about a mile down the road, locked onto Jackie Torrence, and put her in the squad car, and blue-lighted her back up to the cemetery. And by that time the crowd was getting a bit antsy with the stories they were hearing. And we got Jackie on the stage about ten o'clock or ten-fifteen. And of course she's capable of chilling somebody at mid-daylight. And they had come to be scared, and she just wiped the audience out. And they went home happy. But we were right on the verge of total disaster. We had no sound system. Somebody had brought along one of these walking-tour, battery-operated things like you use on the street when you've got fifteen or twenty people, it wasn't a bullhorn, it wasn't a megaphone, just one of those little square speakers, about six inches, it's got a mike and a cord on it. But the crowd was fine.

Ghost story sessions in cemeteries have demonstrated themselves to be the single storytelling revival event with the transgressive potential to draw consistent mass audiences. What rock festivals perform in flouting taboos of gender and sexual expression, ghost tellings in cemeteries perform for social taboos about death. Funerals and wakes having been sanitized to the point of vacuity, there are very few rituals in our society that imaginatively and efficaciously address our fears and fantasies about death. The bringing together of narratives of the living dead with the silently suggestive evidence of their nearness produced an attraction of unsuspected force.

Despite the often predictable repertoire—endless recitals of "Tailypo," "The Golden Arm," or "The Monkey's Paw"—and the prevailing atmosphere of forced and facetious spookiness, the popular need seems inexhaustible. Now and then tellers will come forth with stories of sincerity and sorrow at these ghost tellings, stories that touch chords of real loss in the audience, and then macabre laughter will release it. However, after their serendipitous discovery, some graveyard ghost tellings have ritually devolved in the direction of "Goosebumps" without many objections. As audiences grow beyond what can be safely accommodated in cemeteries, they may be moved, as they were at Jonesborough and Corn Island, to parks in the vicinity of cemeteries—the throngs of scare-seekers hardly seem to notice. Patrons remain as hypnotized by the transgressive lure of creeping flesh as organizers are by the lure of separate admission fees. For many festivals, these ghost story sessions actually subsidize the rest of the weekend. As one organizer told me, "We break even with Saturday night. The rest is gravy."

"The Swappin' Grounds"

The open-mike segment of the first festival soon grew into its own separate performance area, the Swapping Ground (or "Swappin' Grounds"), where anyone could sign up to stand in front of McConnell's Medicine Show wagon and step for a moment into the storyteller's role. McConnell recalled:

> I'd suggested to Jimmy Neil Smith that we have an opportunity for everybody to swap a yarn or tell a story. So we had what we called the Swapping Ground. And I just said, "It won't take anything but some old haybales out there, and I'll sit around and just tell some stories, and we'll swap some yarns." And it started out, and it became just that. And it was so popular that I could go down early in the morning during the festival, and just sit down on the bale of straw and start telling a story, and then ask someone who would like to tell the next story, and then who would be next, and who's next; and that Swapping Ground would run by itself,

spontaneously, all during the day and into the evening. People just wanted to tell a story. And so the Swapping Ground became an important part of our storytelling festival, and it, like the ghost storytelling, became a part of other storytelling festivals across the country. It was appropriate that wherever people gathered to tell stories, even if they were not featured tellers on the program, they'd like to have an opportunity to tell a story. So we really hit on something that was of interest there. (taped reminiscences)

The Swapping Ground expressed the egalitarian idealism that helped drive the storytelling movement. "Anyone can tell a story" was the movement motto that encouraged many a shy person and closet stage-hound to stand before the hay bales and try out an Uncle Remus tale or go on about Grandma's rhubarb pie. One of the psychological benefits of belonging to a storytelling support group was the sense of a safe place to try on new self-images, and this the Swapping Ground provided in an exotic, carnival frame. It could lead to some excruciating half-hours for Swapping Ground audiences but also to some great moments of serendipity.

For a time in the early and mid-eighties, the Swapping Ground at Jonesborough developed into an audition spot, where members of the NAPPS board of directors might have a chance to see and hear emerging professional storytellers' work. There were a few famous episodes of tellers doing a bang-up job at the Swapping Ground in front of Barbara or Connie or Jean Smith and finding themselves on the main stage a year or two later. This audition procedure was sustainable for only a few years before audition hysteria began to swamp the Swapping Ground. As we will see in chapter 6, this growing competition had some dark consequences for the community.

The Storytelling Olio

The year 1975 marked the first storytelling "olio." The term was borrowed, appropriately enough, from the nineteenth-century minstrel shows, a notable predecessor in the American pattern of transforming marginal folk culture into popular entertainment. An olio originally signified a spicy Mediterranean stew in which many ingredients were simmered together. The storytelling festival olio is a variety performance in which the featured tellers have ten minutes or so to introduce themselves and their work to the public or to say farewell after a long storytelling weekend. Olios soon became a ubiquitous part of the festival form. They serve as opening and closing movements, sometimes with an additional olio on the Saturday night of a three-day event like the National Storytelling Festival, each with a different ritual purpose, tempo, and atmosphere. While opening olios are icebreakers, closing olios on Sunday afternoon are valedictory. They have some of the aura of what Richard Schechner describes as "cool-down periods," for both tellers and audience members (*Between Theater* 125). The stories told tend to be trifles, drawn-out equivalents of the trance-breaking formulas that tag onto the ends of wonder tales: "And I was at the wedding, and I drank till the wine ran into my beard, but never a drop did I taste."

Tents

In 1978, the "underground storytelling festival" burst its bunkers. The festival emerged from the local church basements into the autumn sunlight and the glare of national publicity under bright, yellow-and-white, green-and-white, or blue-and-white striped tents.

According to McConnell, the original impulse was unreflective: "I guess it was sheer necessity. Other activities in our area use tents—like, if they have a car show, or a big motor company has an automobile sale they'll have a 'tent sale.' And we just thought a tent would be a good place just to get under. It's *big*, cheap housing" (telephone interview). But the iconography and atmosphere of the tents soon became an essential part of the festival mystique. The obvious associations, of course, for the majority of the audiences are not with auto sales but with the circus and tent-and-sawdust religious revivals. The circus connection emphasizes the aura of liminality, marvel, and fantasy that attends the event and its artists. It highlights the tellers as stage magicians of the imagination, daredevils of verbal dexterity; and it increases the festival aura of time out of time, an enchanted island in which mundane social order is suspended and magical rules of freedom and fancy now apply. The serendipitous connection to religious tent revivals was even more important to the mythos of the storytelling revival. Ed Stivender expressed it well in an interview, from a dissenter's point of view:

> Wallace Stevens, American poet, died in 1955, said that poetry would re-
> place religion; that was one of his adages. And it has not, in fact, replaced
> religion. But some of my storytelling colleagues believe that storytelling
> *has* replaced religion. And for good reason, in a sense. The structure of

NAPPS' festival is pretty much the same structure as a camp meeting, as a Methodist camp meeting, back in 1932. The structure of the event, of going into a tent and having someone up front talk and make us feel good, and then sing together—more and more NAPPS has learned that singing is important at the festival—it does, in fact, replace the experience, the liturgical experience of *Methodist* religion. And that's why it's such a tricky business; because it is so vital in copying this old form and secularizing the old form. (January 7, 1992)

Stivender then added, "Well, I don't think it's a conscious attempt. I don't think Jimmy Neil set out to do a Methodist revival. In fact, he didn't have tents for a long time." When the tents did go up, however, it serendipitously added another important ritual element to the appeal of the festival form.

The tents became an evocative key for other successful festivals as well. Jim May, who returned home from NAPPS to Spring Grove, Illinois, to found the Illinois Storytelling Festival in 1984, was consciously imprinted by the liminal space the tents created:

I think, in terms of how NAPPS affected me back home, that whole format, with the tents . . . there seemed to be no question that when I would do something back in my hometown that it would be in tents. Partly—I'm trying to think whether that was just part of the myth—I think it was. Well, it might have been because there was no place in Spring Grove big enough to hold what we were doing—which was the same thing in Jonesborough.

But I remember putting that tent up in Spring Grove and having that same sense, of, God, we've really arrived! 'Cause it felt like that same thing that happened at NAPPS, you know; the same sorts of smells in the air, and textures, and light, that happen when you put up a tent.

I also remember . . . two things, one is that, the first year at Spring Grove, we had borrowed an old farmer's tent. We had a regular tent, too, a tent that was put up by a state-of-the-art tent guy. We also had one that we rented from a farmer at a low price. And it was an old canvas tent with wooden poles, and we had to put it up ourselves, and it was a real bitch—now I know why they have elephants in circuses. And when we got all done, we sat there in the shade; it was hot. And we looked out away from the other tent, just so we were looking back out across this field, with the woods in back. And all you could see was the wooden tent posts, woods, the place where we had cut the grass to put this tent up, then there were some old, ancient really, wooden fenceposts in the back. And that scene just struck me, as like, this must have been what the chautauquas were like: you came into town, you cut the grass in a field, and you put up these old wooden tent poles to hang this canvas from. And this is what the fields looked like.

And there was that sense too that Thursday there'd be nothing there but a ballfield or a park. And then Friday there'd be all these colorful tents. And then Monday they'd be gone. And there was a real sense of creating something that was very fleeting. And that made it even more magical.

Microphones

One of the late Marshall McLuhan's axioms was that "environments are invisible." He explained that the dominant communications technologies of a culture become so deeply embedded in the sensory experience of its natives that they fail to notice either the source or the effects. Microphones have become such a ubiquitous part of our technological environment that they have become invisible in precisely this sense. It is easy to overlook the crucial role that sound reinforcement plays in the contextual transformation of storytelling. Microphones are an essential tool in shifting from a primary oral medium, as in home or community storytelling, or a print-based, interpretive art form, as in library storytelling, to a postliterate medium of electronic representation, in which prior cultural media are blended, juiced, whipped up, and redistributed. The process of capturing the voice at its acoustic source, transforming it into an electronic impulse to reemerge amplified and reverberant from loudspeakers, is a transformation of scale that parallels the shift from an oral, to a literate, to an electronic community. This shift is an unassimilated, rejected part of the dominant culture for many storytelling revivalists— as Ron Evans's totemic tale "The Storyteller Knows Me" so powerfully demonstrates. The shift breeds alienation, anomie, and blasted roots of identity; and yet it is also an inexorable contemporary presence, a part of our common consensual reality. The storytelling festival's appropriation of sound reinforcement technology for the purpose of restoring ancient fireside tales to instantaneous communities of a thousand families epitomizes the dialectic of resistance and accommodation that sustains the entire movement.

The microphone is a rod of power for the revival performer. Its mastery is a rite of passage that marks the performer's ability to project work on the scale demanded by the social and economic engine of the festival. It has been so from the beginning. Ray Hicks described a near-disaster at his National Storytelling Festival debut in 1973, sitting on the farm wagon stage behind the Mail Pouch Building:

And I got up to the mike. And didn't know, you know. I'd never been to a mike like that, and me just a wild mountain man! And then didn't realize but what the mike would pick me up further from me. You know, when it's outside it don't do as good, like it is in a building.

And [the announcer] said, "Get your mouth up close to the mike." And I didn't hear that, just went right on.

And he said he was gonna kick my butt, if I didn't get my mouth up close to the mike. He said, "If you're gonna *tell* the heifer *tale,* you'd better get to the mike or I'll kick *your'n.*"

And it hit me—God, I hate to think it—I nearly just thought how it would work if me and *him* would put on a show. See who kicked—whichever would kick whose butt, mine or his.

But I guess they'd o' locked me up in jail. And maybe it'd been the worse 'cause I was out o' North Carolina!

Freeman recalled seeing Hicks perform that day:

Ray was so nervous that he looked at the sky the whole time. And that microphone, and his voice, he was just shaking, you know; and his mouth was dry, and he was scared to pieces. And I thought to myself, and Connie I know had the same thought, Boy, this seems cruel, you know, to bring somebody who is a front-porch storyteller out of their natural environment and subject them to a big microphone and big speakers and a great crowd of people. 'Cause this man is miserable. Of course, the next year at NAPPS, he was grabbing that microphone and in full control. In full-tilt boogie; so I kind of readjusted a little bit. I just said that was like growing pains. And people loved it so much; and now Ray loves it so much.

A similar moment occurred at Ron Evans's festival debut in 1979. Jackson Gillman was in the audience and described it:

I went down to Jonesborough the year Ron Evans was first there—1979. I witnessed Ron's debut. And I distinctly remember my feelings watching him, during his first session. 'Cause, he started out sitting down, with all these people in a tent, in chairs, facing him. And did not go for the microphone. And started telling these stories. And people stopped him, and asked, would he please stand up and use the microphone. And you could see this culture-gap making itself wider. And he admitted that he had actually never told stories with a microphone before. He had never told stories standing up—he never even told stories and not been in a circle. So I'm thinking, oh, gosh, this is a really squirmy moment. This was not a good idea, inviting this person into an element so foreign to him, to be a *performer,* you know, on a stage.

And I think it was, first they asked him to use the microphone, and he started, and then they asked him to stand up; and it was sort of a sequential series of hurdles that he had to overcome. And within his first story, he hurdled it all. And told his story so purely and directly, that all that preceded it was moot. And he went on for the rest of that festival to really win everybody.

Evans played a significant, inspirational part in the storytelling movement for a number of years after that. But the gap never really closed between the mediated generality of festival performance and the very specific cultural work on behalf of his tribal and ethnic communities that he felt called to do. He was never fully at ease in an environment in which the storyteller did not have a truly intimate, interpersonal connection with the listening group. As the festival grew, it became less resonant to say from the stage, in a tent that held over a thousand, "The storyteller knows me." By the late eighties, Evans had dropped out of storytelling festival performance altogether.

Many performers came to Jonesborough with full mastery over the techniques of sound reinforcement. Others, including the organizers, learned as they went along by trial and error. Some, as Donald Davis points out below, never successfully adjusted to the amplified context of festival performance and thus never made the jump from local tradition-bearer or aspiring professional performer to integrated professional in the emerging storytelling world.

The Sacred Storytelling

In 1979, a group of storytellers who were disenchanted with ghost stories in the graveyard met in an empty tent on Saturday night to tell "spiritual stories"—stories of otherworldly encounters or intuitions that were meant not to scare but to comfort or to heal. The next year, Stivender and Michael Williams initiated a session on that theme on Sunday morning. Here is Stivender's characteristically flip expression of the serendipity motif:

> I said, "Hey, how about a religious storytelling thing, tomorrow morning at ten o'clock underneath the shed—which is now [1991] the resource

area, the little A-frame on the festival grounds. . . . There was no resource tent at that time, the shed was just sitting there, and I said, "Can we have a storytelling thing in the morning, religious storytelling, maybe a few songs?"

And so they said, "Oh, sure, go, hey, why not, I guess." And so we did. . . . Not too many people showed up. . . . There wasn't a Catholic Church in town and I was looking for something to do for religion; plus I was trying to serve the moment, and I saw that there was this lack, so. . . . (January 7, 1992)

The following year, 1981, the sacred storytelling session was on the official Sunday morning program, dedicated to the memory of Ken Feit, who had died in an accident that summer. Feit had been scheduled to be featured at that festival. The tragic serendipity of his death left a ceremonial legacy at the event. He was an artist whose quest for the spiritual in story performance and life had influenced many in the storytelling community—Stivender included—very deeply. There was a strong impulse of collective grieving over his passing, and this was deepened and released, as it has always been in communities, by ritual performance.

The appropriateness and genuine feeling present in that Sunday morning session was indelible to those who were there. It became the high point or culmination of the festival weekend for the many whose feeling for storytelling crossed into the realm of spiritual seeking. This made it natural that the ritual instrument of a Sunday morning spiritual story session would be repeated and traditionalized at Jonesborough.

Spiritual storytelling sessions in storytelling revival contexts have enabled participants to act out a very broadly defined, nondenominational approach to spirituality, as well as to narrative form. The sessions often feature songs, poems, mime or clown pieces, personal anecdotes and testimonies, along with traditional folktales focusing on themes of unconditional love, generosity, or grace. It became customary at Jonesborough and some other festivals not to applaud at the sacred telling—at first because loud clapping disturbed the worshipers at nearby churches and later because clapping dispersed the emotional euphoria generated by the performances. Instead of clapping, audiences would raise their hands and rub their palms together with a sound like rustling leaves, a gesture attributed alternately to American Sign Language or to the monastic culture of Tibet.

Spiritual storytelling was such a natural expression of the eclectic quest for meaning that had brought most of its practitioners to the art form that it was already central to other storytelling events. Robert Bela Wilhelm's

Mythos Institute, which produced a series of very influential events across the country in the late 1970s, was devoted entirely to the sacred aspects of storytelling. They were essentially conference seminars but had many elements in common with storytelling festivals. Feit's workshops during the 1970s were, in effect, seminars on spiritual storytelling, as were those by other influential storytellers, such as Brother Blue, Reuven Gold, Gioia Timpanelli, Nancy Schimmel, or Diane Wolkstein. Wolkstein inaugurated the National Conference on Storytelling in Jonesborough in 1978 to explore issues of spiritual meaning in storytelling, and this conference became an important gathering place for sharing ideas and inspiration among the revival community. David Outerbridge, the organizer of the North Atlantic Storytelling Festival in Maine, attended Stivender's off-the-cuff event in 1980 and returned home immediately to start his own festival, with a prominent place reserved for the spiritual story session. As festivals began to proliferate in the early eighties, the Sunday spiritual telling spread with them, becoming a standard part of the basic storytelling festival form.

"The Old Man of the Mountain": The Canonization of Ray Hicks

Ray Hicks had been hired to perform on the square in 1973 on the recommendation of the East Tennessee State University folklorist Thomas Burton and on the strength of his old Folk Legacy album. He belonged to a family of folk artists who had been visited by folklorists for decades because of their extraordinary repertoires of traditional tales, ballads, instrumental tunes, and folkways. He had no telephone, and Smith had to make arrangements through a neighbor, Ed Presnell, to talk to Hicks on the Presnell's phone. Like many traditional mountain people, Ray is shy but obliging and dislikes saying no to a personal request. But he had never before told stories outside of his local area or at any kind of outdoor festival. The resulting cultural clash was another kind of crisis/opportunity.

Hicks's special passion is Jack tales—oral *maerchen* from an ancient Western European folktale cycle about the adventures of a youngest, best, everyman hero named Jack. As a group, these are the oldest, rarest, and fullest folktales to survive in North American oral tradition—they are the majestic eagles or whooping cranes of American folklore—and Hicks is the recognized master of the genre, as several essays in William McCarthy, Cheryl Oxford, and Joseph D. Sobol's edited collection, *Jack in Two Worlds*, testify. He was not the only one, however; there were several fine Jack-tale tellers living in the mountains at the time of the festival's founding, most of them related. Ray's first cousin Stanley Hicks, who died in 1989, lived near Ray and told most of the same stories in a terse, high-spirited style. A more distant cousin, Marshall Ward, who died in 1981, taught fifth-grade in Boone, North Carolina, and told the stories in an elaborated style that could incorporate much pedagogy. Maude Long, who passed away in 1984 well into her nineties, lived all her life in nearby Hot Springs, and Woodrow Roland lived near Canton, North Carolina; also related to Ray by a common storytelling ancestor, they, too, could tell many of the same tales. Except for Long, each of these other storytellers performed at Jonesborough at least once in the 1970s, but none achieved Ray's official status. His discovery by Smith may have been serendipitous and triumphantly fraught with cross-cultural peril, but his canonization at Jonesborough is a case study in selective traditionalization.

Hicks's singularity as a folk artist is beyond doubt and apparent to anyone who meets him even casually. His talk is a torrent of personal memories and traditional lore, shot through with natural philosophical speculations and rare, anachronistic turns of phrase, segueing seamlessly into complex traditional fictions. His patience and generosity with folklorists and storytelling revivalists who have trooped to his door over the decades are wonders in themselves. Yet great folk artist as he is, he has also come to function as a Jonesborough icon, and these two roles do not always complement each other.

It can take an hour or more—roughly the length of one of his festival performances—for an outsider to begin to decipher his archaic mountain dialect. This means that much of a typical Jonesborough audience is reduced to staring. There is plenty to stare at. Estimates of his height range from six-seven up to seven feet; he is beanpole thin, and what most take for a costume is only the pair of overalls he wears day in and day out. Most of the time, the force of Hicks's personality and the palpable joy he takes in his heroes' adventures, whether his own or Jack's (there is little difference in the narrative texture), leap the cultural barriers inherent in the context. When they fail to do so, the spectacle has to suffice; and the ambivalent fact is that for much of the audience, for the press, and for the promoters' strictly commercial purposes, it does.

It has often been stated that Hicks has performed at every National Storytelling Festival—the festival programs of 1986 and 1987, for example, read, "Ray has performed annually at the National Storytelling Festival, an honor bestowed upon no other American storyteller." However, this claim was amended in the 1989 and 1990 programs to, "Hicks has been *invited* to perform at every National Storytelling Festival since its inception in 1973" (emphasis added).

These ritual invocations, in which event and storyteller are associated to their mutual justification, are examples of the traditionalizing process at work. Hicks was not on the festival program in 1974—Ward was. Hicks performed at the festival in 1975, but late that year he had a serious automobile accident that has left him in frail health to this day. He returned to the festival in 1977, but not in 1978 or 1979. When he came again in 1980, his fragility added to the aura of reverence that was beginning to grow around him. That aura was increased by the devotions of urban and suburban storytelling revivalists who were beginning to flock to Jonesborough, hungry for icons of pure, frail, but stubbornly enduring tradition.

The 1980 program read, "Once again NAPPS is pleased to have Ray Hicks of Banner Elk, North Carolina share with us his authentic jack tales for a special session of storytelling on Saturday. It'll be a treat you won't want to miss." This year seems to have marked the beginning of the institutionalization of Hicks's performances at Jonesborough, and their incorporation into a finished, ritualized festival form. This, too, still had its element of serendipity. Given his uncertain health, Hicks could not be given the rigorous performance schedule that was increasingly being demanded of other, "professional" tellers. He was given a special exemption that sanctified his status as a nonprofessional "living national treasure." From that year on, he performed a maximum of two, sometimes only one hour-long storytelling session per festival, on late Saturday afternoon.

Since Hicks never drove to Jonesborough, volunteer staff people were designated to pick him up. The staffers would drive to the house on the top of Beech Mountain, ninety minutes from Jonesborough by the most direct route; pick up Ray and his wife, Rosa, along with various cousins, nieces, and nephews; and drive them down to Jonesborough in time for the event. It was not always a sure thing, as one storyteller-volunteer, Steve Sanfield, fresh from the mountains of northern California, found out in 1980:

> I had gotten there early, and I was in the office, which was where the Main St. Cafe is now, upstairs. And I heard somebody say, "Oh, we need somebody to pick up Ray Hicks. . . ." I thought this was a great opportunity. And I got lost finding him. . . . But he played like, "Oh, is today the day? Do we have to go today? I don't know if I want to go. . . ." And I'd

never met the guy! And I'm supposed to bring him back to this festival. And he's sittin' around, and then he starts tellin' me stories, about chestnut trees, and panthers, and Baptists, and . . . and it was fine with me if we never went. It really would have been fine with me if we never did go.

And finally his wife says, "OK, Ray, I got your teeth clean here, here's some clean coveralls, let's go." So we drove back to Jonesborough in the rain. We're very late, we're hours late. And I say, "Ray, I've got to call ahead." So I stop at a pay phone. And the call won't go through. I end up smashing the phone down, "GODDAMN MACHINES!!" It was total frustration.

And at that time I was working on my first book, about John Henry. And I'm sitting in the front seat with Ray, and babbling on about machines. And I happen to say, *"The last man to beat a machine was John Henry—and it killed him to do it!"*

And Ray says, *"Oh you know about John Henry!"* And he and Rosa start *singing verses of "John Henry" that I've never heard.* And I have done two years of research at that point. And I want to stop the car, and write this stuff down! But I've got to keep driving through the rain.

So we drive on to Jonesborough. And I literally pull up at the main tent. And as soon as I pull up, he's surrounded. *The car is surrounded!* And Barbara and Connie were there, and Jimmy Neil. And they literally *drag him out from the car and onto the stage.* It was *like that.*

During these years, honors and recognition began to mount for Hicks. He received a National Heritage Fellowship from the National Endowment for the Arts Folklife Office. According to a subsequent profile in the *New Yorker* magazine, he stunned the assembled dignitaries at the awards ceremony by showing up in his customary overalls and floppy hat and launching into a performance of "Soldier Jack," in which the hero captures Death in a gunny sack (Kinkead). Ray refers to the award in the most pragmatic fashion—he simply calls it "the five thousand"—as in dollars. But for informed cultural tourists, the National Heritage Fellowship is an attraction marker, certifying that it is impermissible to make the trip to Jonesborough and not see Ray Hicks.

Robin McNeill came to the top of Beech Mountain for the PBS series *The Story of English.* The *New Yorker* profile appeared. The NAPPS festival program duly marked the growth of his mystique. These, too, should be regarded as attraction markers, in Dean MacCannell's sense. Through them, we can see the changing nature of the event being marked—as opposed to the person, who, in my own observation, has changed little over the years:

1981: A native of the Western North Carolina mountains, the tall and lanky mountain farmer tells the adventures of Jack in the famed Jack tales of Anglo-Saxon origin in the same dialect of yore. He was the featured storyteller at the first National Storytelling Festival, and he returns often, as his health will permit, to share his stories with us. Ray and Rosa, his wife, farm the North Carolina mountains and dig ginseng and other herbs for their living.

1983: Ray Hicks of Big Beech Mountain spills out a Jack Tale, his six-foot-eight-inch frame swaying to the tale's rambling rhythm. A frequent teller at past festivals, Ray is the father of five children and hails from Banner Elk, North Carolina.

1984: A mountain man from Banner Elk, North Carolina, Ray mesmerizes with his repertoire of authentic Jack tales and backwoods stories that richly reflect his Appalachian traditional heritage. Honored recipient of the American Folklife Center's National Heritage Fellowship Award.

1985: Performing at the Festival since 1973, Ray Hicks is an authentic Jack tale teller from Banner Elk, North Carolina. Ray is a national treasure of the United States and is considered a lifetime honored guest at the Festival. His audiences have laughed and cried . . . his tent is always overflowing with people. This year he will perform two sessions on Saturday to give everyone a chance to "sit a spell and listen."

1986: Ray Hicks is America's best known and most respected traditional storyteller. A western North Carolina farmer, Ray tells Jack Tales and traditional stories handed down to him from his ancestors who settled the southern mountains generations ago. Ray has performed annually at the National Storytelling Festival, an honor bestowed upon no other storyteller.

By 1986, the transition from serendipity to ceremony was virtually complete. Any program guide will have a ceremonial element, since, as MacCannell shows, the act of marking an event or an object for the purposes of cultural consumption is inherently ritualistic. But what was being marked for appreciation in the earlier days of NAPPS was often the serendipitous nature of the storytelling act—the ordinariness and earthiness of an art issuing from the mouths of "little-known people, from all walks of life." By the late 1980s, NAPPS was integrating itself into a national storytelling art world, with Jonesborough as its ritual center. What would be highlighted now would be the dignity and national significance of the tellers and their work. Hicks's markers, in particular, would be adjusted to display the revival transformation in microcosm—from marginal folk art to "national treasure" of indisputable cultural importance.

David Whisnant writes in *All That Is Native and Fine* about the mythic image he calls "the Old Man of the Mountains." This motif repeatedly appeared in the public presentations of Appalachian settlement schools, such as Hindman, Pine Mountain, and the John C. Campbell Folk School. These educational institutions were founded and run by crusading northern lay missionaries, mostly women, who came to the mountains to spread a gospel of progressive education, paradoxically flavored with nativist cultural revivalism.

Each school, according to Whisnant, put forward a creation narrative for itself, involving a gift of land or an emotional plea from a venerable local patriarch, an Anglo-Saxon noble savage, who begged the cultural missionaries to start their school and save the local culture from decay. Whisnant shows that the actual founding histories of the settlement schools invariably involved complex cultural politics, personal motives, and economic alliances. But the mythic narratives of barefoot benefactors, "Old Men of the Mountains" who would give their blessings and their land to support the schools' enterprises, were persistently favored in public relations. Nor was it only the schools that fostered these images—the print media of the day found them far more convenient to receive and transmit than a complex narrative or analysis would have been. This is not to cast doubt on the factuality or the sincerity of the particular local's support of the institutions. It is only to say that the use the schools and the media made of it soon left the realm of reportage and entered the realm of myth. Whether Hindman's Uncle Sol Everidge, Pine Mountain's Uncle William Creech, or J. C. Campbell's Uncle Luce Scroggs, the "Old Man of the Mountains" myth was a collaboration between the settlement school organizers and the popular media, with their strong storytelling impulses.

The continuities between the settlement school movement and the storytelling revival, as it has localized and institutionalized itself in Jonesborough, are suggestive. Both involve complex alliances between local cultural and economic interests and bands of powerful, crusading outsiders (mostly women, interestingly, in both movements), searching for a field in which to exert and express themselves for cultural upliftment. Both use nativistic and vitalistic folk revivalism as the medium of progressive social, economic, and educational agendas. Pine Mountain, for example, made use of traditional Appalachian and imported crafts, dance, music, and storytelling in its curriculum. Richard Chase, who went on to collect the Jack tales from Hicks's relatives, got his start listening to ballads and teaching English folk dance at Pine Mountain. Chase spent his last years trying vainly to be hailed as the old man of someone's mountain. The outbreak of storytelling revivalism should have been his opportunity, but by then he was too transparently the "olde pretender." The coveted role went instead to Hicks, who covets it little.

Ray Hicks is the National Storytelling Festival's "Old Man of the Mountains." His image has adorned its posters and programs. He is generally the first to be photographed and written up for color pieces by the print and electronic journalists, who strive each year to properly mythologize the festival. He shows his support for the enterprise by his willingness to come down from his mountain year after year to bless it with his repertoire—to lease to it, as it were, his narrative landscapes—and the festival supports him by inviting him, sending staff to fetch him, paying him in cash, and providing him with a place where he is personally beloved and his skills revered. Hicks actively dislikes traveling and therefore accepts invitations to few other festivals. His regularity at Jonesborough gives it a special status among storytelling events, the impression of his particular seal.

Ray Hicks's role at the National Storytelling Festival is as the archetypal embodiment of storytelling tradition. He is, in Walter Benjamin's words, "the resident tiller of the soil," the man who has "stayed put" and grown up absorbing the local folklore through the soles of his feet. He is one end of a continuum that runs swiftly in the direction of those traveling storytellers who "come from afar," bringing tales of many lands and peoples, with which they have seldom had direct, personal experience.

It is significant that Hicks's canonization at Jonesborough coincided with the period in the early eighties when the balance of power and artistic prominence in NAPPS and at the festival was beginning to shift toward these cosmopolitan storytelling professionals and away from the parade of folksy, down-home characters who made up much of the festival cards in the 1970s. In the early eighties NAPPS was at a crossroads in terms of membership, funding, and popular support. Folklore agencies at the federal and state levels, which had helped the festival along somewhat from its inception, were demanding in return a conformity to the ideological categories of folkloric representation. "Traditional" artists were to be clearly marked, sensitively presented, and distinguished from (and privileged over) their "revivalist" counterparts. However, the NAPPS membership, its board of directors, and its middle-class audiences of teachers, librarians, liberal ministers, retirees, recovering hippies with children in the minivan, and so forth were more comfortable with storytellers whose backgrounds and agendas reflected their own. These were the storytellers able to hold these audiences, and these were the audiences willing and able to pay increasingly steep ticket prices to support the festival. They would pay for the exotic, sure enough—but not if the exotica couldn't put on a show.

Donald Davis, NAPPS chairman in the mid- and late 1980s when this trend crystallized, reflected on the festival as he found it in the early 1980s:

> That [1981] was the ninth year, in terms of festivals. But it seemed to me that there were still only two little, tiny pieces of the storytelling community in existence. There was a very small number, I mean less than a dozen, who had some credible strength as emerging storytellers. And then the people who were doing the festival every year were trying to find more people, find more people, find more storytellers. And the pattern seemed to be that, every year, there would be a few of those repeat tellers. And then there would be some trying of new people. There were some interesting people, especially in terms of traditional tellers. But they had no appeal to the festival audience. And when you had a teller there in those days, when you had a crowd of, say, two thousand people—not ten thousand, but two thousand—they could all go to one tent, inside and outside. And leave someone they didn't particularly like with a tent with two rows of people in the front. (telephone interview, April 9, 1992)

The "ancient art of storytelling" was in the midst of a transformation, through the storytelling festival medium, from an art of front porches, parlors, and church basements to an art of auditoriums, microphones, and revival tents, with seats for three hundred, five hundred, eventually a thousand. No more "secret society" here—NAPPS was now in the business of creating popular storytelling "stars." The organizers may not have consciously wished to leave their traditional roots behind, but those tellers who could not get up on stage and boogie with the big boys and girls were going to have to stay down on the Swappin' Grounds. Hicks was one certifiable traditional storyteller who had that mysterious something extra: star quality. No two rows in the front for this mountain man—you could put it in the program: "his tents are always overflowing with people." This was a tradition-bearer who could shake some performative booty.

The years of revivalist transformation were a heady and also a hazardous time for members of the board of directors of NAPPS, who then were solely responsible for programming the festival. They were, most of them, trying to manage their own careers as well, which meant that they were responsible for grooming and feeding a horse they were simultaneously trying to ride. It was a powerful, snorting, unpredictable public beast. The ritualization of Hicks's appearances was a way of constructing a soothing and stabilizing tradition for the festival itself. It served the purposes that traditionalization always has—continuity, group security, and solidarity—but it had special meaning in this cultural context of rapid artistic mutation. It suggested that whatever transformations were inflating the event and whatever sacrifices in the values of intimacy and community that had funded the movement from its days as a "secret society," at the very least there would always be Ray Hicks, the "Old Man of the Mountains," to represent a fountainhead of pure storytelling tradition.

Hicks's ceremonial eminence at Jonesborough does raise questions about the role of cultural stereotypes in his presentation and promotion. Certainly Hicks is an anachronism and an anomaly in many ways, a man whose speech and lifeways are a century removed from his audience's experience. It would be easy to look to his manner and appearance for confirmation of regional stereotypes and to cite his accommodation to festival norms as proof of his willing colonization. Some Appalachian storytellers, such as those from Kentucky's Roadside Theater, who consciously and aggressively challenge stereotypes and attack exploitative cultural politics about the region, no longer feel comfortable or welcome at the National Storytelling Festival. Others, like Davis or Michael Williams, whose cultural values are more adaptive, represent at Jonesborough a new generation of Appalachian middle-class professionals, who express their cultural identity through a complex weaving of nostalgia and reinvention. Hicks is left to represent a radical traditionalism that is so extreme and yet so astonishingly detailed and precise that it confounds audiences' wildest stereotypical imaginings. I vividly recall one Saturday afternoon performance, for example, in which he interrupted himself in the middle of a Jack tale to detail mischievously his own experiences roasting and eating potato worms. "They taste good," he concluded, with a grin that suggested that he had us by the nose—"if you cook 'em right."

I would suggest that in the dynamics of Hicks's relationship with festival audiences, organizers, and fellow performers, there is an energetic exchange that transcends simple analysis. It is something that might be called postmodern, in the sense that it explodes and inverts traditional hierarchies. In the collagist context of the festival, in which ethnic and elite artists are placed on level footing or into an "olio" relationship that neutralizes hierarchical difference, Ray is never simply the exoticized other. He is recognized at the festival as a master, a colleague, and an extraordinary citizen among citizens—as a friend and in some surprising, serendipitous ways a colleague. Steve Sanfield told of having a meal with Hicks after the performance in 1980 with a group of New Yorkers:

> Real New York intellectuals. Earnest, sincere folklorists. And he started to put 'em on. He started to tell 'em about *hoopsnakes*. And I started to tell 'em about some snakes from California. And we kind of caught the twinkle in each other's eye. And I would confirm everything he said. And I was more a part of their world than I was of Ray's, in their eyes. And I would say, "Oh, yeah, it's true." And they took notes! It was a great discipline for me to control myself. Because it was such a wonderful put-on. And I saw that Ray was clearly in control of almost any situation he's in. He knows exactly what he's doing.

The hoopsnake is an ancient, traditional tall-tale motif—a snake that can take its tail in its mouth and roll toward its prey at fantastic speed. Sanfield's story shows him and Hicks joining together to deploy their tall tales in the traditional, initiatory way. They are entering into a ritual of "differential identity" (Bauman, "Differential" 31–41), in which they exploit their insider knowledge of nature and narrative at the expense of the "earnest, sincere, New York intellectuals." Until the outsiders grow wise to the act, they will get to play the hicks, on the invert terrain in which a Hicks reveals himself as the consummate sophisticate.

Spalding Gray, a New York monologuist and master of postmodern anxiety, was invited to the festival in 1985, and he, too, responded to Hicks at a level that transcended his cultural constraints. He told me that none of the performances he saw held much interest for him—until he saw Hicks. Then something in him stirred. He thought, "This man is a genuine autobiographic storyteller. He's speaking from the first person, he is also enjoying his stories, he's both in them and out of them." Gray said that despite his difficulty with the dialect, he was surprised to feel a sense of kinship, and he expressed the same sense of connection that storytellers from all over the world have felt on encountering Hicks: "I thought . . . I am doing this in my own kind of weird way."

Hicks has acted as a storytelling father-figure to many who have met him at the festival and gone to visit him at his home, discovering first-hand how stories can function in a traditional community, household, and worldview. I have written about my own experiences of this in *Jack in Two Worlds* ("Jack in the Raw" 3–9). Here is how Doug Lipman described it in our interview:

> When I went to that first festival, I went down a day early; because there was an archive there, and I was listening to tapes and watching videotapes. And somebody said, "I'm going off to drive two hours and pick up Ray Hicks, do you want to come with?"
> And I said, "Nahhhhh, I'm more interested in this stuff here."
> And then Ray showed up. And something really magical happened when I heard him perform. And I went to the crowd of people around him after his performance. And he was still feeling pretty feeble after his accident. And somebody said to Ray, "What was it like for you growing up in the mountains, on the farm?"
> And he started to tell the story about how, after his father died, then his oldest brother was the man of the farm, and it was too much for him, and he left. And a-a-all his brothers left, one after another. And then Ray, at a very young age, was the man of the farm. And it was too much for him. And he decided to run away. And one night, he got as far as the hill where he had his last view of home. And turned back to take his last look. And he got to thinking about his mother. And he went back.
> And then, without a pause, he went into telling "Hardy Hardhead."
> And the unusual feature of his version of "Hardy Hardhead" is an incident where Jack is the only one of his brothers to be kind to the old man. And the old man says to Jack, "There's a river there, you have to turn it into wine."
> And Jack says, "I can't do that."
> And the old man says, "Close your eyes and just try."
> And Jack closes his eyes and *tries*. He doesn't know what to do, he just tries. And when he opens his eyes, the man's smiling at him and the river is wine.
> And that's just kind of inserted there. Most versions don't have that. And it's not central to the plot. But I was struck by the *emotional* similarity between Ray's moment on the mountain, and that faith test in the story. And *that* made me fascinated with Ray.
> And that night, sleeping on the floor of somebody's home there, somebody said, "So when are you going to visit Ray?"
> And I said, "No, I can't visit Ray and nyunh-nyunh-nyuh ... "
> He said, "You were in seventh heaven listening to Ray. People should do what puts them in seventh heaven."
> So I wrote a letter to Ray and Rosa and said, "Can I come visit?" And

that began lots and lots of trips down there, sitting at his feet. And ultimately feeling like one of the family.

For a core of storytelling devotees in the festival audience, then, Hicks's appearances have many levels of artistic and personal resonance. But above all, Ray Hicks has come to occupy a central place in the iconography of the National Storytelling Festival because he epitomizes, in his person and his performances, the border-crossing nature of the entire enterprise. The festival is about the preservation and perpetuation of an art that is ancient and family- and community-centered. In a contextual sense, it is also about the economic preservation and perpetuation of a particular small town (Jonesborough) and the small-town values and scale of life that allow storytelling to flourish. To fulfill those purposes, the festival promoters have had to open the borders that previously defined the scale and values of art form and community and mark each for commercial exchange with the wider, anonymous, popular culture. Like the opening of the Berlin Wall, it was an exhilarating, risky move. For Jonesborough, historic preservation became the regulating ideology that controlled the ways in which the integrity of the town would be negotiated with outsiders. For the storytellers, Hicks's identity and repertoire—so intimately reciprocal, so apparently unchanging yet ever renewable in the ritual of performance, so ancient and strange, and yet so compellingly familiar to a wide range of visitors—have become vital symbols of the ways in which storytelling can negotiate the treacherously shifting borders of self and society.

Gay Ducey, a former chair of NAPPS, told me a story about Hicks that encapsulated for her the complex weave of cultural forces that make up the National Storytelling Festival. She told of watching an eager young girl approach him after his show:

> As I came around the side of the tent, Ray was . . . there with, I'd say, a half a dozen people. Singing "Amazing Grace." And you know how Ray is—he had his great big arm up. And at every beat he'd *whack* his arm down.
> You know, keeping TIME
> to that BEAT
> in that SONG ...
> And there was this young person. I guess she might have been in her early twenties. Very blond, very cute-looking young woman. And she said to him—she stopped and she patted him. And Ray was deeply engaged in singing. She said, *"Ray! Ray!* I'm going to teach you a verse

you've probably never learned!" So of course I snorted to myself. Believing in my heart that there's no verse worth knowing that Ray doesn't know to that song.

And she taught him this kind of new-political version, which was very puzzling to Ray. And gentleman that he is, of course, he accommodated her, and sang away, and sawed away with his arm. And then stopped.

And she said, "Well, goodbye." And his relatives gathered him up and started away.

And she stopped and actually tugged at his jacket. And she said, "Ray, now don't forget, don't forget!"

Ray turned to her and said, "Forgit what?"

She said, "Now don't forget! You remember, you promised! I'm going to send you my video! And I want to be sure you watch it!"

And there you have the festival.

Indeed, there we have the festival in its thoroughly traditionalized form, a ritual performance of the full storytelling revival mythos. Beginning with needs, desires, and serendipitous convergences, the event was rapidly configured into ceremony. Using the mythic narrative of a dying and reviving tradition, the founders of NAPPS exhibited a frenzy of creativity in devising and discovering forms to advance that narrative to its foregone, triumphant conclusion.

The form has never been entirely stable—the quicksilver of cultural-climate change and the pressures of constant growth are always pulling at the envelope. But the three-day form was more or less in place by 1977, completing itself with the establishment of Ray Hicks's Saturday appearances and the Sunday sacred telling in 1980 and 1981. It has remained essentially intact, despite a variety of attempted innovations, additions, and lacunae, ever since.

Recapitulated, the festival unfolds in the following sequence:

Friday afternoon: registration; miscellaneous "warm-up" sessions, sometimes formal, sometimes informal.

Friday evening: opening olio.

Saturday, 10:00–5:30: continuous storytelling sessions, sometimes thematic, sometimes general, featuring one, two, or three featured tellers; Swappin' Grounds running all day; Ray Hicks performing for one or two hours in the afternoon.

Saturday evening: ghost stories, formerly in or near old Jonesborough cemetery, since moved to Mill Spring Park; since 1985, a variety of storytelling concerts and "one-person shows" scheduled concurrently.

Sunday morning: sacred storytelling

Sunday afternoon: "cool-down"; miscellaneous sessions; closing olio.

All of these festival elements have been discovered through serendipity or creative necessity or have been borrowed from a preexisting repertoire of cultural forms. They have been immediately subject to the pressure of formalization and traditionalization to create a reproducible cultural text, one that can be readily scanned by and assimilated into American popular culture.

4

The Storytelling Festival as Ritual

In 1982, having just returned from the Tenth Annual National Storytelling Festival, the storyteller and author George Shannon wrote a letter of
appreciation to the NAPPS newsletter, the *Yarnspinner*. In it, he vividly
expresses the power that the festival exerted over those who were caught
up in the revival passion. The letter also moves, in a kind of auto-ethno-
graphic reverie, toward an elucidation of the dramatic structure and the
liminal atmosphere underlying and enfolding the event:

> Dear *Yarnspinner*,
> "Why are you going to Tennessee?" they ask each year. "To hear sto-
> ries," I answer. "But it's so far away," they say. "Can't you hear stories
> closer to home?" "Yes, but some of the very best will be in Tennessee."
> "But it's so far," they continue. "Can't you find them in books and
> records?" And I try to explain, "In person is better."
> "But it's so far," they continue, knowing only one form of time and
> distance. And out of need for another answer I suddenly heard myself
> saying, "Ritual"—a response which both pleased me and left my inquisi-
> tors puzzled enough to stop their hollow questions. Though my answer
> of "ritual" was serendipitous, after experiencing the 10th NAPPS festival
> I feel that ritual is indeed one of the core elements of the annual autumn
> storytelling gathering and why so many travel so far.
> The entire festival has become for the tellers and listeners a ritual of
> homecoming in the truest sense—a connecting point in the year's cycle.
> We return to a town we know, like Brigadoon, that is filled with magic of
> the finest kind. For the length of the festival (just as when a story is

shared) all else ceases to exist. Time expands and deeper worlds are explored. It is a weekend spent surrounded by one's spiritual kin—past, present, and future. For three days no one has to explain their symbiotic relationship with stories—does not have to explain their vocation, avocation or passion. It is a sharing time with familiar faces in the tent crowd and favorite tellers that make us laugh, cry and sing; tellers who take us back through familiar stories for the umpteenth time as we listen as eagerly as ever, being taken back to favorite images, lines and times; each telling connecting with other festivals and friends. . . . Such familiar stories function as ritual within the ritual, letting us know we are there and all is underway.

The festival is also a time for tellers to share their new discoveries—new prisms of themselves. . . . The entire festival is in ways, a giant folktale: being filled with familiar motifs and events that let us know where we are in the story of the weekend, and of the year—that let us know we are in familiar lands and emotions, and can securely explore new worlds. And by its conclusion, the festival has become a blend of family reunion, the child's favored bedtime story cycle, and the third brother's search through unknown lands that through time, growth and careful listening, brings him back home and richer for the journey. . . . (3)

Shannon's letter begins by picturing an imaginary dialogue between the storytelling initiate and a gaggle of uncomprehending inquisitors. In the face of their hardheadedness, he finds himself in the archetypal role of the storyteller as knower of secrets—things that are not knowable except through the medium and love of the craft. Like the Zen master with his students or Jesus among the Pharisees, he shifts the ground out from under his earthbound interlocutors with his answer, "Ritual," peremptorily lifting the discourse onto a mythic plane. The move appears to them as a dead end but to him as a revelation. It sends him off on his pilgrimage with a traditional metaphor for the construction of identity: the rite of passage.

What he finds at the end of it is a vision of the festival as a story. In his exalted, free-flowing state, he sees his own life as a story and as a festival. The mundane identity of George Shannon of Eau Claire, Wisconsin, immerses itself in the ritual delta of the National Storytelling Festival and dissolves into the Ocean of Story, to reemerge within a new imagining of wholeness.

Victor Turner wrote, "Ritual is, in its most typical cross-cultural expressions, a synchronization of many performative genres, and is often ordered by *dramatic* structure, a plot, frequently involving an act of sacrifice or self-sacrifice, which energizes and gives emotional coloring to the interdependent communicative codes which express in manifold ways the meaning inherent in the dramatic *leitmotiv*" (*From Ritual to Theatre* 81).

In the structure of fairy tales or wonder tales, there is a pattern that reflects the dramatic core of the storytelling revival, as Shannon sensed it and as I have illustrated it so far. Vladimir Propp, the pioneering Russian structuralist, analyzed the classic wonder tale form thus: beginning with a blessed original condition, there follows a transgression and fall from grace, which must be redeemed by the hero's journey. The hero accomplishes the redemption with the aid of magical tokens or helpers, which are gained by inward grace, special virtues, or difficult lessons on the way. The return journey is again beset with trials, temptations, and often further transgressions, which must be redeemed before the final blissful reunion and communal restoration are achieved.

Joseph Campbell showed how myths, sacred narratives, and fireside tales from around the world tend to conform to this same pattern. But perhaps Campbell's most affecting contribution lay in his enthusiastic amplification, throughout his writing and teaching, of the psychological idea that the events of each human life can follow such a mythological pattern as well. As he wrote in his signature work, *The Hero with a Thousand Faces*, "These are the everlastingly recurrent themes of the wonderful song of the soul's high adventure. And each who has dared to harken to and follow the secret call has known the perils of the dangerous, solitary transit. . . . And by a like miracle, so will each whose work is the difficult, dangerous task of self-discovery and self-development be portered across the ocean of life" (22–23).

I would suggest that in the liminal/liminoid spaces of storytelling festivals, where the primary communal mythos of the revival was built, the story is woven again, in deep metaphoric resonance with the stories told from the stage. A powerful subtext of these outward performances is the story of the storyteller, framed by the magic circle of the festival spotlight as the hero of a cultural quest. Through the travels and travails of the performing artist's path, the storyteller seeks to redeem society from its Hamlinesque sin of denying story and the primal unity that is story's gift.

The storytelling festival became, for its most involved participants, a way of enacting a ritualized happy ending to the wonder tale of the storyteller's journey. For the teller on stage, the festival is a homecoming, a redemption, a wedding of teller to traditions and to an idealized community. For the committed audience, the festival is redeeming, too: a home-coming to a kingdom where storytelling is restored to its rightful place at the center of community life.

The ritual form of the storytelling festival evolved to incorporate ech-oes of many other liminal zones across cultures and centuries—the mass, the seder, the Eleusinian mysteries, a brush-arbor meeting, a tent revival, or such American feast-days as Thanksgiving, Christmas, and the Fourth of July. But the death-and-resurrection story implicit in the conceptual framework of "revival" sets the overall metanarrative tone. At its heart, the revival story is a story of redemption, in which storytelling acts as a stand-in for the primal unities we have sacrificed on our journey of civilization. Storytelling pilgrims arrive at Jonesborough predisposed to believe that culture has fallen from grace. Somehow, sometime, we had sinned, by denying ourselves, our heritage, our nature—the sacred "something" that, for lack of more authoritative words, we would now call "the lost art of storytelling."

If we have not yet received the catechism when we arrive, the torrent of stories and exhortations about stories creates a sense of cultic immer-sion, like the all-night chanting of the Mystery School, which immediate-ly initiates us. The mythic pattern is read and enacted in the quickening of our spirits: *"In the beginning was storytelling, and with storytelling was community. In storytelling was contained the seeds of all the arts, sciences, ed-ucation, politics, medicine, and law. As specializations multiplied, storytelling died, sacrificed to the soulless reflections of human skill; it descended into cul-tural oblivion, where it endured as a candle in the houses of the oppressed; on the third day of the storytelling festival, by the Sunday morning epiphany of the spiritual storytelling, the art form will have risen again, to return the world to spring."*

The culture's neglect of the simple communion of storytelling is made to stand in, like a medieval sin-eater, for a multitude of transgressions; and the weekend of resurrecting the art is an occasion for ritual cleansing. We repent and are absolved. *Pax Vobiscum. Go in Peace. Next year in Jonesbor-ough.* In the center of the ritual drama is the celebrant-priest, the story-teller.

The storytelling revival movement added this structuring narrative and sense of vocation to the usual perils of a performing artist's career. It is not so very different, perhaps, from the vocational passion that infuses artists in many disciplines (a word, after all, that shares its roots with *discipleship*). But at the outset of a movement with the revitalistic tone of the storytelling revival, that mythic sensibility reveals itself in individual biographies and the discourse of the emergent community with particular clarity and poignancy.

Revival is never about actual death—that story would be tragic and final. The key plot turn of a revival story is the revelation that death was only illusory, the result of our failed belief. No one believes that storytelling actually died any more than the town of Jonesborough died—if they had, there would be no town, no festival, no story. These precious things are perceived as having been abandoned, turned from, denied, their values obscured by ignorance and neglect (which is sin). We are then invited to repent—gently, indirectly; after all,most of us are good, middle-class, late-twentieth-century adults, who would rather be caught *in flagrante delicto* than shouting and moaning on the mourners' bench. But by Sunday morning at a typical storytelling festival, we may have performed some of those same spiritual gymnastics.

"Liminal" or "Liminoid" Aspects of the National Storytelling Festival

Liminal means of or pertaining to a threshold. In anthropological discourse, it has come to stand for those communal rites in which the rules and forces of order that govern the everyday world are deliberately suspended or inverted so that fundamental creative, psychic, or spiritual powers may be encountered. Because of the gravity of those sacred powers, the ritual threshold is traditionally approached not lightly but according to a separate complex of rules and obligations that differ from those applying to mundane social existence. In order not to shatter our human vessels, the sacred is traditionally quarantined from us by liminal areas both in the physical world and in the social fabric. The mystery of a cave, a mountaintop, a crossroads, a graveyard—or an altar, a theater, a stadium, a festival ground—lies in its separation from ordinary time and space, bringing us by ritual ordeal, contemplation, or spectatorship to the threshold of realms where elemental powers hold sway.

The narrative subtext of a liminal rite is always, to a certain extent, unconscious or occult. It is like a dream that cannot quite be brought to consciousness or, when it is, begins to reveal all sorts of dream-mutations, fault lines where the narrative seems to fissure into a host of associative layers. We can see this tendency in Shannon's letter as he leaps from metaphor to metaphor in an effort to express truths that adamantly resist full revelation. Even in the presence of sacred texts and authorized narratives, such as those of the Jewish, Christian, Hindu, Muslim, or Buddhist faiths, the continual proliferation of denominations, sects, enthusiasts, and schisms, each with its own efflorescence of ritual creativity, reveals a relationship of ritual to core narrative that can never remain fixed but is constantly shifting to accommodate new interpsychic demands. The moment ritual ceases to adapt and becomes frozen in normative behaviors is precisely when it ceases to be life renewing and loses contact with the numinous, playful, mutable, and subjectively dangerous psychic realm wherein we truly experience, rather than simply register, the sacred.

In a complex society like our own, this is one of the functions of what Turner calls *liminoid ritual* and Sally Moore and Barbara Myerhoff call *secular ritual*. These are ritualistic formations generated in the border regions between communally obligatory, sacralized behaviors and voluntary, secular, and commercial behaviors. New formations of these types develop constantly in the fissures where the archetypal dream-narratives underlying traditional social structures begin to mutate and connect with other stories, other dreams. This may come from cross-cultural collision, rapid social changes sparked by new cultural technologies, or both modes of social stress working in tandem. But even in examining preindustrial cultures, Turner finds this creative, homeostatic element to ritual. He writes:

> I began to see performances of ritual as distinct phases in the social processes whereby groups became adjusted to internal changes (whether brought about by personal or factional dissensions and conflicts of norms or by technical or organizational innovations), and adapted to their external environment (social and cultural as well as physical and biotic). From this standpoint the ritual symbol becomes a factor in social action, a positive force in an activity field. Symbols, too, are crucially involved in situations of societal change—the symbol becomes associated with human interests, purposes, ends and means, individual and collective, whether these are explicitly formulated or have to be inferred from the observed behavior. . . . from the very outset I formulate symbols as social and cultural dynamic systems, shedding and gathering meaning over time and altering in form. . . . (*From Ritual to Theatre* 21–22)

This view connects Turner's ritual symbology with Anthony F. C. Wallace's study of revitalization movements. In complex societies, more so than in tribal societies, Turner sees the liminoid realm of "play," including most forms of what we call "art," as vehicles for what Wallace would call "mazeway reformulation." In Turner's words, he sees liminal and lim-

inoid situations as "the settings in which new models, symbols, para-
digms, etc., arise—as the seedbeds of cultural creativity. These new symbols and constructions then feed back into the 'central' economic and
politico-legal domains and arenas, supplying them with goals, aspira-
tions, incentives, structural models and *raisons d'etre*" (*From Ritual to Theatre* 28).

It should be noted that the designation of the storytelling festival as
"ritual" is not imposed from outside as part of a scholarly framework but
is part of the discourse of the storytelling community. It is an "emic" rather than an "etic" term, as Shannon's letter shows (given the number of
participants in the storytelling community with some folklore or anthropology training, even gruesome Latinates like emic and etic are not above
their occasional emic use). The festival is, speaking strictly in terms of
Turner's definitions, a liminoid phenomenon, because of its clear place-
ment in the realm of volitional, leisure activities in a complex, postindustrial society. However, many of its most significant participants are quite
self-consciously seeking to recuperate ritual performance roles, forms, *and*
contexts from preindustrial, tribal societies. For these people, the ritual
and dramaturgical meaning of the event is quite different than it is for
those casual onlookers who have been drawn to the festival through its
listing in *Holiday Magazine*'s guide to the hundred best weekend getaways.

The storytelling festival can serve as a laboratory for testing the adapt-
ability of Turner's concepts. When we do, we find that liminal and liminoid aspects are actually tightly braided in the experience and perspectives of various participants at various stages in their lives and careers.
Much depends on the individual's relation to the festival—whether the
participant comes as spectator, amateur enthusiast, aspiring professional, featured professional teller, local traditional artist or exotic culture-
bearer, NAPPS insider or functionary, aspiring or actual organizer of a sat-
ellite or rival festival, or any combination thereof. Depending on one's
history, feelings, and beliefs about the organization, the festival, and the
art form, each festival can provide various levels of initiation, can generate manifold complexes of meaning, or can be just another gig, just another weekend. Depending on the particular psychological necessity of
storytelling and its ritual enactments in one's own life, a particular festival can operate as a vital liminal rite, a casual liminoid episode of work or
leisure, or a crass commercialization of what is already a sacred process.
As Turner wrote, "'Les symboles sauvages,' as they appear not only in traditional, 'tribal' cultures but also in the 'cultural refreshment' genres, of

poetry, drama, and painting, of post-industrial society, have the character of dynamic semantic systems, gaining and losing meanings—and meaning in a social context always has emotional and volitional dimensions—as they 'travel through' a *single* rite or work of art . . ." (*From Ritual to Theatre* 22).

I will focus here chiefly on accounts from those most deeply invested in the storytelling revival—those storytellers who treated the festival as a rite of incorporation in a storytelling community and as a rite of revival for an art through which they were crafting a social identity. I will concentrate on the experiences of those for whom the festival represented not just an optional leisure activity but a public enactment of a ritual obligation to themselves and to a consciously conceived community. The depth and stability of these obligations and this community are certainly open to question. As in other recent outbreaks of spontaneous communitas (Turner's term for the revitalized communal spirit), they formed quickly, burned brightly, and tended to scatter as social and economic tides washed over them. I take both sets of phenomena seriously: those attendant upon the evolution of a spontaneous storytelling communitas and those attendant upon its possible decay.

The following generalized reading of the festival takes as its chronological reference the period of the late seventies and early to mid-eighties, when the event was reaching its apex as a ritual center of communitas—even as the pressures of increasing popularity and internal competition were beginning to drown the serendipitous ceremonies of innocence that generated that communal spirit.

The Festival Experience

Separation from everyday reality in the storytelling festival experience begins, as we have seen, before the first story is told. At the National Storytelling Festival, and to a lesser extent at many smaller regional festivals, the geographical isolation of the festival site is an important element of ritual separation. As Jonesborough became truly national in scope—that is, as it began to live up to its audacious naming—storytellers and would-be storytellers began to make the journey from all around the country. The effort involved became a part of the ritual and, in turn, part of festival folklore.

Many would drive together, often getting off work Thursday afternoon and driving all night. Jim May would ride down from northern Illinois:

It was a ritual for three or four years there, when I was teaching. We'd all pack into a van. Bring lots of bags of trail-mix. And head out right after school. And drive through the mountains all night—I kind of miss that part—driving through the mountains all night.

I think that's where the myth began. Those nighttime drives, with friends, and sometimes telling stories, and sometimes just listening to music, and napping, and changing drivers. But going through those mountains at night, and you'd pull off the road to rest, and you'd see those lights, down in the mist. If the conditions were just right, you'd just see that mist down there, and the lights of the towns, with these sort of mist-haloes around them. And I think that, as much as anything, gave us the sense of a mythic journey. The fact that it's in the mountains is important, I think. Also there was something about crossing the Ohio River at Louisville. . . . There's something mythic about crossing those rivers, and there's some big factories there, and lots of lights. And we'd usually hit that close to midnight. So you'd be in the Kentucky mountains around two in the morning.

The overnight journeys made a fertile ground for propagating spontaneous communitas. Some groups of storytellers rented buses or vans to make the trip from the Northeast or the Midwest, telling stories and singing songs along the way. The time of isolation in the womblike enclosure of the car, van, or bus allowed for a buildup of shared expectation and commitment that overflowed onto the festival grounds. The all-night drives, too, fulfilled the functions of a vigil. Postural rigors and deprivation of sleep are traditional methods of inducing altered states. With the aid of this potent, nonpharmacological enhancement, the festival parade of narrative imagery could register with heightened intensity.

Even those who flew to the festival would find in the flight a liminal zone of separation from everyday expectations and rules. The out-of-the-way-destination helped. It necessitated at least one change of planes. The last change would put you aboard a bumpy commuter flight into Tri-Cities Airport, in upper east Tennessee—a field that could handle only dwarfish jets and noisy prop planes with a dozen or so narrow, boardlike seats. Spontaneous communitas would often erupt through the natural sorting process of these festival flights. Rafe Martin recalled:

I remember the first time I went to NAPPS, the experience was, it's like I had seen the future. You know, you're flying down on the plane, and people are talking. . . . It was like, everyone on the plane was talking storytelling. In other words, people were sharing who they were. I had been on so many flights, traveling around the country to tell stories, and they're all dead. You know, it's people buried in business work—basically going over figures and files; or sleeping; or reading really dumb books. And that's it. Instead, this was a flight of people—all different walks of life, all different looks, all different ages—and everybody was talking with one another. And there weren't racial issues, there weren't political issues—I mean, it was like, "You've got an interesting story—*Neat!*"

And then you get to Jonesborough, and you felt—this was the future. People from different political backgrounds, nationalities, races, religions—all getting along. And it didn't matter what you looked like, it didn't matter where you were from; what mattered was, if you could tell a story. And if you could, then everyone was going to be there for you.

When the time on the highway or in the netherworld of airports and airplane cabins was over, the moment came when you turned off the divided four-lane highway 11E that runs past Jonesborough's northern flank. You cruised down a road that narrows as it approaches an Exxon station, like a gateway at the foot of a steep hill. Taking a sharp right turn around the gas station, you found yourself abruptly bumping along on cobblestones, gazing up a crowded Main Street vista that had been cunningly recomposed into a living history tableau of which you were suddenly a part. It would not be a closed or complete tableau but an open-ended collage, in which some of the dominant signifiers of twentieth-century culture—power lines and corporate advertising logos—had been conspicuously banished. Others, like autos and tourists, remained in the picture; and still others, like the storytellers in their performing colors and the harvest motifs sheathing the lampposts and spangling the sidewalks, composed a crazy-quilt of temporal references, in which the motley flags of postsixties, eco-gypsy culture were appliqued against a traditional American background, with a sprinkling of pre-Christian accents.

Moving slowly up the street, past two short blocks of brick and limestone shops on the right, past the Mail Pouch Building and the domed county courthouse on the left, and then past the long white clapboard Federal-style porch of the Chester Inn on the right, conspicuously marked and dated 1797, you would arrive at the central example of Jonesborough's floating historical signifiers: the Christopher Taylor Cabin. This two-story, mid-eighteenth-century log cabin was moved from the outskirts to the center of town in 1975 and reassembled on a strip of parkland between the Chester Inn and the 1840s Greek Revival Presbyterian church. The church was still a church, the inn was being restored (through a state grant) to serve as official headquarters for NAPPS, and the cabin sat vacant most of the year, a mossy civic tool shed mysteriously transfigured by the knowledge that Andrew Jackson once slept there.

There you would undergo the first initiatory ordeal of the festival: registration. Fitting yourself into a line that straggled down the flagstone path back toward the street, you would gradually be borne toward the rough-hewn doorposts of the cabin. Stepping across the dark threshold to an interior smelling of damp earth and straw, you would be confronted by tables of cheerful young votaresses, one of whom would take your name, address, NAPPS membership status, and money. In exchange, she would hand you not a ticket but a schedule and a small, jagged-edged, calico swatch, pierced through by a safety pin. If you confessed your puzzlement at this esoteric token, she would affix it to your shirt pocket with a soothing hand and the instruction that this was your weekend pass. You were to keep it constantly pinned to your person, transferring it dutifully from soiled shirt to clean, lest your way be blocked at the breach of a tent by one of the monitors—volunteer staff primed to stand and murmur, "Pass by," only to those initiates bearing the calico swatch.

So, pinned and instructed, you walked out the back door of the Christopher Taylor Cabin into the autumn sunlight and found yourself on the edge of the Swappin' Grounds. If you were early enough, Doc McConnell would be there, dressed up in the stovepipe hat, frock coat, and clipped goatee of a backwoods Mephistopheles, capering about in front of his outlandishly emblazoned wagon and warming up the crowds with comic patter while peddling real bottles of imaginary snake oil. McConnell played (and still plays, to a lesser extent) an important threshold role at the NAPPS festival and other Jonesborough events—the "greeter." As the first performer that many encountered at the site and as chief master of ceremonies on the Swappin' Grounds, McConnell took it upon himself to begin to induce the festival state of imaginative transport and self-forgetting. Being from the immediate area, he acted as a performing host, reaching out to strangers through the medium of his tall tales and hyperbolic patter. He introduced them to a rural, traditional world that was immediately assimilable, because it was composed entirely of inversions and impossibilities, offered up with an enveloping wink of complicity.

"Where I live," he would shout, "in Tucker's Knob, Tennessee, it got so dry one year that the Baptists took to sprinklin', and the Methodists just used a damp washcloth." At the 1982 festival, he told of a Tucker's Knob entrepreneur named Crazy Jim, who opened up a restaurant called "Down Home": "And what he done, he hit upon a bonanza. He got in touch with all them old rangers, and them wardens, and property owners, and sportsmen out in New Mexico, and Arizona, and Texas—where they have them old hard-shell armadillos out there? And they're a nuisance out there, they claim. And so Old Jim had 'em kill all them old armadillos, and pack 'em in ice, and send 'em back there to Tucker's Knob. And old Jim fixes 'em in his restaurant, and he serves 'em, and calls 'em *'Possum on the Halfshell'*" ("Tucker's Knob"). The form of McConnell's story is thoroughly traditional, but its content reflects the cosmopolitan system of social and economic exchange of which the festival itself is one expression. McConnell's Crazy Jim could easily have been Jimmy Neil Smith, importing recontextualized storytellers from all over North America to small-town Tennessee and serving them up to nostalgic travelers who want their narrative possum on the half-shell of redemptive ritual. In the restored performance context of the festival, McConnell's tall tales performed an initiatory function analogous to the one they play in traditional male societies—as narrative riddles, whose solution is betokened by laughter and whose ritual reward is incorporation into the community of knowers.

If you emerged from the Christopher Taylor Cabin after McConnell's set, you might have cocked one ear to a bellowing neophyte while scanning the schedule with one eye and the gathering flood of passersby with the other, searching for old friends and acquaintances while simultaneously straining to plot your course from hour to hour and to prepare for the coming onslaught of narrative overload. Overload is an essential transformational mode of festival consciousness. In the presentational equivalent of the cornucopia baskets splayed across the sidewalks of Main Street, three to six tents would be running at any given time, plus the Swappin' Grounds and the "resource tent" overflowing with storytelling books, tapes, videos, and souvenirs. There would be *too much* to do, to see, to hear (and to buy) throughout the weekend, and the more you wanted to be touched and transformed by the experience, the more that too-muchness would pull on your mind. You would experience the festival activity just out of reach of eye and ear as a kind of half-conscious stimulant, simultaneously a distraction and a spur to renewed intensities of receptivity.

The first formal sessions with the featured performers would be billed as "Family Showcases"—lightweight, mixed programs for general audiences—and "Meet the Storyteller" workshops, in which performers are encouraged to speak in an informal, personal way about themselves and their relation to their art form. These introductory sessions start to melt whatever resistances to the art form we may have brought with us and begin to shape our identification with particular tellers. The more we get to "know" them, the more the illusion is spun in the charged air between us that "the storyteller knows me."

The first olio would be on Friday evening, after a dinner break. In 1985, for example, the tellers lined up, seven in one large tent, seven in another. Each told a ten-minute story. When everyone was finished, there was a break. The little flotillas of tellers switched tents and started over again. Audiences could get a taste of each storyteller's personality and repertoire and could better pick their way among the array of simultaneous offerings on Saturday. The olio serves as a baptism by immersion in the river of voices that constitute the festival in any given year. There is no pretense of closure—since the festival is avowedly constituted of all its members. "We are all storytellers" is part of storytelling movement catechism. As festival director Laura Simms invoked the ideal in the 1985 program: "Storytelling is intimate and reciprocal. Therefore, our audiences are as important as our storytellers. Whether there are three people or three thousand people in the audience, everyone feels included." There is, above all, the goal of breadth and intensity.

The National Storytelling Festival takes upon itself the task of representing not just the national storytelling scene but *a storytelling nation*. It is a nation different from the one represented, say, on the nightly network news, a nation revisioned in the bright silver of the revival mythos. It is a nation *of* storytellers—of individuals, groups, and communities empowered by the knowledge of their stories and by the ability to share them and to be heard by their own and by one another's communities. Before "multiculturalism" became an ideological shorthand for cultural work in the nineties, it was a vision struggling to be born in the gravitational field of the storytelling festival lineup.

The schedule in 1985, for instance, included Spalding Gray, the autobiographical monologuist from New York City; traditional musician-storytellers from Ethiopia (Selashe Damessae) and Bengal (Purna Das Baul); a professor, Robert Creed, whose specialty was reciting Beowulf in Old English; a seventy-eight-year-old retired children's librarian, Alice Kane, born in Belfast and raised in Toronto; a Pueblo Indian novelist and poet, Simon Ortiz; Mary Carter Smith, a self-styled African American "urban griot" from Baltimore; Peninnah Schram, from New York, who specialized in Jewish folktales; a teacher from St. Louis, Lynn Rubright, who had developed large-scale pilot programs for storytelling in schools; Connie Martin, a colleague of Robert Bly in the use of folktales as tools to revision gender roles; revival performers with backgrounds in writing (Jay O'Callahan), theater (Jon Spelman), mime (Jackson Gillman), and music and dance (Heather Forest); and Ray Hicks. "These performers represent a wide range of styles and stories, traditions and cultures," wrote Simms in the program guide. "In 13 years, NAPPS has successfully created a place for storytelling as an important social, political, and healing art."

What Simms meant by linking those three dimensions—social, political, and healing—in her mission statement links it in turn to Robert Cantwell's sense of festival magic. The careful calibration of cultural representation in constructing the festival program became for her and others a potent metaphor for the ritual construction of a peaceable kingdom. Geographic, ethnic, racial, gender, and stylistic balance are not casual matters in this construction but matters of world-shaping import. The actual complexity of that work of sympathetic magic was highlighted over the next few years of strife, retrenchment, and reorganization in the storytelling community and in NAPPS.

On Saturday, the formal storytelling activities would run from ten in the morning until ten-thirty at night, in all the tents and the Swappin' Ground. Each featured performer generally has one one-hour solo slot and then two or three other sessions that are shared with one to three other tellers. Sometimes these group sessions are planned around a theme—in 1985, the themes included "Men's Stories," "Women's Stories," "Stories of the West," "Heroes," "Laughing Stories," "Stories with Music," "True Stories," and "Family Stories"—sometimes the theme is only implicit in the contrasting voices of the tellers. Inevitably, you would be drawn and quartered by your appetite for things going on in many separate sites, until you were forced to surrender to the narrowness of a personal agenda. Apprentice storytellers and fans would pick a favorite, or two, three, or four favorites, and try to follow them from tent to tent, studying and enjoying them under different conditions, large tent and small, alone and in various combinations, watching them work off of one another and off of the energy of different crowds. For apprentices and journeyfolk, it is an opportunity to be imprinted by stories and by telling styles that resonate particularly with their own personality and background—that reach inside and awaken some slumbering sense of personal voice and vocation. Jim May described the transfer of power as it occurred to him on his first visit to the festival:

That first morning, I just remember the cool morning. And going in the Tent in the Park. And being real aware of the smell of the grass and the canvas, you know, under those tents. And Jackie Torrence came out, and told "Soldier Jack." And changed my life. And I remember seeing Doc McConnell sitting on a hay-bale, telling a story. And he actually even looked like one of the auctioneer friends of my Dad that I remembered. And kind of talked like them. Those two things, that first trip. Jackie and Doc. For some reason, I felt real welcome, real at home with their story-telling and their style. And I kind of let "Soldier Jack" roll around in my head all the way back home, twelve hours. And Monday morning got up and told my fifth graders that story. And I would have to say that in ten years of teaching, I had never been in that sort of place . . . of *connection* with the whole class at once, in that sort of place, that *trance,* I guess, that we all know about now. So, I was hooked.

The festival could come as a transforming shock to those who had been working on the craft in isolation, fueled only by a sense of personal necessity. Seeing the myth enacted in a concentrated congregational setting could make the whole story fall into place for the first time. Heather Forest described it that way in our interview:

I was at a coffeehouse in Connecticut, singing my songs and telling my stories—and in that coffeehouse, somebody mentioned that there was a gathering of storytellers down in Jonesborough, and that I should go down there. And I was *totally shocked* that there was anybody else interested in the same thing that I was interested in. And I said, "How long has this been going on?"

And they said, "Oh, for a number of years. There are a lot of people that tell stories."

And I really needed to see this for myself. It was hard for me to believe. I had no contact with anyone who was interested in this kind of stuff. I'd never heard of, or met, or anything. So I went down, in 1979, to the festival, and camped out. And spent a whole weekend with my mouth open. . . . I saw Laura, she was there that year. Jackie Torrence was there. Ron Evans was there; Roadside Theater. I was overwhelmed. On one level, I looked around at what I saw, and I said, "I'm not the same as anybody here. But on the other side, I haven't invented a single thing." That all those years of thinking that I was pushing edges and looking and seeking and experimenting, I was basically just digging down to some roots that preexisted. And that even though everybody there seemed to have roots in different ways, they were all tapping into the same wellspring. And I felt for the first time in *all* of my years that I had found my family. That the poking around, everything from clay to folk music to dance—these were just small branches and leaves on a very strong root, and that root went down into the same place that everybody else was touching into that I met that weekend.

Beth Horner had just begun her first job as a children's librarian in Champaign, Illinois, when she first went to Jonesborough in 1980:

And *I'll never forget it.* I will never forget it. The tents were very small at that time. And there was only one tent going, Friday evening. So it was very small, very homey. It reminded me so much of my grandmother's storytelling. It was the same feeling I got when my grandmother told a story. But it just amazed me that these people could make a living doing this. I was just blown away by it. I remember being in the tent with Brother Blue and Ed. And Brother Blue getting up and telling about his Ph.D. from Harvard. And then he told stories. And Ed got up, and before he sang, he was just strumming his banjo; he said, "My name is Ed Stivender, and I only have a *master's degree."* But Ed told "Jack and the Robbers." And that was the first time I'd ever seen someone *play,* really play with stories.

Horner's experiences at Jonesborough inspired her to work her way out of her library job within three years and into the world of free-lance storytelling.

Milbre Burch, who was trained as a mime and discovered the storytelling world in the late seventies, also had her attitude adjusted by Ed Stivender. Her anecdote evokes the many ways in which a trip to the festival could shift performers' perspectives about their place in the storytelling scene:

I went to the festival in '83. And I met Ed Stivender. . . . And here was Ed, playing his banjo, with a decrepit straw hat on. And Loralee introduces us, and he says to me, "What's your tradition?" And of course I was completely floored. I didn't have any idea what that question meant. And after gasping for air, and talking a little bit, he said, "Oh. Your tradition is theatrical."
And I said, "Oh. Okay. Alright." That was my tradition.

By late Saturday afternoon, the vision (or more precisely, the audition) of revived tradition, or of a polyphony of revived traditions all caroling their anthems under the banner of NAPPS, would be largely in place and the place prepared for the arrival of Ray Hicks. The staff car, covered with dust from the mountain roads, would pull up to the Tent in the Park. The designated driver would jump out to help Hicks unfurl his astonishingly elongated frame. His wife Rosa, tiny and thin, would follow him out carrying bags of ginseng, sassafras, and angelica root gathered from the mountain and some homemade apple cakes, all for sale. Whether Hicks was late for his show or not, he would be instantly surrounded. Children and adults, friends, acquaintances, and strangers, storytellers and tourists would stop to ask him questions, to listen to his torrent of talk, to snap his picture, or just to gawk. Hicks's image has adorned so many posters, flyers, schedules, programs, not to mention newspaper and magazine articles on the festival over the course of twenty years, that for a moment it would seem as if the festival itself had stepped out of a car and stood waving its enormous arms between the resource tent and the road.

This synecdoche remains compelling even though no one could be less typical of the contemporary storyteller bred by the revival and the festival than Hicks. Kathryn Windham recalled her first sight of him, back in 1975, before he had become a traditionalized symbol of the festival; yet the shock that lingers in her memory can give us a clue to why he became so:

> The first time I saw Ray Hicks, he was in the hall of one of those houses on Sisters' Row. And he was squatting down on his haunches; had on his overalls and his cap, his hat, pushed back on his head. And he was just squatting there, telling stories, and there were people standing and sitting around him in amazement. Most of them were from way off somewhere, and they couldn't believe that this man was just *there,* and—he went on for an hour, two hours there. And you know you have to get into Ray's rhythms and speech patterns before you really understand what he's saying. But he was having such a good time, telling them stories. He still does, doesn't he? I mean, it's awfully difficult to get Ray to conform to time limits.

Though the festival would increasingly move toward professional tellers who were quite at home in the segmented world of the weekend schedule, it still needed as its symbol a man whose stories and whose entire consciousness came from outside that world and were subject to being contained within it only for brief, ritual descents one Saturday afternoon a year. The Christian ritual, by analogy, takes as its centerpiece a man who was both born in a manger and immaculately conceived. The incarnation of American storytelling in a cabin on Beech Mountain that lacks central heating, running water, television, telephone, or clocks is a similar boon to the devout imagination.

In McConnell's unofficial Friday appearances, he would act as a fore-runner to Hicks's storytelling messiah, baptizing visitors in Appalachian storytelling traditions in preparation for Hicks's Saturday descent from the Mountain of Transfiguration. The difference in their repertoires is appropriate to this complementarity. Tall tales are worldly and rough; Jack tales, for all Hicks's characteristic interruptions, are most often otherworldly, supernatural, and associated with the Jungian archetype of the sacred child. Tall tales play with exoteric/esoteric code-switching. Hicks's long wonder tales, particularly in his archaic dialect, are purely esoteric, difficult to follow, but they reward the faithful with microcosmic epiphanies of the storytelling revival myth.

Hicks embodies for most of us the sacred "otherliness" of the storytelling tradition—the Other as Past, the Other as Wildman, the Other as Sage. His identification with his ancestral tradition is so profound and startling to the modern eye that he seems to merge with the heroes, the adventures, and the otherworlds of his tales. Even Duncan Williamson, a storyteller from Scotland whose traveler traditions are even richer in Jack tales than Hicks's Appalachian traditions are and who lived in a traveling tent for much of his life (McDermitt, "Duncan"), had this kind of shock when he met Hicks at the festival in 1987. I remember Williamson marveling, during his own session late Saturday afternoon, "I've heard stories about Jack all my life; I've told hundreds o' stories about Jack; but today, I've finally met Jack."

After Hicks and his wife were bundled back into the car and driven away, there would be a break for dinner. Food courts line the parking lot between the big Tent in the Park and the smaller tent on the hill. The resource shed, later to grow into a tent of its own, is open and thriving; all the restaurants in town are full. These free, informal zones in the tightly scheduled weekend are where the web of personal connections are formed that give a sense over the course of the year and the years that there is such a thing as a national storytelling community. Relationships are deepened—sometimes with acquaintances from home who suddenly become, in this liminal space, the people in the world who most closely share your soul; sometimes with strangers from half a continent away who catch your eye and wind up sitting across from you in a heart-to-heart outpouring all the more passionate the further it soars from your daily life. All this occurs in the altered, festival state of emotional susceptibility brought on by two days on a constant roller coaster of narrative movement.

After dinner there would be another scheduled session, a kind of mini-olio, in which two to five tellers play off of one another in each of two to five tents. The sun has set. Stories told would deepen and darken, revealing new comic, tragic, or personal dimensions. There is a sense of immanence, of a premonitory excitement leading up to the ghost story session. The accumulated invocations of ancestors, of otherworldly visions, and of hostile, benevolent, or tutelary spirits thicken the atmosphere of dusk. At this session in 1983, telling after Gamble Rogers, Carol Birch had her revelation of her own stage persona. Five years earlier, in 1978, Gwenda Ledbetter was walking to this session when she fell in step with Rogers. Both were at the festival for the first time. She recalled in a May 14, 1992, interview:

> He was talking out of the depths of the philosophy that was so much Gamble. And my mouth was agape at the wisdom that was pouring out of this "humorist." And the poet that I sensed was in him. And I don't know what caused me to say it—it must have been something in his talk. But I told Gamble, "I've got a story I think you might like." And I told the story of two preachers in a mountain cove that's divided over "sprinklin' or dunking." And the two ministers are so afraid that some of their flock will go over to the other church that they preach agin' each other. And then, there's a flood. And one minister jumps in to save the other minister's grand-daughter. And in so doing, loses his own life. And the community is united, because of that. And they only have one church, after that. And the name of the story is the name of the church: Harmony Chapel.
>
> And that night Gamble—I remember so well—he just sat with his guitar—*sat!* And when did you ever see him sit and tell a story? He didn't use the quiet stuff much, because it was too hard to get down there and then back up to where he carried people. But that night he sat and told that beautiful story-song about Joe, the guy who comes to the doorstep and leaves food for the hungry. And I was caught in the compassion of what Gamble was singing about. This deep compassion.

The story Rogers told that night was his elaborated version of Big Bill Broonzy's talking blues, "Joe Turner's Been Here and Gone," about a mysterious benefactor who leaves food and supplies for the hungry after a Mississippi Delta flood.

Thirteen years later, in 1991, Gamble Rogers drowned trying to save a swimmer caught in a riptide off a Florida beach. Ledbetter, recalling the session after his death, commented, "And so when he died, the way he died, I could understand it completely. I mean, I was *furious* at him—'Why in God's name did you do such a thing as that? With rheumatoid arthritis, and you jump in to save somebody ...' But that was in him" (May 14, 1992). She told me the story to remember and honor Gamble, who was a friend and a hero to many in the storytelling community, but also to evoke the liminal atmosphere of the festival evening, when connections struck between new acquaintances could spark storytellings that would function as prophetic dreams.

Until 1986, all other activities would stop at 9 P.M., and crowds would gather at the foot of the hill northeast of Main Street for the walk to the cemetery for the ghost telling. The seasonal approach of the old Celtic New Year, the divide between the light and dark sides of the year, when the gates between the worlds stand open for a night, would add an atavistic shiver to the natural chill in the air. In the ritual form of the festival, this is the traditional descent into the Underworld, with the storytellers as shamanic guides. It is an opportunity to contemplate the lower, malevolent, and fearsome forms on the other side of the divide of life and death.

In the mythos of the storytelling revival, the ghost telling has a dual resonance. In addition to being the most popular and profitable event of a storytelling festival, ghost storytelling is one of the last living refuges for traditional oral narrative in contemporary American popular culture. Whether on Boy Scout trips, at summer camps, or on junior high school sleepovers, there remains a lively tradition of keeping the darkness at bay with hoary old legends and gruesome new inventions.

So as midnight approaches, the ritual dramatization of the revival myth deepens, in a thicket of subliminal paradox. Through the imagining of death—our own as shivering mortals, paired with the projected death of storytelling as an art form and divine scapegoat—audience and art form are titillated into a state of exaltation. Though repeatedly pronounced dead and buried, here is the art of storytelling risen before us, reminding us that we are alive by leading us to the brink of annihilation—to sites in the imagination where resurrection of the body is worse than death. "Go back to the grave!" cries the father in "The Monkey's Paw," refusing the temptation to wish his dead son back in the flesh. While Jackie Torrence was telling this story in the cemetery in 1985, a drunken fan went wild, shouting, "Jackie, Jackie, I love you, Jackie!" with such mournful exuberance that she fell off the porch of the decrepit old house where she was standing and had to be carted away. It was the last ghost telling in the Jonesborough cemetery and a chilling glimpse of what it might be like to have the art of storytelling resurrected in the hungry flesh of American celebrity worship.

After midnight, the crowd is released. It streams down the hill like a fleet of candles in the dark, burning with the light of an art that has just been struck to life. After a short night of dreams, the festival faithful resurrect into the light of the sacred telling. These two events, ghost telling and sacred telling, are twinned in the ritual structure of the festival, dark giving way to light, yin to yang. The stories told here all concentrate on positive images of spiritual experience. Revenants appear only to wipe a weeping eye and tell their loved ones they are at peace. Wailing and gnashing of teeth are stilled by a kind word or a gentle touch, from this world or the next. Gods and goddesses, saints and bodhisattvas play peekaboo from behind the fleshly masks that appear to the world as bag ladies or simpletons. The holy fool sleeps forever in the divine mother's arms, and the sibilant whisper of palm rubbing palm would not disturb this sleep.

At the height of the revival period, the sacred telling was the climax of the festival for festival initiates, as the ghost storytelling was its climax for the merely curious. Many of those who streamed down the hill from the cemetery would not come back but would go away satisfied with the metaphysical teasing of the ghost stories. Those waiting to find a redemptive vision in storytelling would return in the morning for the sacred telling. The spiritual worlds depicted on Saturday night were exciting precisely because they were sundered from this world by great gulfs of fear. The spiritual worlds depicted on Sunday morning were gently joined to this one by currents of love, mercy, forgiveness, and courage.

Spontaneous communitas could reach its peak at this event. The sacred telling was initiated by Stivender and Williams as a loosening in the hierarchical structure of the festival. Originally unscheduled and congregational, it gradually grew more ceremonious, as did every regular feature at the festival; but for a while, at least, it maintained some of that sense of spontaneous and egalitarian play. Featured tellers and other performers in the festival community would participate according to the spirit of the moment—as that spirit was interpreted by the presiding elder, the M.C.

Some illustrative anecdotes are in order. In 1984, the high point of the festival for me came Sunday morning, when a spontaneous, wordless jam session erupted on stage between Ephat Mujuru, a traditional teller and *mbira* virtuoso from Zimbabwe, and Horace "Spoons" Williams, an elderly black percussionist and poet from South Carolina. As a festival volunteer, I had talked with Ephat early Saturday morning about his passion for sharing African traditions with his African American brothers and sisters and had heard his frustration at the apparent indifference or hostility he sometimes encountered here. But that changed when he met Spoons. A statuesque, very dark man nearing the end of his days, Spoons had fled a lynch mob in the thirties, lived most of his life in Philadelphia, and was just now receiving recognition as an eloquent bearer of African American verbal and musical traditions. As their rhythms locked together in the expectant atmosphere, a wordless narrative was woven among the listeners. A prodigal son of the African American diaspora and a long-lost brother seemed to reunite, through rhythms that had been preserved and passed down through their divided ancestors for three hundred torturous years. Little was said about it during or after, but the sheer joy of the playing itself was not enough to explain the emotion of the crowd, the tears rolling down faces, the standing ovation that would not stop until they had told the story over again.

On a Sunday morning in 1987, I awoke in the house where I was staying, a few miles west of Jonesborough, to the sound of a terrible crash. I looked out the window and saw a station wagon in the middle of the two-lane road, flipped over and resting on its roof. Expecting to find a bloodbath, I ran toward the crash scene, only to find a single woman rising unsteadily to her feet beside the wreck. Alone in the car and unhurt, she had unhitched her seat belt and crawled out the window. Now she threw herself into my arms and wept. "I know you understand," she cried. "You're a *storyteller!*" Assuring me that she needed no further assistance, she walked down the road toward town to look for another ride home to Cincinnati. I, meanwhile, went back in the house, got dressed, had a cup of coffee, and caught a ride from my hosts to the sacred telling, where I asked for and received the M.C.'s permission to go up on stage, tell the story of the morning's encounter, and ask the assembly to send the dazed and carless storyteller our prayers.

Perhaps the story that epitomizes the flavor of the sacred telling as a liminal zone of rededication and ritual climax to the festival is this one, told to me in 1992 by Doc McConnell:

There was a time there, two years ago, that I showed up at the festival. And I met this lady, walkin' down the street there. And she says, *"Oh, Doc, here you are, here you are!* I want to introduce you," she says. "This is my daughter. And this is her new baby. And we want you to be the baby's godfather."

And I said, "What?"

"We want you and Rex Ellis to be it's godfather." She said, "We want you to christen it Sunday morning at the sacred telling."

I said, "Well, I'm not a minister."

And she said, "Well you can christen it for me."

And I said, "Well, I'm not sure," I said. "But I'll do what I can."

And then she saw me later and gave me the details. This young girl was not settled. She was a rambunctious teenager that was not doing well in school, and was not happy at home, and was just having all sorts of problems. Her mother is a psychologist of some kind; she has a doctorate. And so, she was trying to tell me, this girl became pregnant. And had the baby, just a week or two before the storytelling festival. On the eighteenth day of September 1989.

And she said that this girl was still distraught and didn't know what she was going to do. And her mother was tryin' to tell her, "This is your baby, and it's your responsibility."

Said, "Why don't you go to the National Storytelling Festival?"

"What, I don't want to go to that."

Said, "Well, why don't you go with me, you might like it."

"Well, alright, I'll go with you."

And she came. And her mother said, "After she got here and was here for a day or two, like on Friday and Friday night and Saturday, she listened to Rex Ellis and Doc McConnell tell stories." And she said, "She found something at the festival, from people who came to the festival, that she had never experienced before. She found love, and concern, and caring. She heard them folks talking about love, and care, and understanding, and responsibility, and those things. And she got a sampling of that, and she said, "This is real. I've never had this before in my life. I never found anyone who loved me just for who I am. I never found anybody who seemed to have love and caring and concern in their heart for their fellow human beings. And I want to be a part of this, and I want my baby to be a part of this, in the very beginning of its life."

And so she wanted me to present that baby, in such a way as that they would know that baby and know that she was committing that baby to those things that storytelling stood for.

And so, I did it. I went over, and took her, Rex Ellis and I—Rex didn't know what to do, and I told him we would just kind of do *a* ceremony— and we went over to the big tent where they were having a sacred telling, at the beginning, on a Sunday morning. And I was the first thing on. And I got up and told 'em this story about this lovely girl.

And I had her there. And said, "I would like to present to you, this beautiful baby here. Who was born only two weeks ago, and is now at the festival. Her mother has found something here that she's never found before. And she wants you to know that, and she wants you to share in the joy and the love that she has for this baby. And we want you to share in the joy and love of this baby, too.

And I presented the baby and passed it to Rex, and then Rex passed it on to its mother—and made a beautiful ceremony.

In fact, I have the pictures in front of me right here now. And it was a beautiful little girl. And so, she's doin' fine. And her mother's goin' back to school now, and the baby's doin' fine; and turned that young girl's life around. And storytelling did that.

The trajectory of the festival, like many other liminal rites, moves downward into the dark to push the spirit up into the light. The revival preacher takes care to draw his eager audience into the steaming pit of hell before raising it into the dawn of salvation. The tribal initiate may be symbolically buried or dismembered before being reincorporated into a new status. At the storytelling revival event, once again, the symbolic protagonist of the festival's ritual narrative is storytelling itself. Featured tellers and committed audiences celebrate the sacrificial death of the folk art, its harrowing of the hell of our haunted imaginations, and its resurrection as a tool of social connectedness and spiritual healing. By our identification with and dedication to the storytelling form, we are moved to shed fears and doubts and take on some of the power demonstrated at the festival, for reincorporation into our own lives and home communities.

The Storyteller's Sacrifice

Sacrifice, it has often been said, is the dramatic core of most ritual events. Schechner quotes Michael Bristol's paradigm: "A substitute victim is murdered in order to ward off a more terrifying, indiscriminate violence among the members of the same community. This sacrificial murder is the partly hidden meaning of all religion and thus of all social life" (*Future of Ritual* 47).

At the core of the storytelling festival drama is a sequence of sacrificial acts. The first order of sacrifice exists prior to the assembly, as a referential constant, an article of faith: society's sacrifice of the storyteller's unifying importance to the community. As noted in the introduction, the community storyteller has been dismembered by the complexity of modern life and the parts parcelled out among representatives of myriad media and ceremonial outlets. This sacrifice is linked to a larger, mythic theme, which resonates on the personal, sociological, and even cosmic planes. It is the theme of loss of innocence—conceived of personally as the loss of childhood, societally as the spread of alienated labor and alienated art, and mythologically as the Fall of Man or even the Death of God. There is a core of grief and guilt in individuals and society for these inescapable passages, a core that provides an energy deposit to fuel a great panoply of ritual expressions.

The second order of sacrifice dramatized by the festival is a converse and corollary of the first. It is the sacrifice the storytellers on stage and in the audience undertake by devoting their working lives to the restoration of that lost state of aesthetic grace. Where the Christian ritual of mass celebrates, alongside the prior sacrifice of Christ on the cross, the corollary sacrifice of the priest or minister and, by participatory magic, the congregants—who renounce the world and the flesh to consecrate themselves to the host—so storytellers in the seventies and eighties offered themselves on the festival stage as those who had renounced the fallen world of Reaganomics and network news to elevate a vision of preindustrial artistic communion. In that sense, the storytelling festival represents a zone of inversion, where "the last is made first": where a supposedly lost art form could be anointed lord of misrule; where self-confessed fools like Brother Blue, Ken Feit, or Ed Stivender could celebrate and be celebrated in a kind of fool's mass; and where powerful women like Connie Regan-Blake, Laura Simms, or Jackie Torrence could lead congregations of former or would-be dropouts toward reincorporation into the world.

In connection with the storyteller's sacrifice, it is interesting to note the recurrent constellation of sacred attributes that Turner in *The Ritual Process* calls "the powers of the weak," or "structural inferiority." Turner defines these as "the permanently or transiently sacred attributes of low status or position." He points out that in highly structured societies, marginalized or subject groups and peoples often come to symbolize for the dominant groups the neglected or lost potentials of the psyche. He points to "the cult associations whose members have gained entry through common misfortune and debilitating circumstances" among such tribal groups as the Ndembu and Lamba of Central Africa, as well as "the role of structurally small and politically insignificant nations within systems of nations as upholders of religious and moral values, such as the Hebrews in the ancient Near East, the Irish in early medieval Christendom, and the Swiss in modern Europe" (109). He also associates this sacredness with the medieval fool, or court jester, who was given license to upend dominant value structures in his verbal play, and with the holy beggars, youngest sons, and simpletons of folktales, "who strip off the pretensions of those of high rank and office and reduce them to the level of common humanity and mortality" (110). He continues:

> Members of despised or outlawed ethnic and cultural groups play major roles in myths and popular tales as representatives or expressions of universal human values. Famous among these are the good Samaritan, the Jewish fiddler Rothschild in Chekhov's tale "Rothschild's Fiddle," Mark Twain's fugitive Negro slave Jim in *Huckleberry Finn,* and Dostoyevsky's Sonya, the prostitute who redeems the would-be Nietzschean "superman" Raskolnikov in *Crime and Punishment.* All these mythic types are structurally inferior or "marginal," yet represent what Henri Bergson would have called "open" as against "closed morality," the latter being essentially the normative system of bounded, structured, particularistic groups. (110)

We could also point to the revitalizing symbolism that African American music has assumed in American popular culture, through the influence of minstrelsy in the nineteenth century, jazz from the twenties through the fifties, and blues, rhythm 'n' blues, soul, and rap in the decades since; we could also cite the romantic allure of gangs or drug subcultures. All these associations go far in explaining the predominance in the storytelling revival repertoire of folktales drawn from "structurally inferior" lineages, such as the African American, the Native American, or the Appalachian, and of such figures of sacred weakness as Br'er Rabbit, High John, Jack, or Coyote. They represent the potential for psychic renewal that lies hidden in the marginalized or repressed aspects of society and the self—which are encompassed and epitomized by the redeeming image of the storyteller. Turner concludes, "In closed or structured societies, it is the marginal or 'inferior' person or the 'outsider' who often comes to symbolize what David Hume has called 'the sentiment for humanity,' which in its turn relates to the model we have termed 'communitas'" (111). The storytelling revival deliberately identifies with these types, features them in its repertoire, and elevates them in its rituals, all to evoke "the sentiment for humanity" and to weave a fabric of storytelling communitas.

Happily Ever After: "To Work Nationally as a Storyteller"

Some pioneer storytellers of the revival period, such as Brother Blue or Gioia Timpanelli, established their storytelling careers long enough before their encounter with Jonesborough that it did not mark a major passage or change of status. But for many storytellers who came to vocational consciousness in the seventies and eighties, their appearance (or failure to appear) at the National Festival was experienced as a definite rite of passage or, contrarily, as a block to their advancement in the storytelling world. Peninnah Schram, a teller from New York who specializes in Jewish folktales, expressed the transformation succinctly when she told me, "It was the highest point in my professional career, to be recognized and invited as a featured teller. It meant that I was recognized and appreciated by my peers, by professionals of all the different cultures, and it wasn't just an in-group that was appreciating me, in a sense."

Several of the personal narratives I recorded on this theme were structured along the lines of traditional journey tales, emphasizing the trials or the terrors of the passage and culminating in career-transforming triumphs. Jackie Torrence described the fear and uncertainty that accompanied her to Jonesborough in 1977, heightened by the fact that she was one of very few black faces in a crowd of strangers:

> People who took me there weren't going to the festival. They were going to their people in Johnson City, going to visit. And they weren't interested in the festival. They just said, "We'll take you there." They took me there, put my bags out on the street, and left me. And I was scared. I didn't see a black person anywhere. And I was already frightened. Because, this was Tennessee, you know. And Tennessee had a bad rep. For, you know, racial prejudice. And I looked all around, and I thought, "I am scared to death." Happened to look up, and there was NAPPS, that was the office. And I drug my luggage all the way upstairs. And, oh, they were just so glad to see me, and they said, "Well have a seat. Somebody will be with you."
>
> And they left me sitting. And I was just sort of quiet, because I didn't know anybody; and everybody seemed to know each other. And I looked up, and up the stairs came this one black fellow. He was on the crew, the film crew. And it was like, "Oh Lord—" I was so glad to see him—"It's another one here!" But he was so busy, that he, you know, he didn't have time to pay me any attention. And I think I scared him. I just sort of jumped on him—*"Hello there!"* Because I didn't know anybody. You know, they treated me alright, but people knew each other, and they didn't have time to be bothered with me.

In a scene emotionally reminiscent of Cinderella at the ball, Torrence describes the impact of her performance that weekend, as it elevated her to instant prominence in the revival scene:

The first time I got to tell a story was at the Methodist church; they had the olio. And I remember Kathryn Windham and Doc McConnell were M.C.ing. . . . And I was at the back of the crowd. 'Cause I didn't know where to go; nobody had told me you're supposed to be up front. So when they called on me, I'm sitting there scared to death. And they called my name two or three times; when a lady looked round at me and said, "Aren't you—" I said, "Yes." So they helped me walk through the crowd to get up front.

And I was so frightened. Doc said, "Jackie, tell us where you're from."
And I'm standin' there grinnin' at him—I didn't know where I was from.
And he said, "Well, you got a story to tell us?"
And I said, "Yes."
He said, "Well, tell us one."
Well, I had decided to tell all of these stories, you know; and couldn't think of one of 'em. And I ended up telling a story that I wrote as a child, "Elvira and Henry." And that's the way that story got away from me, because, you know, instantly, everybody just grabbed it. . . . Well, that was my first performance. And that weekend, from Friday to Sunday, I booked about fifty appointments. And that was the end of my being at home. That was it. It was like, you know, my career went wild. It was like I was on a buckboard. And I had lost the reins to the mule. And they were just runnin'. And all I could do was hold on.

Heather Forest described a similar anxiety upon her arrival at Jonesborough for her first weekend as a featured teller and gave a touching account of a moment of inward surrender:

It all kind of fell apart for me the minute I walked into Jonesborough. I thought, Oh, no! I can't do this! People will think I'm strange! They'll think—I don't do what people do here! It's the same, but it's different. So I remember coming early and going to one of those yellow and white tents. And I went into the tent. And it was empty. And I just stood there. And I looked at the empty space. And I just stood there for a very long time. Trying to realize that I was home. And that it was going to be all right. And that the only thing that I could do would to be true to myself and to try and express my heart in the best way that I could. And that if people enjoyed what I had to share, then that would make the circle come round. And if I wasn't welcome there, I would find that out too.
And I really did want to feel at home.
And I think that was really a powerful centering time for me—just standing in that empty tent and telling myself it was all going to be all right. And it was.

There was one presentation that I did . . . kind of what I thought was full-out. Where I went and I changed into really comfortable, baggy pants and a leotard. Which I would wear if I was really going to use the space and move through it. Not be limited by a stand-up microphone. It was the only such thing that I did the whole weekend. But I wanted to share with people the full range of what I thought storytelling could be, with movement, poetry and song. And it was the only presentation like that I did that whole weekend; the rest of the time I shared the space with other tellers, and I used the microphone the same way that everybody else did. But in this one, I brought my radio-microphone, and I remember kind of cautiously creeping in with my leotard on. But it was, you know, nothing like a dancer would look—I had a pair of baggy pants on and a vest—it was just that my arms were in a black leotard so I could create shapes with my body and it would be visible. And the intentionality of my motion could be perceived. And I did a story with a pair of bamboo sticks, and I did a story with masks, and I did a story with motion—I told the story of "The Stonecutter," and I did "Heaven and Hell." I did a lot of very physical pieces, and . . . when it was all over, there was kind of like a pause and then, I got a standing ovation. And—I couldn't have been more dumbfounded . . . I really had no idea how people would take it.

Forest, like Torrence, clearly links the two passages, the ordeal and the overcoming, in her memory—her moment of silent dedication providing the courage to overcome her fears and "go all out" with her gifts, to draw on her training in dance, theater, and music to express fully her vision of "what storytelling could be." The result, again, was a true rite of passage for her, through which at the end of the weekend she was reincorporated into her world with a transformed status both inwardly achieved and outwardly confirmed.

Ed Stivender's account of his first appearance at the National Festival also contains motifs from the traditional wonder tale journey. Like such male-protagonist stories as the Jack tales, as contrasted with such female tales as "Cinderella," Stivender's account plays down his inner doubt and suffering in favor of the comic business of personal foolishness or ingenuity. He describes how he bought an expensive pair of cowboy boots for the event. "I bought them because I was going to Tennessee, you know, I had to be dressed. They were nice boots, they were just ... small. Just wore them that one time. I mean, I wore them maybe four times at the most otherwise, because they really were uncomfortable. So what I was doing was, I was carrying around these boots, wearing sneakers between the tents, and then I would get to the tent, put on my boots and go on the stage" (January 7, 1992).

With a customary irony that only heightens the wonder tale motifs, he then described how a conscious attitude of service to the festival staff put him on the path of both worldly opportunity and supernatural assistance:

> But the next great thing that happened to me was, when I arrived at NAPPS, I set up my relationship with NAPPS for the rest the time, and that was the relationship of *porter; roadie;* person who was there and available to do whatever needs to be done. Very important role. So that when Cynthia Orr's plane was late, Barbara or Connie said to me, "Ed, will you go over there and take her place?"—in the opening tent, Friday. So I went over to take Cynthia Orr's place in the opening thing, and as I began my routine, which was going to be real simple, "Jack and the Robbers," cute stuff, there was a thunderbolt that shook the tent; and I took this as a sign from God to do my "Reverend Ed" material, which I didn't expect to do because it was too, um, tricky, I figured, for that community. But, ahh, go ahead. So I went ahead and did it. And it was a great moment for me. It was from that tent that I got real nice work for the next couple of years. And also got a review, it was from that moment in the tent, I got a review in the *Village Voice,* which called me "blasphemous and sacrilegious." Which is a *great* honor, I think, to be called blasphemous and sacrilegious by the *Village Voice.* And that was the beginning of my work nationally as a storyteller.

To begin to "work nationally as a storyteller"—this was the happily-ever-after ending of many storytellers' vocational narratives. But the growth of the storytelling world created a bottleneck of performers who wanted to add that story to their repertoires. The National Storytelling Festival had crystallized its form around a schedule of twelve to fifteen featured tellers per year. Of those slots, fewer than half might go to new tellers, and the rest would be reserved for popular performers from years past—"favorite tellers that make us laugh, cry and sing; tellers who take us back through familiar stories for the umpteenth time," wrote George Shannon, in another expression of the traditionalizing urge. The members of the NAPPS board of directors who made up the festival card had become a kind of priesthood, determining who would or would not receive the coveted initiation. Like priesthoods before them, they thus became targets of resentment and ultimately, as we will see in chapter 6, of a reformation movement.

The Storyteller's Homecoming

The side of Jonesborough that made it seem a ritual sanctuary and zone of reincorporation for a particular late-sixties brand of cultural carnivalesque was pointed out to me by Jim May, describing his first journey there in 1978:

> That was in the seventies, so there were all these . . . young-middle-aged hippies. Or strange, wonderful people from all corners of the country. That felt just really good. That felt like a political homecoming or something. I think having left college, there was a big vacuum for me, at least, in the early seventies. And coming and finding a group of people whose lifestyle seemed to indicate that they were more flexible and open than most people that I was around since college. That was part of it too. When you think about it, I would guess that . . . *a lot* of the people that fueled the revival, both in the telling and in the audience were pretty close to the same age—I would bet. The majority at least, were in their mid-thirties then. It was a way, in terms of self-expression and lifestyle, a way of untying the Gordian knot for a lot of us, I think. Suddenly you could live sort of a vagabond lifestyle and philosophy and be world-embracing.

His comments recall Harvey Cox's remark about "the gap between the world-changers and the world-celebrators." The storytelling movement, like Cox's image of the Feast of Fools, allowed its participants to close the gap. It allowed them to perform a double sacrifice: through inverting the media hierarchy of the dominant culture, they publicly sacrificed their indoctrination in the values of that cultural set; yet in crusading to bring the restored image of the storyteller out of folklife and back into the dominant culture and its media extensions, they were simultaneously sacrificing their own alienation from that dominant culture.

This dialectical process of resistance and accommodation is one we have already seen at work. The storyteller archetype became a mediating image by which creative, searching, alienated spirits could find their way in society on terms that felt like their own. For some, like Robin Moore, who gave up his "straight" job to pursue the life of a gypsy-entrepreneur, storytelling could be a vehicle to take them on the journey out—for others, it was a way back in. Yet by the transformation of that folklife image into what John D. Dorst calls a "vignette" against the field of popular consumer culture, professional storytellers were accepting the terms of that culture, in critical ways, as a setting and measure for their accomplishments.

"Vignette," in Dorst's usage, is a printer's term: a graphic image shading imperceptibly into the text of a printed surface. He turns this into a metaphor for the postmodern indeterminacy of historical or artistic figurations and their contemporary consumerist background. By the late eighties, many revival storytellers who had long expounded on the spirituality of storytelling were becoming equally adept at comparing fees and booking agents. In the effort to create a social identity out of the once meaningless conjunction "professional storyteller," NAPPS had helped produce similarly indeterminate shadings of homespun art and consumable, professional presentation: which was now the figure and which the ground?

This leads us to another sense in which sacrifice is incorporated into the ritual action of the National Storytelling Festival. The figure of the storyteller is hoisted aloft on the field of festive commerce precisely on account of its colorful, "homespun" quality. "Homespun" is a ubiquitous image in the discourse of the revival. It became the title of Jimmy Neil Smith's first book of stories from the festival, and it is even betokened physically in the calico swatch that every festival-goer must wear for admission to the tents. Literally, homespun is cloth made from fibers grown, cut, spun, and woven in a self-sufficient household economy. Figuratively, it is an image of what Jean Baudrillard calls "symbolic exchange" (quoted in Dorst 131)—a community in which production and consumption are internal to a group, which is conscious of the circle of obligations flowing from that estate—as in the totem tale "The Storyteller Knows Me." Dorst comments, "Whether symbolic exchange accurately describes actual pre-capitalist social/economic formations is a vexed question. For immediate purposes it is enough to claim that an *image* of such formations does exist in the discourse of our Site" (131). His remarks were originally made about another artistic school connected with a local civic revival, the Brandywine River School in Chadd's Ford, Pennsylvania; but they can be applied as well to the storytelling movement and its enshrinement in Jonesborough. Dorst continues, "What most characterizes this imagined social order is the inseparability of the objects, instruments, and processes of production from the concrete social relations through which they are enacted and deployed. In other words, the image is of a non-commodity or pre-commodity economy of symbolic exchange in which production, exchange and consumption are unalienated from the participants in these social activities" (131).

This is precisely the form of community that most of us have sacrificed to participate in the fallen pleasures of modern consumer society. The vivid representation of this form of integral culture in the performance of festival storytellers is an important element in their reception and consumption by the cosmopolitan audience—particularly when the commodities represented as organically grown from communities of symbolic exchange are the stories that make up a performer's repertoire. In the contemporary world, of course, anywhere this economy might be said to exist, it is usually accompanied by cruel poverty and social marginalization—which amplifies its powers of weakness and increases its appeal in the revival mythos. Ray Hicks and Ron Evans are paramount examples of this at Jonesborough, but the same hunger is built into the festival charisma process at many levels. This is not to say, however, that any good traditional storyteller will find a place at the festival. On the contrary, those performers who are able to abstract themselves from their native contexts—to reproduce their cultural experience in performative quotation marks for the synthetic community of the festival—or those, like Hicks, who lend themselves to being so abstracted by the festival promoters are most likely to make the transition from culture-bearer for an integral group to celebrant of the revival mythos.

Another striking visual representation of symbolic exchange in the festival spectacle is the storyteller's costume. The alert ethnographer walking down Main Street in Jonesborough at festival time will witness a floating exhibition of loose, flowing, woven clothing from tribal peoples around the globe—particularly from Guatemala, Mexico, Ecuador, the Bolivian Andes, the American Southwest, Bali, West Africa, and India, supplemented by designs from contemporary American craft weavers. The common denominator of storytelling costumes is the image of the handwoven garment, italicized by bold, prismatic color schemes. It is an image out of the life of symbolic exchange—though the costumes themselves are mostly purchased on the import/export market, on tourist excursions, or at resale shops. The exhibition stimulates a kind of hypnotic suggestion for wearers and beholders, associating the weaving of costume, performer, and performance with the dream of a restored, handwoven world. Robin Williamson expressed the connection in our interview when he said, "As society became increasingly mechanized, increasingly silicon-tipped, people turned to sources of eternal verities, and particularly things that had a really handmade touch to them. And there's nothing quite as handmade as the mythical and traditional tale. Which is in the same sort of language as the language of the human dream." The storyteller and folklorist Kay Stone, who at festivals also dresses the part, told me of being approached at Jonesborough by a friendly neophyte who dreamily remarked, "I hope I can dress like that when I'm a storyteller."

Folktales, like folk songs before them and like traditional crafts and folk arts the world over, are forms in which images and impressions out of the life of symbolic exchange can be packed up and exported to inhabitants of a very different cultural economy. The folklife image is resettled in an economy of tourism and the import/export of cultural properties. When the "homespun" storyteller mounts the festival stage, the image of symbolic exchange is sacrificed on the altar of consumer culture. We are offered wine in the place of blood and, in later dilutions, grape juice in place of wine. We can make it real for ourselves by imaginative projection—or else we may just sit back and enjoy the taste of alcohol and sugar.

The most dramatic manifestation of this level of the storyteller's sacrifice is the growth of the NAPPS "resource tent." At the beginning of the 1980s, there was no such thing. The few commodities crystallized from the oral life-stream of the early revival were handed around from trunks of cars and the beds of pickup trucks. By 1982, the A-frame shed that was the site of the first sacred storytelling had become the first "resource area," where professionally produced cassettes, books, and videos were sold on consignment by NAPPS staffers. By 1992, that small area had expanded to fill a tent, and "resource sales" had become a significant part of the profit margin of the festival for both storytellers and NAPPS.

For free-lance performers, the production of commodities has become a primary aspect of the business of storytelling. To have reproduced oneself by means of books and tapes has in significant ways supplanted membership in a community of symbolic exchange (such as the storytelling support groups that are examined in chapter 5) in the process of generating charisma for oneself and one's professional status. For NAPPS members who mainly *use* storytelling in the performance of other professional roles—as teachers, librarians, ministers, or therapists—the commodity process is secondary but is still an important part of their participation in the revival. These are not the producers but the consumers of storytelling resources; and because of this, the programming and merchandising efforts of NAPPS have shifted dramatically in their direction. One storyteller, who had cut his teeth on a populist strain of Appalachian nationalism, told me:

> I think that they probably did a demographic study, realized that they were pretty much getting teachers and librarians, and that those people all had some source of funding to permit them to travel the great dis-

tances required, and to pay the fees required to stay in a hotel and feed yourself in a restaurant for three days. But I saw the price of the ticket quadruple. And I said to myself, what's really going on here is that these people have recognized that they have an audience amongst professionals who can get their trip funded by their institutions. And so they have decided to earmark the dollar-price for that singled-out group of people. And my own perspective was that storytelling *is* a useful tool for librarians and schoolteachers to know about, but it is absolutely the People's art form. And if John Q. Public can't come there because they can't afford to pay . . . then I figured what they'd basically done is, they'd cut themselves off from the man in the street, the man for whom this single art form is probably the most accessible art form. And they'd just sort of elevated it to something that was more and more for the white-collar establishment.

There are other prominent revivalists who take oblique, ironical stances astride this development. Others swim gracefully with the tide or struggle against it; still others jump in and muddy the water, like the novice whom Carol Birch met at Jonesborough one year who told her, "*I figure I should be able to make a killing.* I think I'll be able to make more than Gamble Rogers and Donald Davis and stuff. I figure about two more years." Birch said, "It was disgusting. He was some man who used to be a boat salesman in Florida. Power boats."

Kissed by the Dog

The wonder tales, too, give us images of this late phase of the revitalization process. The hero's homecoming can be as perilous, in a subtler way, as the dramatic trials and ordeals of the journey. How does one share the blessings of the other world, so that those who have never left can receive the benefits? In one Jack tale (Chase, *Jack Tales* 135–150, annotation 198), the hero makes his true love from the other world wait outside by the gate, while he goes in to reunite with his family. She warns him not to let himself be kissed by anyone in his former household until he has told them about her. He tries to heed her and fends off his entire family's onrushing lips. All of a sudden a little dog leaps up and licks his face, and he forgets everything he has been through. The next thing he knows, he is engaged to be married to a local girl, while his true bride, the daughter of gods, has to hire herself out as a servant to an ugly shoemaker, until she can finally bring him to his senses.

The task of reuniting with the culture from which one has turned away to go on a quest for authentic experience can be equally perilous. If some storytellers are kissed by the dog and find themselves engaged to commercial models of success, it is a story we might have heard or told before. The true bride will be at the wedding in disguise, or so the story has it, with a talking fox in a magic box that will open to remind him, before it is too late, of everything that was ever owed, or earned, or given, or loved.

5

Alternate Models of Community

The nurturance of storytelling communities is an essential part of the revitalization effort: the concerted attempt to create the elements of a more satisfying cultural life. This is the natural urge toward completion of Anthony F. C. Wallace's revitalization cycle—the phases of communication, organization, adaptation, cultural transformation, and routinization in which the seed, having sprouted, rooted, and climbed to daylight, now attempts to reproduce. In Joseph Campbell's terms, the call has been answered, the journey taken, the homecoming achieved. The storyteller is now faced with the task of transferring the boon to the home community and making a place for the home community on the map of an emerging art world. In the storytelling revival this meant coming together in groups and networks of groups around the country to ceremonially welcome the fugitive art form home to each locality and to anchor it there.

Communities of storytelling enthusiasts built a variety of alternative cultural events, and the events in turn built revival communities. *Culture* and *community* are intimately linked, reciprocal terms—culture grows from community, and community from culture. They are also terms—like *nation, family, religion, home, tradition,* and *ritual*—that have particular empirical applications but in generic usage quickly slip into a mythic dimension. *Community,* in the storytelling movement, is a term of virtually unchallenged good. It is a key element of the revival dialectic, in which an imagined past is invoked to summon images of a restored future in order to bring hope and fervor to a troubled present. In the idealized past of the revival mythos, communities were strong, satisfying, and inclusive, and they were infused with energy and joy by traditional arts, such as music, dance, crafts, and especially storytelling. To restore these arts, through regular gatherings committed to the revival program and practice, is to participate by transference in the restoration of those ideal communities of the past. Out of this wellspring of utopian imagining flows the peculiar pneuma that attends, for its members, the phrase "the storytelling community."

Beneath this one-hair bridge of fervor from utopian shore to shore, however, roars a chaotic present, polluted with the debris and despair of broken communal ties. In the revivalist critique of American culture, community, like storytelling, is a sacrificial victim—a dismembered god. Rafe Martin expressed it this way: "There was a study recently done, where people were asked, what was most prevalent in American life. And the underlying feeling was: loneliness. That is, the lack of community. And I think that's partly what the whole storytelling network, and structure, is about. You know, traditional tales *imply* community. You can't have the one without the other. And in a sense, by going into the territory of traditional tales, we restore in our minds the space of community." Because of the intimate reciprocity of the storytelling act, storytelling revivalism positions itself as an answer to the American dilemma of broken community—as Heather Forest asserted in our interview:

There's something missing in media, that happens in storytelling. And the thing that's missing is communication. And communication has the same root as common, and commune, and community. So what happens that's so pleasure-full in the storytelling experience, is a sense of community and connection with the teller and the listeners. And the history, or herstory, of this encountering, is so ancient, that it really doesn't seem to matter much if the teller is technically proficient or not. It just has to do with setting up the situation where *a* person is *communicating,* with language, to conjure images in the imagination of the listener. The connection between the teller and the listener is so interwoven, that the feedback is creating language for the teller, and the teller's language is creating images of response on the part of the listeners, and a very powerful, circular relationship begins to happen. No teller, in the most ancient sense of the word, would tell to the air. It's people. And community is definitely at the heart of that experience.

What the storytelling critique tends to avoid are the negative sides of community—conformity, fixed hierarchies, and the stifling of individual difference. Yet the widespread American sacrifice of community is at

least partly based on a cultural reaction against those negative qualities—
and on a fetishistic growth of the opposing qualities of personal freedom,
democracy, and individualism. The storytelling revival imaginatively rec-
onciles that contradiction by setting up an alternate field—a community of self-made renegades, vagabonds, and dreamers, truth-telling liars at
home with paradox, colorful misfits enamored of tradition, bohemian
entrepreneurs from an incorporeal village where it is always the first weekend in October. One recalls Jim May's comment on his discovery of Jonesborough in the seventies: "Suddenly you could live sort of a vagabond life-
style and philosophy and be world-embracing." He continued, "And I can
do that by celebrating horse-trading stories from Spring Grove, which is
a place that I had become pretty alienated from, in terms of its politics,
and its small-town narrowness. So now I get invited to go to Paris to tell
stories about Spring Grove."

The storyteller Bill Harley gave me a revealing Jonesborough memory:

[We were] standing one year, it was probably like '85, '86, saying goodbye to people on Sunday afternoon, standing on the corner with Jim,
downtown. Saying, "Could you imagine if we all lived in this one place?"
Because of that sense that the whole place had been transformed. And
there were all these people that I just really liked and cared about.

And somebody said, *"Yeah, we wouldn't be workin' very much, would we?"*

It's kind of like a fairyland, you know it's kind of like Disney World—I
mean, I hate Disney World—but it's got that sense of, "What a theme
park!"

Certainly we are not talking here about a community in the quaint,
endangered sense of a place one shares with others. Rather it is a form of
virtual community, an extremely low-tech theme park, which was easily
packed up and carried to every region of the country—a carnival of performative rides.

The question worth raising is whether the term *storytelling community*
is descriptive, illusory, or mythic in the sense that we have been cultivating all along—a magical word, invoking a wonder tale of loss and redemption that can never be fully told. The drumbeat persistence of the term in
storytelling movement discourse expresses the romantic revivalism at the
movement's heart. It is an affirmation of desire, a courtship of community; and like much courtship, it is bound for disenchantment in particulars. Still, just as courtship cannot be adequately explained without reference to "love"—carefully as we may wish to sort through the levels of
self-interest and intoxication loaded into that term—so we cannot exam-

ine the storytelling revival without looking at the forms generated under the sign of *community.*

As an alternative sign, meanwhile, the more neutral *scene* presents itself. A scene is implicitly a function of the imagination at work, recomposing reality against a painted backdrop. Scenes assemble, play themselves out, and change when their part in the human comedy is done. Communities, by contrast, generate traditions precisely to protect themselves against change—they replay the same scenes over and over with changing casts. Communities have difficulty accepting change, inspired from within or without, lest the specter of disunity, community's nemesis, arise in the midst like blasphemy—even though the sacred tradition may itself have been put in the place of some failed tradition only a few cycles ago. In the accounts that follow, I will balance the two terms—*community* and *scene*—against each other, not as impermeable categories but for their contrasting connotations, to express the volatile blend of innovation and traditionalization that marked the emerging storytelling revival.

Communities Organize Events/Events Organize Communities

The revival was powered in the main by energetic individuals in widely scattered areas, who banded together into local and regional, formal and informal networks, story-swaps, performance collectives, classes, conferences, and guilds. These local and regional gatherings created their own communal rituals, which tended to be less hierarchical and more egalitarian than the national festival. They also created a loose network of local and regional festivals, which imitated Jonesborough in many respects but diverged in others. These local and regional communities provided the close support and nurturing necessary to launch local storytelling careers, which eventually bloomed into the national spotlight.

Although the obvious sequence would suggest that communities organize events, again and again in revival contexts where community has grown from the ground up, we see that events also organize communities. Storytelling communities tended to organize themselves around the ritual frameworks of festival, concert series, conference, guild, and support group. Of these models, the conference, guild, and support group are "esoteric"—meant to build a community of tellers. The festival and concert series are "exoteric"—meant to build a community of listeners and exercise tellers' abilities to hold the focus of large public gatherings. The models that predominate in a given locale, as well as the ideologies, relationship styles, professional goals, strengths, and weaknesses among key organizers, all have powerful and reciprocal effects in generating community tone.

Festivals and concert series are also implicitly hierarchical, in that many levels of responsibility and prestige are built into their structure. They are constructed of small groups of featured professional (or would-be professional) performers in celebrant roles, larger bands of staff and volunteers performing vital support roles, and the largest groups of listeners, whether they are neophytes, congregants, media, or the merely curious. Regional festivals often show distinct levels among the tellers as well, with a few "national tellers" given top billing and fees, usually because of prior appearances at Jonesborough, while other performers are stamped with the caste marks of "regional" or "local" tellers. Although, as we have seen, the festival form itself has deep roots in religious feast days and community celebrations, the storytelling festival model can nearly always be traced, either directly or indirectly, to the National Storytelling Festival. Before NAPPS, there were "Liars' Contest" components at other local festivals; but compared to what developed later, these were as jokes to a full-fledged myth.

Conferences, retreats, and support groups are less hierarchical, because there are fewer formal levels of status and responsibility. Everyone present is presumed to have a committed interest in the art, at least by virtue of having surrendered large amounts of time and/or money to participate. There are teacher/student or master/journeyman status distinctions, but these are within a closer circle of confraternity. The conference model descends from an ancient pattern of sequestered, esoteric, small-group instruction and exercise. Its contemporary forms derive partly from the National Storytelling Conference at Washington College Academy (on the outskirts of Jonesborough), which was founded in 1978 by Diane Wolkstein and the board of directors of NAPPS and was held there until 1986, and partly from other models, such as Robert Bela Wilhelm's mythos conferences of the late seventies or a host of breakaway institutions, intentional communities, human potential centers, and adult education camps—such as Esalen in California, Naropa in Colorado, Omega and Lindisfarne in New York, Augusta Heritage Workshops in West Virginia—all of which were coming into existence in the same period, in response to the same basic cultural hunger.

Support groups, rehearsal groups, retreat groups, and guilds are natural ways for small, committed bands of amateurs and emerging professionals to pool, sort, and focus their resources to cultivate the art. All these in combination formed the matrix in which a new art world grew, bound together by its own occupational lore.

In what follows I will explore the dynamics of some of these local communities and how they influenced and were influenced by the direction of the national movement. The currents of revitalization stirred up the scattered bones and bade them join together, first locally, then regionally, then nationally. What follows is a small but, I believe, representative sampling—each selected, too, to add a piece to the emerging portrait of the revival movement as a whole. There are many others that could have been included; stories would vary in colorful, personal ways, but the patterns and motives would be strikingly parallel. This point has been confirmed in interviews and experiences with tellers and communities in southern California, the Pacific Northwest, Texas, Oklahoma, New York City, Florida, Canada, England, Ireland, France, and Australia. All these and many other places have fostered storytelling revival scenes—my sense is that each represents a vividly local and regional response to common cultural conditions and common spiritual hungers.

Jonesborough, Tennessee

Though anomalous in important ways, because of its imperial pretensions and the seminal role of local business interests, Jonesborough was in many key respects the center of a prototypical local/regional storytelling revival community. For several years at least, its major public event, the festival, was staffed primarily by local volunteers and office workers. It featured mainly tellers from within about a hundred-mile radius, several more from within two to five hundred miles, and, to add variety and prestige, a few who were funded to travel from outside the region. The nucleus of the NAPPS board of directors was at first primarily regional (southeastern) and then superregional (northeastern and southeastern). It was not until the late eighties, under considerable pressure from other regional groups, that the board and the festival achieved full national representation.

Jonesborough had significant advantages, some natural, some contrived, over other local storytelling scenes. On the business and artistic sides, it had more specialized personnel; it had its mythic geography, enhanced by partnership with the historic preservation movement; and it had its national ambitions. Still, the dynamics of its community growth set a pattern for other areas.

The community came together around an event (the festival) and a program (the revival of storytelling). It quickly developed a core group of committed activists with close local ties, who combined varying measures of idealism, ambition, and public skills. This core group consisted at first of Jimmy Neil Smith, Connie Regan, Barbara Freeman, and Doc McConnell, with Ardi St. Clair and Harriette Allen (of Nashville), Kathryn Windham (of Selma, Alabama), and Lee Pennington (of Louisville, Kentucky) joining them from the surrounding region. They reinforced one another's efforts and supported one another's individual goals, which in turn contributed to a common goal—the success of the event and the program. Shortly after the third festival in 1975, for example, Smith wrote to the board, "Quite by accident, I heard that the producers of *Hee-Haw* were interested in adding more storytellers to their weekly program. I contacted them a number of times, and we were finally asked to send some storytelling folks to Nashville to tape some *Hee-Haw* shows for the winter and spring. Lee Pennington and Doc McConnell and his medicine show folks went. Though I was there only during Doc's performances, I heard very favorable comments on both our offerings. This may mean something really big for both Lee and Doc."

The significant value for Smith was that his ability to help the two storytellers and their ability to help the TV producers would both reflect favorably on NAPPS, on Jonesborough, and on storytelling. He commented, "The nice thing about it all is that NAPPS was helpful to both the *Hee-Haw* producers who wanted storytellers and to Doc and Lee who were able to possibly advance their careers and gain new exposure and experiences" (NAPPS Correspondence, November 9, 1975).

Those who did not share the common goals or did not feel they "fit in" with the prevailing group personality soon directed their energies elsewhere. Though each member developed distinctive performance styles and repertoires (even Smith, as we saw in chapter 2—though his was for the press, not the stage), they learned a great deal from one another about public presentation and the possibilities of the art form. In a sense, then, the early NAPPS board of directors was a prototypical storytelling revival support group.

It was a community of proselytizers, preoccupied with finding new members who could bring complementary talents and add to the group's public profile. This was what Ed Stivender would later call "the bush-beating era" (telephone interview, January 7, 1992). Storytelling at the time was a new and uncertain professional and artistic affiliation. Its votaries instinctively sought to identify themselves with a critical mass of gifted colleagues. Though revivalist ideology placed great stress on the community-building nature of the art, this simple factor should not be overlooked: there is safety and strength in numbers. As they pass certain thresholds of association, a few lonesome dreamers become a vibrant band of comrades, become a movement, become a world.

For many years, the chief evangelists of Jonesborough were the Folktellers. Even before they built a camper on the back of their pickup truck and quit their library jobs to go on the road full time, Barbara and Connie were traveling from festival to festival around the region, recruiting kindred spirits and sharing information and enthusiasm. David Holt was a young folk music revivalist who had tried his hand at a few traditional tales when he met the pair at the Fiddlers' Grove Festival in Union Grove, North Carolina:

> They would go down there, and I was always down there playing in the banjo competition or just down there playing. And they came with their little yellow truck. Just down for the festival. They were just starting, they were really just starting. And I remember just talking about going out on the road and all this—it was very new. And then, I was at Warren Wilson [College, where he had organized the Appalachian music program], and I invited them to come do a workshop. For my students, or anybody who was interested. That was like my first year, so that must have been ... '75 or '76, something like that. Right before I knew there was such a thing as a *storyteller*. 'Cause I was *telling* stories in my music program—but I'd never heard of *storytellers!* And then they invited me, and I went to this thing in '76, and my God, there were all these people doin' it . . . and that really made me get my stories together. Because I was kind of doing them in school programs and such, and I didn't really have enough for a whole storytelling *event*. Especially like a national festival. So when I got invited to that, I guess I had a year, or eight months to prepare, and that really caused me to pull the stories together.

Holt's comments show how the existence of the festival gave potential performers a framework around which to organize a repertoire and a performing identity. It offered a range of role models ("all these people doing it"), repertoires, and performance styles broad enough to pick one's influences, while leaving plenty of room to establish individual contributions. All this made it a uniquely auspicious time and place to be an aspiring storyteller. Holt told me:

There was so little back-biting in the organization from the beginning. And so little need to push somebody down to get your way up. I was really attracted to it. Because I saw that in the music, I saw a lot of that in the music, every level of music, from the lowest level all the way to the Nashville scene, a tremendous amount of rivalry and back-biting. And this has never been the case in the storytelling world, at least in my experience. I think that people who are getting into it now feel some of that, because, you know, it's harder to "break in" or whatever; but in those days there was no "breakin' in," it was just, "Come on in!"

Because of his combination of musical, verbal, organizational, and business skills, Holt was a valuable addition to the fledgling movement. Since he lived just over the mountains from Jonesborough—in Fairview, North Carolina—he was easily incorporated into the local scene and was swiftly added to the NAPPS board. So was Jackie Torrence, after her triumphant first appearance at the festival. She lived in High Point, North Carolina, a three-hour drive. When the Folktellers met Donald Davis, then a Methodist pastor in Charlotte, at a weekend festival in Berea, Kentucky, he, too, was immediately adopted, and he eventually succeeded Regan-Blake as NAPPS board chair.

The extent to which NAPPS seemed to newcomers to be "pushing southern" and promoting the careers of its local core group over those of the wider membership became a vexing question. As we will see, NAPPS at first acted no differently from any other local and regional storytelling support group in trying to promote its own members' careers and the public profile of its small association in the most cost-efficient combinations. It was only its stated mission as the preeminent national storytelling organization that eventually created conflicts of interest and internecine struggles analogous to those in transitions from tribes to nations.

In 1975, the Folktellers did move into their pickup truck for three years of full-time traveling on a circuit of folk festivals, schools, libraries, and coffeehouses. As they went, they gradually expanded the Jonesborough-based storytelling revival community. During that time, the two had no home except a post office box in Atlanta, where Regan's sister lived; "D'PUT," the name they gave the truck; and Jonesborough, where they regularly returned for board meetings, festivals, special events, hot showers, and a semipermanent guest bedroom at Carolyn Moore's house. Their performances, and their very presence around the folk circuit, were entirely devoted to and dependent on the idea of storytelling as a way of life. The closest friends they made on their way, such as Marshall Dodge, Gamble Rogers, or Ron Evans, were those who, on some significant level, had taken similar vows. By the time Freeman and Regan-Blake first met Marshall Dodge at a show in Connecticut in 1976, they had been seeing each other's flyers on coffeehouse walls for months. Freeman had barely to introduce herself when Dodge grabbed them each in his arms and twirled them around, crying, "WHOOO-WHOOO! MY LITTLE SOUTHERN COUSINS!" She said, "It was like meeting a long-lost family member or something."

When the Folktellers invited these friends and revival family members "home," then, it could only be to Jonesborough. The reunions there were invigorating to all parties. Freeman explained how Dodge's encounter with the storytelling movement gave his career not just a new direction but also a new definition:

> Marshall had been doing it for so many years that when we met him, he was on the verge of burning out and quitting. And I think NAPPS really recharged him. Because of the whole new audience down south. See, he had mostly done Massachusetts and Maine, and Canada. And he put out these wonderful records, called the *Bert and I* records. But he was getting so tired of it, 'cause he had done colleges, mostly; almost billed like a stand-up comic or a Mark Twain-type thing. He wasn't necessarily even *called* a storyteller, although he certainly was.

The storytelling community made a place for a number of maverick artists, in the sociologist Howard Becker's sense: performers whose work did not conform to standardized expectations of previously established art worlds. Maverick verbal artists such as Dodge, who may have been constrained by the labels "comedian" or "humorist," or Rogers, who confounded the mere label of "folksinger," found a more open field at Jonesborough. There they could reveal more of the philosophical depths beneath the entertaining surfaces. Rogers could sit down and expand Big Bill Broonzy's sepia snapshot of a Mississippi Delta flood into a full-color poetic landscape of restored community ("Joe Turner's Been Here and Gone," recorded on his LP *The Warm Way Home*). And Dodge could peel back the oilskin Maine-humorist stereotype to reveal an aesthetic philosopher. Doug Lipman remembered Dodge at Jonesborough two years before his early death:

> The first time that I got to spend any time up close [with him] was at the Jonesborough conference. And there he was doing this thing, present-

ing—you know, he was working on a book of philosophy when he died. I don't know if you knew that. I guess he'd been working on it for a long time. And it was a kind of unifying theory of philosophy, based on an *S*-curve. An *S*-curve on it's side. So first it goes up, then it goes over and down, and then it goes down below its original place and goes back up again. And the first half of the loop is tragedy, where you rise and then fall; and the second part of the loop is comedy, where you fall and then rise. And the tragedy part looks like a frown, and the comedy part looks like a smile. And he had everything in the world fitting into that little diagram.

As the Jonesborough-centered storytelling scene expanded, it began, through its rituals, to internally differentiate itself. This was first expressed in the birth of the National Storytelling Conference. "Workshops" had been a part of the festival from 1974 on, though in the days of the "secret festival," it was hard to distinguish educational presentations from the storytelling concerts simply by size or content. When things were so new, it was nearly always necessary to "workshop"—to educate audiences (and tellers themselves) a bit in each performance—in order to establish frameworks of meaning and purpose around even the simplest revival event. But by 1978, the first year of festival tents at Jonesborough, audiences had expanded so much in size and receptiveness and so many eager apprentices were emerging from their ranks that a closer circle of ritual gathering was required.

Wolkstein and the NAPPS board initiated the National Storytelling Conference in 1978 to focus more deeply on "the meaning of stories." It was held every June until 1986 at Washington College Academy, a 180-year-old prep school in the rolling hills a couple of miles from Jonesborough. The Washington College conferences represented perhaps the height of the storytelling revival's "blessed community" (and eventually, as we will see in chapter 6, they witnessed key scenes of the blessed community's undoing). Beth Horner told me, "I loved those conferences at Washington College Academy. One, because you got to see so many different styles and different workshops, and two, because it was such a nice group of people, a fun group of people, and it was an intimate setting, as opposed to the festival, which was now getting bigger and bigger. I wouldn't have missed those for anything, those summer conferences. Those days are gone. Those NAPPS days are gone. And they actually ended before those conferences ended." May remarked, "I don't think I went there until about 1983, maybe. I think one time Hemingway was supposed to have said that there were ten books that he'd rather be able to read again for the first time than to have a million dollars? Well, I think there's a lot that I would give up to have those early days at Washington College again. Or the times I didn't go."

The conference was an opportunity to sit in small groups with some of the most experienced, passionate, and profound teachers and performers in the storytelling world, absorbing the heat of their ideas and commitment. For a time, NAPPS held its board meetings at the conference, and it seemed the entire inner circle of the revival scene was there, whether giving workshops or just "hanging out." It was also a place where, because of the beauty of the setting and the close, spartan, dormitory quarters, one could strike up immediate, relaxed, and unstructured relationships with these mentors and comrades. Yet such relationships came to have a structuring effect on the growth of individual careers and of local and regional communities.

Because of the sequestered setting, compared with the teeming downtown festival, there was an even more complete separation from the mundane world. Room and board were provided and were the same for the storytelling lion or lamb. Activities, such as cafeteria meals, informal story-swaps on the porch, or morning and evening walks, could carry weight in the ritual passage of the weekend equal to or greater than the workshops themselves—because of the equal opportunity for exchanges that would ignite a smoldering sense of vocation. If festivals ritualized the reincorporation of storytelling into the wider national, regional, or local communities, conferences ritualized the creation of a specific, nonlocal brotherhood and sisterhood of storytellers. In effect, it gave its participants blessing and journey-cake and bade them to return to their far-flung places in the world with a transformed status, as a "member of the tribe." As May explained:

> If you were sort of interested in storytelling on a deeper level, or wanted to become a storyteller, or wanted to get more involved—that was an incredible, enriching, sort of mythical place. That little spot. And the quiet. It felt like going back in time—the little narrow roads, and the honeysuckle blooming. It was an amazing place. And there was a time there, three or four or five years, when just *everybody* would go. And then there was a whole other level of people who would be there with them, and that level, those people became real active storytellers. There was a whole bunch of us—Syd [Lieberman], and Bill Harley, and me, and Beth, and Jon Spelman, Len Cabral, Milbre Burch—it was a whole corps of

people that got to be friends and went there because we were interested, and obviously really got nurtured there.

Robin Moore recalled:

> There are some people I met at those conferences when they were down there on that campus that I still keep in touch with. We were all sort of coming up at the same time together. We'd sit up at night, and really talk about our dreams, of what we wanted to do with storytelling. . . . There were a lot of magical moments. And I remember coming back from one of those weekends of sitting up at night telling stories, and really feeling that ... it almost felt tribal to me. Like you were part of a tribe, or something. And you came back from that, and you said, You know what—this is *really living*. I was working in a pretty traditional job then, as a journalist, and when I went back into the office, things seemed very gray and lifeless. And I said, "Ah! I don't want to spend my life like this! I want to be—like it was down there!" And I've been able to carve a little bit of that out for myself.

Boston, Massachusetts–Providence, Rhode Island

The storytelling revival community in the Boston, Massachusetts–Providence, Rhode Island, area contributed one of the largest concentrations of prominent professional storytellers to the national festival in the 1980s. Between 1980 and 1989, a dozen tellers were featured at Jonesborough—including Jay O'Callahan, Dodge, Brother Blue, and Maggie Pierce in 1980; Michael Parent in 1981; Doug Lipman in 1983; Milbre Burch in 1984; Jackson Gillman in 1985; O'Callahan, Blue, and Pierce again in 1987; Bill Harley and Len Cabral in 1988; and Judith Black and Susan Klein in 1989—whose careers had been significantly nurtured by the vigor of that New England revival scene.

How it coalesced makes an instructive study. Once again, it began when a number of talented individuals, who had serendipitously discovered storytelling on their own, came together to concentrate their efforts to foster growth for the art form and for themselves. More potential members were attracted by the group energy. Quickly, the structures of a local community emerged.

O'Callahan, a much-loved central figure in that scene, began his artistic career with the intention of writing stories and novels. But in the course of writing his first two, never-published books, he found that what were really "coming alive" for him were the stories he made up and performed each night for his children's bedtime. He volunteered to tell stories at a local library and then at local schools. After five years of experimentation and buoyed by his gift for language and vocal and physical characterization, he was ready to turn professional. He recalled, "After this five years, I really had a sense that I could do this *very well;* I had the amateur's total confidence. I just didn't know enough to be frightened. I thought I could do it *anywhere,* and if *anyone* had asked me to perform before ten thousand the next night, well, I'd have whipped up a story and done it. I've learned too much, unfortunately. I thought I could do it better than anyone in the world—and I'd never heard anyone do it. . . ."

O'Callahan began to work as an artist in the schools around the Greater Boston area. Lee-Ellen Marvin was a fledgling radio producer at the time, working at the local public radio station, WGBH, where she helped produce a popular children's literature program called *The Spider's Web.* She recalled:

> I started getting a couple of letters in the mail, saying, "There's this wonderful storyteller, you really ought to think about him." And then [Jay] sent a letter. It might have been that he had a little campaign going. But people in Boston who were interested in children's literature knew about *The Spider's Web.* So, he ended up sending a tape, and I completely fell in love with it. And we started putting on segments of Jay's stories. And before that, I had already been working with Brother Blue. Brother Blue had been a figure on *The Spider's Web.* Doing occasional stories. And other than that there hadn't been any really remarkable storytellers. Jay and Brother Blue together got me real excited about the storyteller as performer and as artist. Not just interpreter, but someone who had something to say, and could comment on the contemporary world.

Doug Lipman was still negotiating the transition from folk musician/educator to professional storyteller when he met O'Callahan. To learn more about the craft, he signed up to take a storytelling workshop at a place called Birdsong Farm in Maine. The workshop leader was O'Callahan. As Lipman recalled:

> I said, "I'll do it." And rode up with these two people I'd never heard of, Elizabeth Dunham and Judith Black. And there were seven of us who came to that weekend. . . . And we had an important experience there. Because several of us were professional performing storytellers by then. And there were several others who had an interest in storytelling. And this was our first time to really sit down in a group defined as storytellers. And we had the most wonderful time! I mean, the dinners went on for

like four hours. 'Cause here were all these people who loved to talk and were good listeners. And as we were leaving, Art Shurcliff said, "When are we going to meet again?"

And I said, "That's a great idea, let's do that some time."

And he said, "No, no, no, let's choose a date now or we'll never do it." So we chose a reunion a month later. And since meals had been part of it, we made it a potluck dinner. And then told stories.

A storytelling support group was formed that would serve to focalize its members' artistic and personal growth. Support group members met regularly to try out repertoire and share critical feedback; they participated in group performances, where the variety of voices helped compensate for individual shortcomings of technique or repertoire; they traveled together to storytelling concerts and seminars and helped each other assimilate new impressions and inspirations; and they provided a group solidarity that helped individual members gain a sense of their own worth and the worth of their craft. The circle quickly widened, according to Marvin:

Jay, at one point, mentioned that he had held a little weekend-long re- treat with some other storytellers. And I got excited about the possibility of people coming *together*. And that there were *more* people and possibly other kinds of voices from Jay and Brother Blue. I was hoping to find *women* who could tell stories. You know—is it just the boys who get to tell stories? And the weekend gathering that Jay had had included Doug Lipman, Judith Black, and a woman named Elizabeth Dunham. And Jay had mentioned, sort of offhand, you know, "Gee, yeah, I'm getting to- gether with storytellers, and we're thinking of meeting regularly." So that group formed a private—what they called "rehearsal group."

And then more storytellers were identified, and in that process we learned about Jackson Gillman, who was pulled into the fold. And be- cause a bunch of us, including myself, were very interested in that re- hearsal group, a larger storytelling group was formed in '79, based partly on Jay's retreat, with a lot of other people from the Boston area that were interested. And I became a major player in that. I mean, I was there all the time; hosted once or twice, even though I had barely any space. They were potluck dinners and then storytelling sharing sessions. And lots of crazy things were tried out. People telling about real-life experiences, and dreams, and literary stories, and folktales, and ... odd stuff that they were cooking up themselves, and ... just a lot of stuff. And people would drop in one time and then never show up again. And come from com- pletely different contexts. But slowly, a sense of a Boston community was being formed.

As a local community identity solidified, ambitious individuals within it, led by O'Callahan, chafed for wider opportunities. For these tellers at the time, NAPPS was a gateway to such opportunities but one whose gatekeepers were not hearing them knock. Their alternative was to use what their own dense, urban area offered them in the way of audience resources and to create what was then the first storytelling performance series specifically for adults. Lipman remembered:

That smaller group continued to meet every month for five years. And for the first three of those years, we had a weekend reunion every year. Where we all went away for a weekend together. And somewhere in the second year of that, Jay called together a meeting of all the people who were professional storytellers from that group, and other people that he knew, including Lee-Ellen Marvin and Jackson Gillman. And Jay had been down to NAPPS. And he felt that NAPPS was pushing southern and didn't have much interest in him, at that time. And so, he wanted a *real* national storytelling organization. That was what he called this meeting for. And jokingly referred to what *he* wanted as the Inter-Galactic Association for Storytelling and the Lesser Arts.

And we were kind of sitting around and griping and saying, "Nobody hires us to tell stories for adult audiences."

And one of us, I think it might have been me, said, "Well, then let's hire ourselves." And out of that, the Storytellers-in-Concert Series was born.

Marvin agrees, except that, as happens often in the theater of memory, her version gave herself the pivotal line:

One day Jay gathered a bunch of people who he thought had real professional ambitions. And he said, "I'm sick of nobody knowing what storytelling is. And we need to do something to get it established. *And* I want to perform for adults. It's fine when I perform for kids, but I've got so much more in me. And so do the rest of you!"

I was invited, Doug Lipman, Judith Black, Elizabeth Dunham, Jackson Gillman, and a few other people. And I think I was the one who said, "Well, hey gang, let's put on a show." 'Cause I'd been involved with a little nonprofit radio group that put on a lecture series. I saw how simple it was—you rent a space, you write some press releases, you put out some posters, and people show up. And so I said, "So *what* if we only get thirty-five people the first few times. Let's start putting things out there."

Elizabeth Dunham was the one who found the space that we first used, at the Institute of Contemporary Art, in Boston. I really like the sound of that! *"Storytelling at the Institute of Contemporary Art."* And it was in a small room that was also used for screening films. I mean it was just white walls, gray institutional carpeting, and chairs. And that was all we had. And then we got *real* postmodern about it, because we started getting these romantic images of rocking chairs. And I think we put a couple of rocking chairs on a truck and brought them in and put them into the Institute of Contemporary Art.

And we planned to do four concerts. We ended up putting a pretty good mailing list together. And did this four-part concert series in one month. May or June of 1981. Once a week. Like to killed us. But we had a great time. The opening night was Jay, Judith, Doug, Elizabeth, and Jackson. And we sold out, we had to turn away about fifty people. The room was small. And they said, "Why didn't you rent a bigger space?"

We said, "Well we had no idea what was going to happen."

And as I remember a few, very sophisticated theater-going people looked at us and said, "What kind of jerk are you, you didn't think we would be coming?"

With the growing visibility of storytelling in the Boston area and nationwide, an enterprising dean of the new Lesley College Graduate School in Cambridge, Richard Wylie, was interested enough to fund a storytelling center on campus (the college eventually offered a master's degree program in storytelling, which made good use of local talent and also helped certify it). Marvin was hired as part-time paid coordinator. She remembered:

We did the concert series at the Institute for Contemporary Arts. And that all fed into Dick Wylie deciding, yes, we'll hire Lee-Ellen part-time, twenty hours a week; give her a room, a desk, a filing cabinet, a phone; and see what she can do. And that was essentially it. I said, "What exactly do you want here with this 'Storytelling Center?'"

And he said, "Well, we just think it's important."

I'd never experienced anything like that before. It was like, carte blanche. Well, I started calling up everyone I knew in storytelling. And the list of contacts that I had was significant at that point, and I talked to a lot of folks. And I said, "If there was a Storytelling Center in the world, specifically in New England, what would you like it to do?" And so we came up with the newsletter, some workshops, some classes, and we started "Sharing the Fire" [the New England Storytelling Conference] . . . I developed the list of storytellers who were available for hire. I did my best to stay in touch with people, and know what people were doing, and network for them. I considered myself something like the spider in the center of a web.

Lipman described the effect that the center had on the local community:

Lee-Ellen's presence meant, basically, we were the only storytelling community, with the possible exception of Jonesborough, that had a professional community organizer. And so, we took off—our level of organization increased very quickly. And right away, had the first Sharing the Fire Conference, which is still going on, strong. And not too long thereafter had the first Three Apples Storytelling Festival. And the Storytellers-in-Concert Series, which was *very* successful, especially in its first year. We didn't even know what to do with ourselves, we were doing so well.

The Boston area storytelling revival scene, within a period of roughly five years from its first stirrings, had developed the full range of ritual enactments: a festival, a performance series, a conference, and a variety of support groups, rehearsal groups, and retreat groups, as well as an institutionally based educational program and professionally staffed organizational clearinghouse.

Meanwhile, a short train ride away in the smaller city of Providence, a similar process was going on, transmuting a scattered group of idealistic and ambitious performers into an energetic storytelling scene.

Bill Harley, like Lipman, had been caught up in the folk music revival in college, with its questioning attitudes and vaguely leftward political slant. He and his wife moved to Providence in 1980, because, as he said:

She had a job and I didn't, and I wanted to perform—and I kind of got this hot idea about being a storyteller. I thought, there must have been people who did this. And I really didn't know that it was out there. I mean, I figured there were probably some people out there, but I thought, "I could do this!" You know, it seems like something I could do, and it was kind of different. And I could do the music to go along with it. . . . I was disenchanted with the way things were going, you know, and I wanted to do something that would express it, in a not-really-intense way, but a way that would draw people together, bring people together.

Like O'Callahan, he managed, through a blend of talent, chutzpah, and serendipitous timing, to find his way into the local Arts-in-the-Schools Program. The director of that program told him about O'Callahan—the first storytelling colleague he knew by name. "So I called Jay up. And said, 'I'm thinking about doing this. And I'd like to talk with you.' He said, 'Well, come on up.' So I drove up to Marshfield and had lunch with him, and I played him some of my songs and told him what I was thinking about doing. And he said, you know [imitating O'Callahan's auditorium voice], 'I THINK IT'S A WONDERFUL IDEA! GO DO IT!'"

O'Callahan gave Harley some back issues of the NAPPS *Yarnspinner* newsletter, along with his blessing. Soon afterward, the new storyteller got a call from Cambridge, from the new New England Storytelling Center at Lesley College:

> Somehow the people at Lesley, Lee-Ellen, and Doug, and all those people who were working on forming a storytelling center at Lesley College, got my name, maybe from Jay, and they called me up—called me up and invited me. I didn't know Len, but I said, "Could I bring this other guy, who's doing storytelling?"
>
> They said, "Sure."
>
> So I called up Len, and I said, "Listen, I got this invite, you know, do you want to go up with me?" So we drove up. They were forming a storytelling center. The college was providing a space for them and kind of welcoming people who did storytelling. And actually they gave us this great dinner, a lobster dinner—we couldn't believe it. I mean, we were both dirt poor, and we got up there and they had lobsters, and steamers, and corn and stuff, and it was like, "This is amazing! What a great gig!"

Harley continued to find that storytelling and the institutional settings in which it found its niches could be far more professionally rewarding, in both the artistic and financial sense, than folk music alone:

> An amazing thing happened in New England in the eighties, in the early eighties, before Reaganism really took hold—was that there was *so much support for the arts in schools!* There was just so much work! And compared to, you know—I'd be going out, I was still kind of trying to be folky at night, I'd be going out and playing for thirty-five bucks a night, you know, in bars. Or fifty bucks. And, you know, people wouldn't be listening. Or just really scrounging for the coffeehouses—everybody and their brother wanted to play, and how frustrating that could be. And still learning my chops, you know, as a songwriter, and I was getting there, but, you know, I was just another guy with a guitar. *But there was all this work in the schools!* And I learned how to perform in the schools. You know, there was this audience that was right there that you had to appeal to, and you had to find stuff that appealed to them; and that amazing thing that happens in live performance with a story, that would happen there. And the interesting thing is when you take it into an adult audience in the evening. I can kind of tell somebody who's worked with

kids, because generally their stuff is much tighter. They know how to work, it's not all this kind of wandering stuff that can drive you crazy in the folky world. So I was really lucky. And I wasn't charging them what I do now, but it was a decent amount of money.

Milbre Burch had also moved to Providence in 1980 to be a part of a burgeoning New England performance scene. She was trained as a mime, but under the influence of the charismatic teacher Tony Montanaro, she began opening up her style to incorporate elements of clowning, story-telling, and dance, blending into the emerging genre of performance called New Vaudeville. In Providence, she formed a company with two other Montanaro students. Serendipitously, she found herself being pulled into the gravitational field of the storytelling revival:

> It was really within the auspices of the vaudeville company that I had to come up with a name for what I did. And since I had moved from South Carolina and left my company members behind, and I had these stories and this choreography, but no people to put it on, I started rechoreo-graphing the material for me as a solo performer and speaking the sto-ries. And once that I happened, I realized I could no longer *just* use the word mime. Because people, especially people who don't know about mime's history, think of it as a very silent, very structured art form. So I began to call what I did "mime-storytelling." And as soon as I used the word *storytelling,* I became aware that there were other storytellers in Providence. That there were other storytellers in New England. And eventually, that there were other storytellers nationally. So, it was sort of by mistake that I even found out that there was a movement afoot. And my discovery was local-regional-national, just like that, sort of, splish-splash, around a great big pond.

Burch also found herself drawn to the storytelling activities in nearby Boston, for personal artistic models and for models of a storytelling com-munity in action: "I remember starting to go to the series, very much for my own edification; the Storytellers-in-Concert Series. I don't think I got there before '83. And one of the first performers I saw was Judith Black. And it was terribly, terribly important for me to see a woman doing it. And Judith of course has a very theatrical flair. It wasn't far away from the kinds of stuff I was drawn to do. And that series became a kind of a continuing ed class for me. A chance to go up and study other people's styles."

Soon Providence had its own storytelling group, the Spellbinders, and an ongoing concert series for adults, modeled after the Storytellers-in-

Concert group in Boston. It began, in part, as a reflex of community self-preservation. Burch recounted, "During that time I also met Len Cabral, and Marilyn Meardon, Bill Harley, Marc Leavitt, and Sparky Davis. And we put together the Spellbinders, as a way to do some work together and avoid only seeing each other as storytellers when we were competing for the same residency."

Working in the Providence schools, Harley had discovered that he was being pitted against Burch and other performers with the storyteller label. He recalled:

> We went through one real weird experience where Milbre and I were up for a residency in a school. And I had kind of been given the impression I was going to get it, and then they brought all these other people in. And they brought Milbre in, and it turned into a competition, and Milbre got the job, and the whole thing just felt really crummy. And I went to her afterwards, and I said, "This felt really, really terrible. We're being pitted against each other, you know, and that's a really terrible thing." And so, with all that, kind of decided to get a group together . . . we formed it around a performance. I had started a coffeehouse at that time, with a couple of other people. And so we did a show at the coffeehouse. And we started to meet, and we started to do performances. We had this idea that we could put together this ensemble, and maybe get jobs—you know, we knew there was much more money in college audiences and things like that, but we were too anarchistic to carry that off.

The Rhode Island storytellers never, to my knowledge, organized any serious labor-management job actions—they were "too anarchistic" to carry that off either. But it was important to them, in the context of the emerging storytelling revival ethos, to construct some medium of community solidarity. Typically, this also involved opportunities for furthering their own work as well as the public profile of their art. In the revival support group context, as we have seen, these were linked quantities. The Spellbinders continue to do occasional group performances locally to this day, having matured into presiding elders of the Rhode Island storytelling scene.

The result of all this activity in the Boston-Providence area was to raise the stakes for all of the active members and the art form as well. O'Callahan can be said to have set the pace, by releasing a steady stream of original stories on tape, by creating full-length solo storytelling programs for theatrical venues, and by becoming an important force on the NAPPS board of directors, a popular festival performer, and the director of the national conference for several of its halcyon years. But O'Callahan himself was clearly borne aloft by the community he had gathered around him and by the expanded performance opportunities they helped him create. Before he had the material for his full-length solo shows, the Storytellers-in-Concert Series gave him many chances to explore the possibilities of longer original storytellings for "sophisticated theater-going people." His successful experiments gave support group colleagues clear models of performances that stretched the boundaries between conversational folk art and elaborated one-person theater.

In the years following the breakthrough NAPPS festival of 1980, when four New England storytellers were featured and became among the most popular attractions, a steady queue of Boston and Providence tellers made their way to the Jonesborough stage. Their arrival, following that of the powerful New York City area tellers Wolkstein, Simms, and Forest in 1977, 1979, and 1980 and Philadelphian Stivender in 1980, marked the beginning of a shift in NAPPS's programming emphasis. The shift paralleled the earlier shift in the folk music revivals of the fifties and sixties from rural "roots" performers to young urban revivalists, inspired by folk materials to create their own synthetic, blended forms. The new professional storytellers, like the earlier wave of singer-songwriters who carried the folk music revival to its crest, developed what folklorist Ellen Stekert called a "new folk aesthetic." They adapted folkloric forms, themes, and styles to accommodate their elite arts trainings as well as the ideological currents of contemporary social, artistic, and spiritual movements (Stekert 99–100). It was natural that this new aesthetic emerged most powerfully not from the Southeast, where oral traditions were still a predominant influence, but from the intentional storytelling communities of the Northeast, where elite cultural forms and popular societal ferment became infused with this new strain of folk revivalism.

Nevada City, California

The storytelling movement, as I have shown, grew out of a much wider wave of cultural revitalization in American community life. The inchoate, dissident communes of the sixties had given way in the next decade to a panoply of intentional communities, structured around nativistic, revivalistic, vitalistic, millenarian, or messianic spiritual and political programs. Sometimes these communities spawned their own revival storytellers by a natural chain of associations. Rafe Martin's storytelling awakening as "the Sleeping Sage" at the Rochester Zen Center is one example. Steve Sanfield's experience in the mountains of northern California is another.

The area around Nevada City, California, had become home to a number of alternative communities in the late sixties and seventies. Some were directly organized around a spiritual teaching, such as yoga or Gurdjieffian self-work. Others were more anarchic and ecological in character. Many families and individuals had located there to be near the poet Gary Snyder, who had enunciated a philosophical blend of Native American reverence for the land with Buddhist self-awareness, even as he blended romantic self-expression with the values of frontier communalism.

The lore of Snyder and his settlement on the San Juan Ridge is explored in depth in Jon Halper's recent collection, *Gary Snyder: Dimensions of a Life*. Sanfield was an early member of the Ridge community. He told me:

> Basically, it's a community that doesn't really need a name. A community made up of people who do recognize each other. I guess it's based on a whole value system—or was then. An alternative way of living to our society at large. A way of living where money or material goods were certainly not the most important thing. A commitment to the land and to the people who lived on it. A kind of *re-inhabitation* of a part of California. Very ecologically minded, very socially minded, in helping each other—we were all raising young families at the time, when we started. So, schools and education were real important to us—we ended up building our own schools here. The community—well, I can't say it was initially all writers and artists, because it wasn't. Proportionately there are a lot of writers and artists and craftspeople that are a part of this community. But there are other people, too, all sorts of people: there are farmers, there are carpenters, there are teachers. . . .

Sanfield himself was working in the state Poetry-in-the-Schools Program, when the cultural hunger for stories began serendipitously to impact his work:

> I soon discovered that most kids weren't too interested in *most* poetry, that spoke of the poet's own trials and tribulations in the world, you know, the poet's own heart and vision. But what they really liked, what they really reacted to, were the poems that told stories—were the narrative poems. So I began to introduce more and more narrative poetry into my sessions in the school. And what that led to was the discovery that there was a deep-seated need for stories themselves. That's what the kids were after, not the poetry so much. And so I began to introduce more

and more stories into my programs in the schools. So much so that I was asked to leave the Poetry-in-the-Schools Program. Because I wasn't doing very much poetry. That was about 1976.

Sanfield gives credit to Jerry Brown—the Zen-influenced governor of California at the time—for the innovative state arts council programming that allowed him to redefine himself as a storyteller in the schools:

It was a great gift they gave me. I live here in the mountains of northern California, and it was in a small community. Working in this small school I wound up going into each classroom at least once a week. So over a period of a year, one has to come up with a lot of different stories. I certainly didn't have those in my repertory at that point. So . . . all my nights were spent reading, studying, researching, pursuing stories. It was almost on one level like a sabbatical they were giving me. Just to study. And then during the day I would go out and try to tell these. And I did it for three years. And it was a remarkable three years—for me, anyway. I did it all the way into '80, I guess. And I didn't know about any other storytellers at the time. I thought, "Gee, am I the only one doing this?"

In 1980, he happened upon an article by Rex Weyler in the magazine *New Age,* featuring the Folktellers, and it led him to the National Storytelling Festival and NAPPS. At the festival in Jonesborough that fall, he was introduced to his peers from his own region:

When I was at NAPPS, I met a guy named Floating Eaglefeather. And he floated up to me . . . and he said, "Look, when you get back to California, you should check these people out." So I did. When I came back to California, the American Storytelling Resource Center [ASRC] was having a small festival at Cabrillo College. And I went and I met some of those people, and shortly after that I ended up on their board of directors. And worked with them for a number of years. . . . And for me personally, going to NAPPS and meeting Eaglefeather and having him suggest these people, led me to connections to some of my closest colleagues, and more important, my dearest friends. People like Bob Jenkins, Patrick Ball. These are guys I met through ASRC, and we sat together on that board of directors.

The American Storytelling Resource Center was an organization founded in the early seventies in the Santa Cruz area by Ruthmarie Arguello-Sheehan. Its conferences and festivals at Asilomar and at Cabrillo College in the late seventies and early eighties made it the center of the regional storytelling scene at that time. NAPPS and ASRC began independently and were unaware of each other's existence for several years. When they did come into contact in the late seventies, there was a certain amount of wariness—and jostling for national position. The ASRC folded in 1984, because of the personal difficulties of its founder. But the regional storytelling politics simmering between NAPPS and the ASRC during the early eighties broke into a boil in the effort to expand the NAPPS board of directors later in the decade (explored further in chapter 6).

Sanfield's story shows the pivotal role played by NAPPS in connecting storytellers around the country with organizations and networks in their own areas. Often in the early days of the revival, storytellers labored alone, with no support system, in Simms's words, but their own passion for it. Journeys to Jonesborough strengthened the web of connections and inspired enthusiasts to return home with concrete ideas about how to organize ritual enactments of community.

Sanfield first created an ongoing storytelling performance series called Winter Tales—a reference to the Native American practice of telling their sacred tales only between the first frost and the first planting of corn. The series had a historically evocative site—a schoolhouse that had been built by the first settlers of the area and restored by the recent settlers to serve as a cultural center. It featured regional friends and national touring performers. Like a festival, it had the exoteric function of building a community of listeners and the esoteric function of providing a stop on the underground railway of storytelling performance venues, helping to solidify the emerging storytelling world. After a few years of Winter Tales, the local storytelling audience had grown to the extent that Sanfield felt confident initiating a festival for each July. The Sierra Storytelling Festival at first filled the void left by the demise of the ASRC conference but eventually became one of a small circuit of California storytelling festivals, including Sonoma in January, the Bay Area in May, the Summer Solstice Traditional Music and Storytelling Festival in the Los Angeles area, Mariposa in August, Marin County in September, and occasional events and series throughout the state and the year.

As Sanfield told it:

> Storytelling, by that point in my life, had given me so much—it had given me a way to make a living too; which was a lot better than poetry; it had given me so much on a personal and a spiritual level, as well as an economic level. And so had my community; so had this community that I live in, a community of like-minded souls—that I wanted to give back

to them. So I began this series here called Winter Tales. And every winter we would have three to four storytellers come, one a month through the winter months, and tell stories at this 120-year-old schoolhouse, which we use as a cultural center. And after about four or five years of that, this community became so enamored of, and educated in, storytelling, that I felt it was time to start a festival. And that's how the Sierra Storytelling Festival actually started. This is 1991, and this was the eighth year of the festival . . . so the Winter Tales probably started in 1980–81. . . . And this is one of the greatest storytelling audiences in America. And part of that is because a lot of these kids here who are now grown up, grew up listening to stories. There was nothing unusual or special about it. It was just part of their lives.

Alternate Festivals, Alternate Communities

The pattern of returning from Jonesborough to start a festival on one's own home ground began early. According to Lee Pennington, a charter NAPPS board member, it was a practice deliberately fostered by that board. He recalls:

It wasn't too long after that [first board meeting in 1974], that we came up with the idea of establishing regional festivals, at different times from Jonesborough. And I think one of the things we had in mind then was places where storytellers, on a regional basis, could come in, perform, and even then could be directed interest-wise or whatever toward Jonesborough. I remember that we had about half a dozen such festivals that we focused on. This would have been probably about the third year. And Corn Island was one of those regional festivals that came out of that concept. And we established that here in Louisville. . . . I think that of those we attempted to get off the ground, Corn Island was the only one that survived.

The first Corn Island Storytelling Festival took place in April 1976. It took its name from the legendary site of the first European settlement of Louisville—an island in the middle of the Ohio River that had long since sunk under the waves. The festival thus entered into the revival tradition of turning toward an imagined past that preceded the fallen state of civilization, an origin place that is "no place"—which is, of course, the root of the word *utopia*.

Corn Island was sponsored until 1983 by Jefferson Community College near Louisville, where Pennington and his wife, Joy, were professors.

It was only after the college let go of the festival and turned it over to a volunteer organization headed by the Penningtons that the festival gained a major public profile. The volunteer organization became known as the International Order of EARS, a regional yet globally welcoming storytelling guild that gained a devout following. EARS went NAPPS one trick better in initiatory ritualization by devising an evocative acronym, the meaning of which could not be revealed except to members. New members receive the full name inscribed on a scroll, in return for their solemn promise not to divulge it to noninitiates. It therefore cannot be further analyzed here, save to say that it, too, balances an imagined past and a hoped-for future.

The first ghost storytelling at the Long Run Cemetery, described in chapter 3, was in 1983, and it soon became the largest single event of any storytelling festival nationwide. Corn Island has since developed a flexible format from year to year, which reflects the Penningtons' background as poets and artists. It has resisted the full weight of traditionalization and professionalization that has encumbered the national festival, while maintaining a close regard for the quality of tellers' experience of communitas. Corn Island invites five featured tellers per year, for example, but each year it also features five additional "new tellers," performers who have never before been featured at a major festival, and it gives these new tellers equal time on the main stages with the other featured performers. Aside from the mildly fanfarish "new teller" designation in the program, status is not an issue, as it tends to be in Jonesborough's "Exchange Place" segment—where tellers are not only bracketed in the inferior status category of "regional showcase tellers" but also are offered only cursory exposure on the main stages.

Corn Island has positioned itself as the next oldest, next largest, and next most prestigious festival of its kind in the country and as a significant arena for tellers wanting to step into the national storytelling spotlight. Since 1983, with the founding of EARS and the expansion of their own festival, the Penningtons have shifted their efforts away from NSA toward the cultivation of their own storytelling community. On the organizational front, they are conceding little to the national association. They have secured the donation of a headquarters building from the local water department and have restored and equipped it up with donations and volunteer labor. They have created an archive of Corn Island festivals on tape and have developed a computerized cataloguing system that exceeds NSA's in efficiency. Their newsletter is expansive and passionate and has recently expanded to a tabloid format with nationwide distribution and corresponding advertising space. It is clear that, should NSA falter, the International Order of EARS has positioned itself deliberately to catch the storytelling revival banner.

All over the country in the late seventies and early eighties, storytellers were returning from Jonesborough and forming partnerships with local business interests, educational and cultural institutions, and arts agencies so that they could establish their own local and regional festivals. Lynn Rubright, creator of a pioneer storytelling-in-education program, Project Tell, in the St. Louis area, described the origin of the St. Louis Storytelling Festival in 1979:

> Driving in my little red Honda towards St. Louis with the light shining against the Arch, I said to Robert [her husband], "We need to have a festival in St. Louis." And I said, "I know where to have it. It needs to be underneath the Arch in the museum. That's where it needs to be." And the funny part about that is that Ron Turner, who's now on the board [of NAPPS], at that time was associate dean of the [University of Missouri–St. Louis] School of Arts and Sciences, the Extension—I did not know him, I did not know anything about him—and he called me at my office. . . . He had read about Project Tell in the newspaper. And he said, "We need to get together," he said, "I want to have a festival." And I said, "How odd. Because I just came back from the festival in Tennessee, and I think we should have a festival, too, and I know just where I want it to be, under the Arch," and that's how our festival got started.

An experienced corporate fund-raiser, Turner was able to put together alliances with institutional and corporate sponsors all over the region to create a significant alternate model to the Jonesborough festival form. The St. Louis Storytelling Festival also features an evocative historic site—the Jefferson National Expansion Memorial, which is the museum under the Gateway Arch. But the festival form is integrally based on the community partnerships that have come together to produce it.

Thursdays and Fridays of the four-day event are devoted to busing in large groups of schoolchildren for performances at the museum under the Arch, as well as to outreach performances scheduled in institutional settings all over the city. Saturdays and Sundays are open to the entire community and again feature a combination of festival performances at the Arch and outreach performances at remote locations. In return for these free community outreach performances, local school systems, libraries, service and recreational agencies, arts councils, and corporate foundations all join in cosponsoring the event, along with essential in-kind contributions from the museum and the university. Turner said:

> It's kind of like a Chinese fire drill, you know, just people going everywhere. It took lots of volunteers to get things organized at outreach locations, to get people where they needed to be. Crowd control at the Arch was handled by the park rangers; bus parking and all that was taken care of for us, and that was part of the Arch contribution, as well as the cash contribution they made. So it became an institutional commitment on the part of the libraries, the parks, the schools. The museum made an institutional commitment to it; the Missouri Botanical Garden provided outreach locations for us. The thing just grew, to the point where we have now, typically, twenty to twenty-two thousand people per year at a four-day event.

One significant advantage of this broad cosponsorship is that all the performances are offered without charge to their audiences—a major contrast to Jonesborough's soaring ticket prices. The St. Louis festival model has been utilized by organizers in other communities. It is most appropriate where the institutional infrastructure for a storytelling festival cannot be sustained by a storytelling organization alone (or where the local storytelling organization does not depend, as NSA does, on festival revenues to sustain its year-round operations) but can be created by these sorts of resourceful and complex community alliances.

Yet another alternate model of a storytelling community has been provided by NABS—the National Association of Black Storytellers. As its acronym implies, NABS was founded in 1982 as an ethnic counterpart to NAPPS. NABS cofounder Mary Carter Smith wrote her own creation story for NABS, setting it at the Tenth Annual National Storytelling Festival, where she and Linda Goss, an African American teller from Philadelphia, were performing:

> They were walking through that storybook town, meeting people and enjoying the experience. As usual, there were large crowds attending to tell stories and to hear stories. As the two walked along, they noticed how few African-Americans were among the hundreds of people there.
> "Mary," said Linda. "This Festival is an excellent idea. I think it would be a benefit to also have an organization of Black Storytellers."
> "Yes, Linda, I agree wholeheartedly," Mary answered.
> And that was the way it was conceived. (M. C. Smith, n.p.)

Smith is careful to give precedence to NAPPS in her account: "The two founders both have remained members of the National Association for the Preservation and Perpetuation of Storytelling, which is recognized as the parent group. Its founder, Jimmy Neil Smith, has always been there to advise and give guidance" (M. C. Smith, n.p.). But this filial deference stands alongside a perception that all NAPPS's children may not be equally at home at the feast.

As Jackie Torrence's story in chapter 4 shows, coming to Jonesborough could be intimidating for lone black tellers. As they came together there and elsewhere, they felt the need for a festival and an organization that would focus on their own traditions and provide a vehicle for showcasing and developing the full range of African American storytelling aesthetics. Their concerns were much like those of New England storytellers or other regional groups that felt they had insufficient opportunity in the national spotlight. But in place of geography as an identifying principle, African American storytellers put an ethnic history inflected with the narrative of diaspora, struggle, and cultural survival.

The National Black Storytelling Festival, first held in 1983 in Mary Carter Smith's hometown of Baltimore, would be quite different from its "parent" national festival. The first major difference was that the Black Storytelling Festival would move to a different location each year: Philadelphia, Chicago, Oakland, New Orleans, Milwaukee, Kansas City, and even the tiny coastal hamlet of Georgetown, South Carolina, near the Gullah communities of the Sea Islands. Not only did the festival never attach itself in an ongoing way to the interests of any single local group of organizers, but it actually changes form from year to year depending on the notions, organizational abilities, and mojo of each successive anchoring group. With more workshops, less distinction between featured and nonfeatured tellers, more open story-swaps, and open-ended sessions called "Love Circles," which can feature drumming, dancing, singing, and even prayer, the Black Storytelling Festival cultivates some of the inclusive aspects of a storytelling conference while maintaining an improvisatory tone that is distinctively a cultural style. Like the asymmetries and leaping colors of an African American quilt contrasted with the muted geometric consistency of their Anglo-American counterparts, NABS festivals are less enamored of regularity than of spontaneity and celebration.

Politics also have a place at NABS in a way that is not often welcome at NSA events. At a panel session I attended at the 1996 NABS festival in Philadelphia, Dr. David Anderson, a storyteller and teacher from Rochester, New York, who performs under the African name Sankofa, stood up to read a polemic, which went in part: "*Blackstorytelling* (one word) is that body of traditional stories, and stories new as today, that informs and energizes the African American struggle to preserve and perpetuate the humanity of African American people. *Blackstorytelling* (one word) is an emerging concept, a tool for those who wish to both critique and praise African American culture. Necessarily then this tool can be used accurately only by the creators of African American culture, African American people themselves. . . ." With each emphatic reiteration of his theme, *Blackstorytelling*, Sankofa would add the parenthetical note—"(one word)"—using the oratorical tools of an African American sermon to fuse the rhetoric of the storytelling revival with the ideologies of contemporary identity politics.

National organizations of both Jewish and Native American storytellers have followed NABS's lead in founding floating storytelling events that conform to the needs of historically embattled, geographically dispersed, and yet traditionally vital ethnic communities. In the next chapter, we will see what happened in the late 1980s when those communities' sensibilities clashed with those of NAPPS's idealized storytelling melting pot.

The Northlands Story Network

The storytelling scene in the Upper Midwest began to coalesce in the late seventies, along by-now familiar lines. A group of storytellers from the Madison, Wisconsin, area got together to rent a van and take their first trip to the National Storytelling Festival in 1978. On the way back, they were inspired to start a festival of their own—the Northlands Storytelling Festival. Set in the old Cornish mining settlement of Mineral Point, Wisconsin, it was modeled, according to Reid Miller, one of its founders, "after the *festival* side of NAPPS, and other festivals round the country where we attract an audience because it's a gathering of storytellers who are there to tell stories *to an audience.*"

The Mineral Point gathering also attracted performers from the emerging storytelling scenes around the region, particularly from northern Illinois and the Minneapolis–St. Paul area. Storytellers from the Twin Cities had their own distinct ideas about what they wanted a storytelling community to express. Many of them had been imprinted not by NAPPS so much as by storytelling of a more explicitly transformational, political, or New Age bent—by Jungian analysis, community organizing, or workshops with Ken Feit, Reuven Gold, or Gioia Timpanelli—pioneering pre-NAPPS revivalists with a radically ecumenical basis to their work. Several had been "converted" to the storytelling movement at the Mythos Conference held in St. Paul in 1979, which featured such sessions as Feit's "The Fool and His Vision: A Ritualized Self-Realization"; Gestalt therapist Joan Bodger's presentation, "I Am Vishnu Dreaming the Universe"; and Timpanelli's small-group workshop, "The Storytelling Way." Loren Niemi, who was there, remembered, "Gioia Timpanelli, at the end of a session, said to me, '*It would be a sin for you not to be a storyteller. You would be denying your Grace.*' And that statement made a real impact. I mean, having been a former Catholic, I understood the notion—I understood where she was coming from. And having been part of a religious structure, I understood the idea of vocation. And at that moment I came to the notion of storytelling as life-work."

A local Twin Cities support group formed, called Storyfront. Larry Johnson, one of the organizers, mused on the warm embers of cold war paranoia packed into the name: "That name came . . . in some meeting we were talking about what do we call our group. And I think Maren Hinderlie threw out that, we're sort of a *front* for ... We were talking about how we were doing this but didn't know about it, and she said we're a *front* for something or other, and then Storyfront became the name of it. We were just playing with words." For the populist Minnesotan contingent at Northlands, the ritual enactment of community that best fit its ethos was the conference or workshop format, because of its egalitarian character and its transformational intent. Miller told me, "As soon as the first Minneapolis coordinator took the reins, the shift went decidedly away from performance to conference." There was a sense on the part of some in the Twin Cities group that the festival model promoted what was derisively described as a "star system"—associated with hegemonic forms of mass-produced entertainment. As Johnson told me, "I think it's very fair to say that the people who perhaps had the most power or at least organizing ability on that early Northlands board were pretty much in agreement that storytelling was—that word *cultural worker*. Storytelling was something that you did in the world to help make the world a better place—not something you did to be elevated as a media star. That sort of distinction from the thing that tends to drive a lot of modern entertainment." Or, as Niemi put it only half-jokingly, "For some people it just rubbed against their Lutheran grain."

Soon the workshop elements were taking on more importance at Mineral Point. A regional organization began to develop, dubbed the Northlands Story Network, at first revolving around the Mineral Point festival. But that base was not secure. Support from the townspeople never materialized to anchor the event there, the way Jimmy Neil Smith and his associates were able to do in Jonesborough. Storytellers who were organizing the festival and simultaneously trying to manage their own careers began to tire. The Northlands board decided, according to Niemi, "that we should float around the Midwest for awhile, and take people to different parts of the area. So in '85 it went to Elkader [in northeastern Iowa]. But then it sort of got stuck in Elkader. And it's been there ever since."

The Northlands Conference at Elkader, Iowa, (and since 1997 in Dubuque) has remained clearly modeled on the conference/small-group workshop format. It has striven to maintain its egalitarian rules; there is a shaggy-dog-story aura of screwball camaraderie that modulates at intervals into self-conscious transports of ritualization. The host towns have been welcoming and have provided some infrastructural support without doing much to promote the event either regionally or nationally. It has therefore remained entirely an in-group affair, and that seems to be comfortable for all concerned. Meanwhile, several storytellers in the region with festival-scale performing ambitions have formed community partnerships to found their own events—such as Jim May's Illinois Storytelling Festival in Spring Grove, Illinois, and Michael Cotter's Stories from the Heartland in Austin, Minnesota. The persistence of both models of community expression shows the importance of each to a flourishing revival scene.

Toward a Storytelling World

Heather Forest, who founded the Long Island Storytelling Festival in her own home base of Huntington, New York, spoke of the network of local festivals created by storytellers, working in their home communities, as the building blocks of a storytelling world. Her comments can serve to sum up the braided impulses of storytelling community–building in the seventies and eighties, in which the spirit of service to the art and to the community was so tightly bound with the spirit of personal enterprise— with the struggle to create support networks that would sustain independent, alternative, performing careers:

> By creating a festival locally, I was able to raise the consciousness of people in my own community about storytelling as an art form—because

now instead of just seeing me, they were seeing people of diverse technical abilities, diverse ethnic backgrounds, diverse stylistic approaches—
and the palate of the art form was just broadened, and people's respect
for it increased over time; such that people around here now conclude
that storytelling is an art form in and of itself—and in many of the cultural arts resource catalogs around here, storytelling is its own category,
it's not tucked into theater, or folk arts, or something else—it's accepted
as an art form. And I think our local festival had something to do with
bringing storytelling to public consciousness. . . .

When I tour nationally, at this point, it's primarily to other places
where venues have been created by other storytellers. If you look at the
storytelling festivals around the country, primarily the movers behind
them are storytellers or storytelling enthusiasts. We have our own network. And it's not the same network as other touring venues—which
would be more along the lines of college concert series and community
concert series. It's sort of an underground, independent network.

The sixties, seventies, and eighties saw the gestation, birth, and growth
of an integrated national storytelling community—a revitalized storytelling world. That world grounded itself in a basic repertoire of ritual gatherings—festival, conference, support group, concert series—all of which
had existed as formal potentials prior to the revival period. The revival
brought them together in a social movement, giving them new tones, new
intensities, and new personal, political, and even religious significance.
The importance of alternate models within that repertoire of gatherings
lay in broadening the possibilities for participation by a range of communities, localities, and alliances within the wider cultural fabric. The
breadth and depth of alternate models of community revealed the web of
connections between the storytelling world and the world it existed to
celebrate and to critique, to serve and to consume.

I leave open the question of whether the term *community* or *scene* most
accurately portrays these coalescences of storytelling revival energies.
From a strictly sociological perspective, *scene* would seem more apt, because of the geographic and professional mobility of participants and the
consequent tendency in all the key ritual events toward rapid turnover of
personnel—often toward evanescence of the events themselves. It would
seem that the sense of community remains strongest when events are
most stable—as in New England's Sharing the Fire Conference or the Louisville and St. Louis festivals—or else when a support group is anchored
by one or two stalwart members who maintain a continuity of memory

and vision. Otherwise, scenes can easily evolve into organizations—bureaucratic structures for which consistency of power and product becomes paramount—or into cliques, whose members have developed set styles, repertoires, and business networks, with one another's help, but have little energy or interest in inviting newcomers to share the fruits of their labor. When scenes do evolve in either of these ways, the revitalization cycle, locally at least, comes full circle, to mimic the cultural forms from which the pilgrims of the revival originally departed.

Mythologically, however, *community* remains the storytellers' term of choice—even if the group and its rituals have changed forms and personnel many times since their inception. Once again, events organize communities as powerfully as communities organize events, but the desire for community remains a shaping force in revitalization activity—even when conflicts with the dominant cultural ethos of individualism and careerism may stunt its realization. We might well ask how much of the energy of these scenes is devoted to the specific, goal-directed tasks of cultivating professional careers and how much is dedicated to cultivating the kinds of intimate, "high-context" interdependencies by which folklorists recognize traditional communities? How do local communities change as one or several of its founding members grow in their careers from energetic local enthusiasts into touring professionals on the national circuit? And how does a storytelling organization, a community, or a scene constitute itself to endure in the face of pressures from the outside and from within?

The first two of these questions would have be answered case by case, through ongoing reflection and discovery. The third we will see dramatized in the chapter to come, and this will lead to reflections on the relationship between spontaneous and normative communitas, between cultural revitalization and its progression (or descent) into social structure.

6

Blood on the Porch

There must always remain, however . . . a certain
baffling inconsistency between the wisdom brought
forth from the deep, and the prudence usually
found to be effective in the light world. . . . Martyr-
dom is for saints, but the common people have their
institutions, and these cannot be left to grow like
the lilies of the field.

—Joseph Campbell, *The Hero with a Thousand Faces*

Cathryn Wellner's first NAPPS event was the National Storytelling Conference, the sequestered gathering at Washington College Academy in the
rolling hills outside of Jonesborough, at the height of the movement's
"blessed community." She recalled:

> In June of '83, I was so taken with storytelling, so caught by the storytell-
> ing bug, that I thought, I'm going to go down to my first NAPPS event.
> And so I went down to that NAPPS Conference, in the spring of '83. And
> I was really excited about it, because by that time I'd been reading the
> *Yarnspinner* faithfully, and I'd developed this pantheon of storytellers.
> And among them were Jay O'Callahan. . . . And Jay was there, and the
> Folktellers, and Gioia Timpanelli, and John Langstaff. . . . Everyone was
> so generous, with their time and their comments. There was a real spirit
> of community there, in that particular weekend, that was a good way of
> getting started with NAPPS. I made some friends that weekend that have
> stayed with me. And I went away thinking, "My God, these storytellers!
> They're a pretty fine bunch!"

The next year, 1984, I made my own first journey to the National Storytelling Conference. I recall the atmosphere of spiritual openness and
immanence on the wide porch behind the dining hall, in the golden glow
of early summer twilight. People took their plates out on the porch and
lingered long after plates were empty. David Holt, Bill Harley, and I broke

out a banjo and guitars and picked old-time tunes—"Liberty," "Over the Waterfall," "Whiskey before Breakfast." As dusk deepened, the story-swap began. The session was electric, as tellers incited one another to new levels of skill. The entire NAPPS board of directors was there looking on—and for several of the tellers who stood up that night there was a sense that their stars in the storytelling firmament had just come shining out.

The next year, the Saturday evening story-swap at Washington College Academy became widely known among those who attended as the "Blood on the Porch" night. Ed Stivender named it in an improvised song, the refrain of which ran, *"Storytelling nightmare, blood on the porch."* As Stivender recalled it in a January 7, 1992, interview, "The event was two individuals at the end of the night, in fact the last storyteller and the person who *wanted* to be the last storyteller, confronting each other. One had a chair in her hand. And that was the 'Blood on the Porch' moment." How had we gone from blessed community to "blood on the porch" in the span of three summers?

Festival, concert series, conference, guild, support group—the combination of esoteric and exoteric models of ritual celebration, and the power of affirmation that went into them, made for powerful leverage in expanding the community. Yet tensions between the different models also opened fissures in the community as it grew, and familiar conflicts began to appear in the cracks.

As we have seen, the festival and concert series are hierarchical in that they elevate an elite group of performers above a mass of listeners. The conferences, guilds, and support groups are more egalitarian in principle. But the hierarchies of reward and respect projected by the public models cast their shadows on all the community events. The transcendent boon had crystallized into coin of the realm. The footfalls of unslain giants began to sound around the edges of the camps, and wicked stepmothers dressed as peddlers wandered through, offering sweets.

The growth of the NAPPS festival and the storytelling world it supports was steady. In 1978, the estimated attendance for the weekend was 500; in 1979, 800; in 1981, 1,400 (NAPPS office). For the 1982 festival, the tenth one, director Connie Regan-Blake had the inspiration to invite back every storyteller who had performed there over its first decade. More than sixty tellers came. It was a dramatic enactment of the movement's communitarian ideals and also a kind of public annunciation of "critical mass." The impact was felt nationwide. In 1983, over 3,000 people attended. By 1986, attendance had doubled again. Organizers regularly had to add more tents. In 1978 there was one, in 1979 two, in 1980 and 1981 three; in 1982 through 1985 there were four tents, which themselves grew more capacious each year. By 1988, there were six tents or open outdoor sites, which could hold between 500 and 1,000 people; the Mill Spring Park site, where the ghost storytelling was now held, was an open meadow and accommodated several times that number.

Meanwhile, regional and local storytelling festivals sprang up in Jonesborough's wake: the 1983–84 NAPPS directory listed twenty-five, the 1986 edition forty-two, and the 1988 edition sixty-nine. The number of practicing professional tellers also multiplied dramatically. As late as 1980 the festival was a loose enough affair that Heather Forest could phone the NAPPS office secretary and find herself casually invited to stop by and be a featured teller the following year. The 1982 festival marked the end of "the bush-beating era"—when revival activists like the Folktellers had to hunt up and down for colleagues to fill the festival bill—and the beginning of an era of stampede.

By the end of the eighties, the main stages of the NAPPS festival were guarded by multitiered national selection committees. The NAPPS board, once a casual clique of local boosters from the South and Southeast, had grown into a representative body with a constitutional mandate from regional storytelling associations covering all fifty states: Jonesborough as Global Village. But the transition was not without its agonies and its sacrifices.

"We are all storytellers"—this was a key article of the revival catechism. "Everyone is welcome, everyone has a story worth telling, worth hearing." It is a powerful, universalist message that infused the infant storytelling communities with the rosy glow of sanctuary. But it began to be discovered in the eighties that while everyone was called, not everyone was chosen. Blocs began to form, based on geography, ethnicity, or status, to articulate, challenge, or protect the emerging lines of structure and authority within the national movement. An irresistible tide developed that would transform the spontaneous communitas of a revitalization movement, and the ideological communitas of revival discourse, into the rationalized organizational structure that Victor Turner called "normative communitas." Anthony F. C. Wallace called it the phase of "routinization" of a revitalization movement. Ed Stivender would call it "the Federalysis of NAPPS" (telephone interview, January 7, 1992).

The folklore arising from NAPPS's rapid growth and from the political struggle to "open up the organization" portrays a movement's awakening from the spell of remedial childhood that lay upon it in its early days. It shows confrontations with some of the basic mythic conflicts of adolescence—the breakup of the family cult or the sacrifice of the small to the greater, of intimacy to power, of innocence to experience. The development had a painful, even tragic aspect to some who had experienced the "magical" bliss of spontaneous storytelling communitas, only to find it riven with mundane divisions. Egos, which had expanded in the encounter with the archetype of the storyteller to embrace all of humanity, now found to their shock that not all of humanity, even all storytelling humanity, were always eager to embrace them back.

There were parallels with the developments of other social movements of the sixties and seventies. Movements and gatherings as diverse as the civil rights marches of the early sixties, rock festivals of the late sixties, feminist collectives of the early seventies, gay rights parades of the late seventies, and a myriad of meditation and personal growth groups may have taken various political, spiritual, artistic, or life-style issues as their rallying point, but they were based at least as much on the natural craving for a medium of radical human community. And all at some point had to face the limits of spontaneous communitas in providing an environment for sustainable community life and growth. By 1985 or 1986, it was dawning on the storytelling world that the "blessed community" (activist John Lewis's phrase referring to the civil rights movement before the alliance of blacks and liberal whites collapsed) of early movement days was transforming itself into a professional community, with competitive pressures and corresponding ecological limits. The carnival, as always, had to keep moving on.

In what follows I will examine some of the ways that rival segments articulated themselves within the growing storytelling community and how the community sought to restructure its rituals and associations to accommodate its segmentation while striving to remain, in some sense, a community. I will begin with a look at the dynamics of the storytelling scene in the Upper Midwest, where critical friction emerged that directly impacted the national organization.

"We're Not Thirteen Colonies Anymore!"

By the early eighties, the smoldering conflicts of status and prestige within NAPPS that were expressed in New England and northern California were heating up in Northlands, too. Larry Johnson and Elaine Wynne, his wife and storytelling partner, told their side of the story in a joint interview:

Elaine: Larry had had some contact with Tom Nankervis, who used to coordinate the conference on Storytelling and the Religious Message. And Tom had asked us to be a part of that. And it was in Milwaukee, at a retreat center.

Larry: '82 was in Chicago, and that was the first year we went. '83 was in Milwaukee. But we began to recognize in that thing that "we weren't as good as some people because we were from here." I mean, that's oversimplifying—

Elaine: Well, yeah, there was that attitude. And we had already started the Northlands Network by then, because of wanting to create something in the region. We didn't feel that NAPPS was really representative of the whole country. We felt like they chose most of their tellers from the East Coast and that they were very East Coast and Southeast United States–oriented. So we were already a little rebellious.

Larry: But we started talking to Tom, telling him that there were many very good storytellers in the Midwest, and that, even if they hadn't been on the NAPPS festival didn't mean that they weren't very good. And so that second year he invited Mark Wagler [of Madison, Wisconsin] to also be a part of it.

Elaine: We actually felt somewhat put off—maybe snubbed would be a closer word—by some of the people who were there who were NAPPS featured tellers. And we had come out of this populist tradition. And were all very political, and we had already started this regional organization, and we weren't really prepared for that. And we just kind of got together brewing on that, and we decided, well, we're going to create our own fun here! And we did, the three of us. And as we did that, then we found that more and more people were interested in what we were doing, because ... Northlands has a kind of free-wheeling, raucous style, in a way. People like to dance, and late-night parties, that was all a part of that revival here in the Midwest.

Larry: Part of the thing, too, was it seemed like there were some people that you were supposed to kind of fawn over, or at least lots of people were doing that. And we decided that we weren't going to participate in that. We knew lots of good storytellers that were from here.

Elaine: It really was a recognition issue. And so we went back from there—

Larry: And it was at a Northlands board meeting here—that all hell broke loose. We started talking about this, and lots of people felt that way, about really having a national organization that represented everybody. I think there were two different meetings of the Northlands board where this was vociferously discussed. And there was the one where this language got created about, "We're not thirteen colonies anymore!"

But there was also a meeting where people started saying, "Wait a minute! NAPPS is not us and them! *We* are NAPPS—most of us belong, so we *are* NAPPS! And if that's the case, then—"

Elaine: So we really began pushing NAPPS about having a congress.

A letter, featuring the notorious "thirteen colonies" broadside, was sent from the Northlands board to the board of directors of NAPPS, protesting the concentration of power and public opportunities within the organization. The letter demanded a geographically representative national body and suggested a national forum, which was eventually called the National Congress on Storytelling, for working out the political ramifications of the changes.

These feelings and ideas were not new. As we saw in chapter 5, the New England storytellers, led by Jay O'Callahan, had sounded similar rumblings when their own ambitions first collided with the mythic bastion of recognition and prestige that was NAPPS. They were only quieted by NAPPS's prompt acceptance of O'Callahan as a performer and board member and the reliable openings for New England performers that followed. The idea of a national storytelling congress had first been floated by the American Storytelling Resource Center, which had even attempted some grantsmanship through the National Endowment for the Arts and the Smithsonian Institution for the project. NAPPS remained cautiously neutral about these ASRC efforts; the project eventually collapsed, and subsequently so did the ASRC. But the challenge from Northlands would not subside. When Beth Horner was elected to the NAPPS board in 1985, she took it as her mandate to work at "opening up the organization." She recalled:

The organization changed so fast, from being a very informal, small organization to being a large organization, with people wanting to be on the inside track. And feeling that they were not on the inside track; and that there was an inside group that was *trying to keep them out.* And I, of course—when I came on the board—that's how I felt. Although I had gotten to know a lot of people on the board and had a lot of respect for them, it was very clear to me that these people did not understand that there were other storytellers in the country. Because when they started the organization, they were the only storytellers they knew of. And putting the festival together was just, "Oh my God, do you know anybody that could come to this place and tell stories each year?". . . . And it just changed so rapidly. Because the festival was so wildly successful.

The "Blood on the Porch" Moment

The transition between the "bush-beating era" and the stampede that followed was disorientingly swift. In a very few years, the old Jonesborough support group went from a scrappy, collective effort, which was amateur in tone if not in tendency and had plenty of room for volunteers to enter and find a niche, to an exploding professional scene, where nearly everyone's career was on the line. Nothing epitomized the changes in the aura of the organization more than the change in the Washington College Conference. Horner remembered the evolution of the after-dinner story-swaps:

> Before, I remember, it was a very informal thing. And it didn't even happen every year. And not everybody even went to the porch. I remember being in groups that just kind of took a blanket and went off in the dark somewhere and told stories. . . . Doc or Chuck Larkin would just start the storytelling going. And people would sort of join in or not. It wasn't a big thing. But that changed, quickly. And then those conferences ended. Because it became apparent that this had become a big thing; a big competitive thing. People needed to have an avenue to be seen for the festival.

The very attribute that made the Washington College conferences so magnetic—the presence of the entire NAPPS board and a host of up-and-coming storytellers eager to make their mark—also spurred the encroaching audition fever that would doom it. In 1985, it went over the competitive edge, with traumatic results. Cathryn Wellner, then a member of NAPPS board of directors from Seattle, reflected:

> There are a lot of theories as to why it happened. I think the main thing was, there were so many people who were starting to get hungry. People who were coming up as storytellers who were desperate to be known. And people kind of figured at the time that the only path to stardom was through NAPPS. Now there are so many more things happening around the country that people are more sophisticated about it. But it looked to people as though that was the route: you had to get featured by NAPPS. And only a few people could get featured. That's the name of the game. You know, there's only a few slots.
>
> And another interesting dynamic of that particular conference was Michael Parent did a very effective workshop on performance anxiety. And he left people with the thought, *"By God, better get out there and do it!"* And I think that was another factor. Because people were really pumped up to by God, go out and do it! And it got ugly.

One person got up. And instead of telling *a* story, which is *the* rule, and everybody knows it—it doesn't have to be restated—we thought—this person got up and told *three* stories. Not short stories. And people are generally polite. So nobody really could believe that this was really happening. And when the second story ended and this person went on to do *another* story, the tension began to build until it became almost explosive. And by the time that person sat down, feeling, I'm sure, as if they'd done a good job, because everybody was listening—what was really happening was, there was this *burn* going on. A smolder around the group. And the next person to get up, kind of *rushed* up, because, my gosh, the time was getting late, and if I don't tell my story now I'll never get another chance like this—and so, the listening stopped. Because there were so many people who wanted to get up and tell a story, and such an awareness in the group that this was happening, that there really wasn't anybody listening to anybody. But there was this tension about *having* to get up and tell a story. The body language was wonderful—people began to physically move forward. And try to edge forward to get position, so they could be right up there ready to—*LEAP!* onto the stage, and tell their story.

And it got ugly. There wasn't any violence, but it was probably as close as you're going to get. Because there were some people who were clawing, literally, for space. It was, "My audition, my God, if I don't get this audition I'm never going to make it!" And the irony of it was that the board members had all buggered off. And there was nobody to audition for. What happened was that people went off with their friends—which is a perfectly legitimate and wonderful thing to do. But those people who should have felt some responsibility for what went on there, relinquished it. And just walked away and let it happen.

And so it shouldn't have happened. But certainly everyone learned a lesson from it. And maybe it was good that it happened, on that level. But it was a frightening experience. The good spirit left. It let people know that storytellers are not all sweetness and light. The dark side of human nature reared its ugly head. But after all, why not? We're telling stories about the dark side. *Did we really think they were just stories?* That was a demon we needed to deal with.

As Wellner so aptly perceived, the "Blood on the Porch" story-swap showed the dark underbelly of the bright, shining body of revitalization—what Jung would call the movement's shadow—and aspects of this shadow would continue to surface in dramatic ways.

Save perhaps for those who had to travel the longest distances to get there and so could rarely if ever attend, no one really wanted the conferences to leave Washington College. Only two years earlier, the entire gathering had clasped hands in one large circle inside the college gymnasium, swaying gently as John Langstaff led them in singing, "Will Ye Go, Lassie, Go . . . (And we'll all go together . . .)." In 1984, the song was tried again, on the sloping lawn outside the gymnasium, out of the instinctive urge to formalize traditions. Without Langstaff, there was no one to lead the verses—so the circle just sang the chorus over and over. The memories were fresh and poignant. Yet already the storytellers were squeezed together so tightly at Washington College that they were turning the circle into an unruly crush.

Jim May recalled, "Lynn Rubright used to say that she was *going home to America*. That's what she called Washington College. *Going to America*. I was part of that move to kind of open up NAPPS. But I sure never wanted Washington College to end." Stivender, who had been trained in Catholic theology and who, as a member of the NAPPS board, fought hard to keep the conference in Jonesborough, responded to my questions about it this way:

> The loss of the Washington College conference I think was a grave mistake. Because, there's another religious factor that made the conference special in a way that St. Louis or Santa Fe were not special. And that was: pilgrimage. Pilgrimage is a very important aspect of the Jonesborough festival experience; and pilgrimage was a very important aspect of the conference. And the Protestant Reformation lost that. Once you get rid of Rome, there's no reason to go to Rome. And the Protestant Reformation has lost that element of pilgrimage, by which the community defines itself. And I'm not sure if it was worth it. (January 7, 1992)

It was becoming increasingly clear that, in the view of the national membership, NAPPS had simply outgrown Washington College. But in another sense, it was like an old homeplace that had to be sold off to pay the tax— the cost of what its own desirability had done to property values.

"A Buyers' Market": Fear in the Tents

The 1985 National Storytelling Festival was, in some respects, Laura Simms's crowning achievement as an organizer of storytelling events. But it also brought out further lines of stress and division in the storytelling community. Under Simms direction, between 1983 and 1985 the Jonesborough festival became for the first and possibly the last time an international festival. She invited the Australian tellers Moses Aaron in 1983 and Kel Watkins in 1984 and the French teller Muriel Bloch in 1983. In 1984, she programmed the Zimbabwean mbira virtuoso Ephat Mujuru; the Canadians Ron Evans, Bob Barton, and Alice Kane; and Maggie Pierce from Northern Ireland. Simms was also inclined to eclectic traditional and modern selections, which challenged the community's assumptions about what storytelling was or could become.

In 1985, these programming inclinations came together to make the most diverse and controversial festival lineup yet. It included two performers, Seleshe Damessae from Ethiopia and Purna Das Baul from Bengal, who spoke little or no English and only sang in their tribal languages, to the accompaniment of exotic stringed instruments; another performer, University of Massachusetts professor Robert Creed, who told no folktales as most of the audience understood the idea, only chanted *Beowulf* in Old English; a distinguished Native American writer, Simon Ortiz, who seemed unprepared to perform in front of large, boisterous, festival crowds; and Spalding Gray, who wryly described his Manhattan home as "an island off the coast of the United States" and whose dark, autobiographical monologues came as an unpleasant shock to some. Gray recalled doing a section of his three-hour monologue *Swimming to Cambodia*. It included a four-letter word quite routine on the New York stage or the Hollywood screen—but which had not yet made its festival debut. He asked the woman in whose house he was staying about it, and she told him that her nine-year-old and eleven-year-old children used the word regularly, for all her best efforts to stop them—so that it probably would not "be any kind of shattering thing."

But it was. He recalled beginning his piece, coming to the forbidden word, and finding that the entire tent seemed to quake. "And women grabbed their children and ran for the edges of the tent. And then a lot of young people moved down closer, so it kind of polarized the whole tent."

The reaction of the storytelling community was similarly polarized. Some of my contacts still regard the 1985 event as a high point in their festival experience. Some called it a worthwhile, stimulating experiment. Others were not so charitable, especially at the time. Donald Davis remembered, "That 1985 festival was one where I got over one hundred and fifty letters of complaint about the festival. I mean, *violent* letters of complaint. I wish I had those. That would be interesting. Not in terms of the names of people they came from. Just in terms of the kinds of reactions that were coming out of people" (telephone interview, April 9, 1992). Regan-Blake told me, "People don't tend to sit down and write unless it's something that they're upset about. So there was more feedback saying, 'Where're the ones we're used to seeing? And where are the *American* storytellers?' I think there were a lot of fears that jumped up in people's faces" (telephone interview, January 21, 1992). And Wellner thought "that the community—and I mean the story-listening community, that comes to the festival, wasn't ready for it. . . . It was just a matter of people being pulled out of a set idea of what storytelling was before they were ready to be pulled out of it."

But Davis, who became the chair of the board at the beginning of 1986, took a hardheaded business point of view toward the artistic issues involved. His comments reflect the struggle to balance the demands of structure and communitas in an environment shaped by market pressures:

The test was, who was going to define storytelling? The test was, does the audience define storytelling, or does the presenter define storytelling? Is this a sellers' market or a buyers' market? And, as with all things, it's a buyers' market. That's gonna be true, through and through. A sellers' market might work the first year. But then it's defined by the consumer. And I think that was proved out, in that we had during some of those years, some big financial losses. And some membership drops. The '86 festival went way overboard in the other direction, to try and recoup financial losses. And there's a lot of misunderstanding of that by artistic people, who felt that their judgment was being excluded, that they were being excluded, that there was a sort of a star system in operation. But I was sitting on a board there, looking at a twenty thousand dollar financial loss, and a drop in membership. And saying, "Are we going to stay in business or not?" And so, it was like, all feelings aside, we've got to do something to restore the organization, immediately. And then start to ease out toward the edges again. . . . And there were people who said, "Well, let's make the right artistic decision, and not even worry about the money." Well, we would have been gone. NAPPS would have been gone. Or in bankruptcy with that. That's what happened to the old "Storytelling and the Religious Message" event. That event's position was, "Let's do the very best thing, artistically, we can possibly do, and trust that the money will come up." And it went into bankruptcy. Total bankruptcy. . . . So that was sitting there beside us. And NAPPS had lost members and was sitting there, way financially in the hole. And there were people knocking on the door, saying, "Me, me, me, me, me!" And I was sitting at the place of saying, "If we hurt feelings, that's too bad. What we've got to do is survive at this point, and *then* redirect." So I made a decision at the moment, in terms of what to push for. And there was a price to pay for that. But that's what happens. (telephone interview, April 9, 1992)

For the 1986 festival, NAPPS received substantial grants from the state of Tennessee's bicentennial celebration, Homecoming '86. The program was extremely conservative—only one new storyteller was featured, the mild-mannered Scottish ballad-singer Norman Kennedy, who resided in Vermont. For the rest, it was all familiar NAPPS veterans from the Southeast and Northeast. Eight current or former board members were on the bill, along with Ray Hicks, Linda Goss, Elizabeth Ellis, and Gayle Ross, all of whom had been born and raised nearby or had descended from natives of the Tennessee mountains.

One of the prices to be paid for that was Simms's resignation from the board. Another was Horner's fury. She had been elected but had been unable to attend her first board meeting, in February 1986. So she kept in touch with Smith, now executive director of NAPPS, by telephone. She said:

> That February board meeting, I was on the phone constantly with Jimmy Neil, telling him who I wanted at the festival; and telling him that this congress, which had been proposed by Laura Simms and Connie, really was important, and it needed to stress regional development. And after the board meeting he called me, and he was giving me a rundown of what had happened. He told me the festival lineup, which was Homecoming Tennessee '86—there was not a new face on there. I was furious! And I railed and railed at him. And then he said, "Well, it was decided that the congress—it wasn't the right time." I said, "If we don't have a congress, there's going to be a revolution. People are going to leave this organization in droves." I was so angry. I was, you know, very emotionally involved with it all then. But I could not believe that this board would pass on the congress. And I was furious! And about a week later, Jimmy called back and said, "Beth, maybe we should go ahead with the congress." And we started planning it.

The planning for the first National Congress on Storytelling involved more than a mere redesign and relocation of the National Conference on Storytelling. The process would demand greater changes in the structure of the board and staff and the working relationship between them. The first step was the formation of a national advisory council, with representatives from each of ten regions of the country. This would eventually be incorporated in an expanded board of directors, which would feature proportional regional representation. For NAPPS to generate a national congress that could justify the name, such changes had to be set in motion; and in turn, the perspectives generated by the congresses would demand further nationalization and rationalization of NAPPS.

The process was emotionally charged for those involved, because of the inevitability that it would also lead to changes in the mystique of the organization, of the board of directors, and of Jonesborough itself. With the best of intentions, the Jonesborough support group and the group of northeasterners who joined them in the early eighties had created a feedback loop of mythic charisma that flowed from the Jonesborough events to the board, to themselves—and around again from themselves, to the board, to the events. They had accomplished this by virtue of being the ones who had chiefly represented the ritual catharsis of the storyteller's journey during the years of the events' great public expansion at the same time that they were performing the role of directors and programmers of the events. The power attached to each of the three vital functions—performer, director, and site—became passionately identified in the iconography of NAPPS and in the imagination of the community.

It was a mythic and magical stage of the revival community's development. It was heightened by the array of references to archaic shamanic beliefs that permeated the repertoire and the ideology of the movement. The NAPPS directors were in the center of this magical operation. There was nothing particularly sinister about it. But the energy and imagery of a revivalistic revitalization movement evoked an atavistic set of cultural terms. It thrust this talented group of storytelling pilgrims for a short time into a role that resembled royal priests and priestesses of an ancient cult. And then, so swift were the forces of modernity by which the revival was encompassed, it almost immediately tore them out of it.

For those in the national community who felt excluded and disempowered by the magical identification of Jonesborough, the board, and storytelling, the concentration of power could, and did, backfire. It created a groundswell of righteous resentment directed at the board and NAPPS. Northlands's "We're not thirteen colonies" salvo was more than ringing rhetoric—it was a statement of historical fact that was irresistible. Ed Stivender, the storytelling Jesuit, called it "the Protestant Reformation of NAPPS" (telephone interview, January 7, 1992).

Norma Livo was the advisory council member from the Rocky Mountain region. She recalled an exploratory visit from Jimmy Neil Smith:

Out here in the West, we're separated by space. But it's a very close community that really helps each other, supports each other, *cares* about
each other. And at one point there was the feeling that—"NAPPS didn't
care about us!" So there was a little rabble-rousing that got started.

I remember Jimmy Neil—he came out when we were scouting the territory to put on a regional conference out here. And he was asking, very
honestly, about how important *is* NAPPS to us out here. And honestly, it
wasn't that important, except to those of us that went to the festival.
And not everybody had the money to go do that. And I said, "NAPPS
needs us. But we, maybe, don't really need NAPPS."

And I have to say: that man gets kicked in the teeth and comes up
thinking. He is amazing! He just sat there and said, "Okay. I hear it." And
that's when that advisory board got formed.

Horner was an apt choice to enunciate the truth to the board, because
her allegiance was dual: she had been transformed from a librarian to a
free-lance storyteller by the touch of the Jonesborough revivalist wand,
but now she was living in the midst of the Northlands backlash:

I had met a Northlands person at one of the [NAPPS] School of Storytelling things, and they told me about Northlands. And so I started going to
Northlands events. And boy, talk about people angry with NAPPS—
those people were angry with NAPPS, at being passed over. Which I always thought was so strange. I was a NAPPS person. I was a NAPPS person from the word go, and these people were angry at NAPPS. And I
remember saying to them, "Have you ever gone to a NAPPS workshop?
Have you ever volunteered to do any work for NAPPS? How are they supposed to know you, if you don't make yourself known to them?"

Yet when she found herself on the board, a crucial distinction of status was
immediately apparent to her:

I was the poor relation. I was only the second person who had been
elected to the board who had not been featured at the festival. Lynn Rubright [who was subsequently featured in 1985, while still a board mem-
ber] had been the other. They hadn't heard of me! They sort of knew
who I was, but they had never heard me tell stories. And at that time,
that's how you got on the board, was by being a respected storyteller.
That was our only way of relating to each other—that was our only way
of knowing each other, was through having heard each other tell stories.
And I remember the first year that Gay Ducey's name, and my name, and
Cathryn Wellner's name were brought up as possible people to be at the
festival. And we all refused to be considered. And that was just incredi-

ble! The three of us decided we did not want to be considered for the festival, it was a conflict of interest. And when Milbre Burch came on the board, she said, "Alright, let's make it policy, then."

Wellner recalled:

It was a fascinating time to be on the board. A period of tremendous transition and growth. And not a little anguish. . . . The transition was from those people who had really become known as storytellers, in part because of NAPPS, to people who were not in that sort of star category but were sort of the workers—worker ants. And I'm not saying that because the other people weren't workers—my gosh, people worked hard on that board. It was a very small group of people doing an incredible amount of work. . . . At the time Beth and I came on the board, board members were doing program planning. . . . Everybody had responsibility for planning one event. And for volunteers to plan a national event— that's a pretty major commitment. So people were putting in an inordinate number of hours, to do that.

And I think that the reason that it felt like such a transition from old guard to new group was that there was a perception among the NAPPS community that unless you were one of a handful of people that had been featured at NAPPS, NAPPS didn't know you existed. And wasn't going to do very much for you. You know, that there were certain people who got invited to the festival, and certain people who got invited to do workshops at conferences. And that was NAPPS. Well, that was never the intent. Nor, really, what was going on, entirely. There was a certain amount of that, because people who were on the board also put themselves on the festival. And that had to be cleaned up. But that was in part because how many people were out there that people knew about?

Davis described the issue this way:

One hard thing to do was the point at which it was decided that no board member would be featured at a festival, while they were on the board. And I said, "We've got to get out of the self-interest position. *If* we're going to feature strong tellers. Because if we feature strong tellers, and have board members on there, the point of view is, we feature *board members*. And so we've got to say, 'No board members.' So that when we feature strong tellers, that accusation can't be a part of it."

Because it was very clearly perceived that people came to a festival because there were a few names of people they recognized, that they wanted to come and hear. And once they were there, they would hear other people. But if you didn't have, say, a Gamble Rogers, and a Folktellers, somewhere up there where the names could be present—or say, a Jackie Torrence and a David Holt—then you weren't going to get an audience. So those strong people had to be people who were not on the board, to avoid that perceived accusation by people who wanted to come and weren't getting to come. (telephone interview, April 9, 1992)

"Bad Storytelling"

It became politically necessary "to avoid that perceived accusation," in part because of another shadow element of the storytelling revival that was becoming more difficult to avoid by this time: the problem of "bad storytelling." It was clear that the storytelling marketplace, like the porch at Washington College, was becoming crowded, and a fair proportion of what was crowding into it was trite, derivative, pretentious, narcissistic, or dull—sometimes all at once. This should not have been surprising in an art form that was undergoing a sudden surge of popularity among people for whom it was very new—it might surprise us more that so many powerful and distinctive voices emerged in so short a period. But "bad storytelling" presented a troubling contradiction in terms for the revival community. According to the prevailing ideology, such a thing should not have been possible.

Heather Forest was speaking from the heart of the revivalist creed when she said, "It really doesn't seem to matter much if the teller is technically proficient or not. It just has to do with setting up the situation where *a* person is *communicating,* with language, to conjure images in the imagination of the listener." However, in particular situations that were being set up, starting with and stemming from the National Storytelling Festival, it really did seem to matter a great deal if the teller was technically proficient. Regan-Blake recalled her experiences on the road with people who had been prejudiced by exposure to "bad storytelling":

I think when anything is in that kind of stage—I mean, when someone hears a piano player who isn't very good—that doesn't mean they're never going to hear another piano player. They make an assessment, and they say, "Well, whoever recommended that person I'm not going to listen to their recommendations any more, but I'm certainly not going to stop going to piano concerts." But with storytelling, it was different. And we were hearing this out on the road, you know. Because then, as people started telling stories, there was such a rash of people that said, "I can do that! I can *do* that!" And they went out and got their cards the next day and started doing it, and advertising as being a storyteller. Then we would hear from people at a workshop who would say, "I had told myself I was never going to come to another performance." And probably, on the percentage-wise, that was probably a pretty small percentage. But still, we were hearing that. And I think that gave us even more of a zealous commitment to NAPPS and to ensuring the quality of it. (telephone interview, April 9, 1992)

The storytelling revival emerged in the seventies from a fusion of worlds: the unself-conscious world of home, family, and community talk, where its folk roots lay; the world of libraries and schools, where its official status in support of literary culture had long been established; the artificial families of revival support groups, where the idea that "we are all storytellers" was fostered; and voluntary or involuntary castaways from other established art worlds, such as theater, music, or literature, where high levels of training were generally required and the strictures of critical standards were pervasive. Regan-Blake reflected on the confusion of judgment and desire that prevailed as these worlds intersected in NAPPS:

I think that people have an amazing amount of creative ability. And if they have that *desire,* then they can tap into whatever level their creative ability is and be able to do something. And that's why I think that anyone can paint a picture, or sing a song, or tell a story. But as far as being a performer, or a musician, or a storyteller that people would want to come to—as far as being an artist as a storyteller, I *don't* think everyone can attain that. And that was a lot of confusion. Because I think, in the storytelling movement at that time, we were all saying, "We've got to take back storytelling." And I'm still saying that, and most people are too, that we want everybody to be out there telling stories, in their families, and in their communities, and in their homes, and in their churches—but not necessarily out there on a stage. I've always felt that when you get up there in front of people, that that's a different quality then. . . . And I think that that was probably a confused message. Because we were all saying, "Anybody can tell a story." And yet all these people were trying to perform at the festival, and they were not necessarily of that same quality for that kind of staged performance. (telephone interview, April 9, 1992)

Perhaps, according to some, technical proficiency came to matter too much, for there was a growing body of technically proficient work that went under the now fashionable and fundable name of storytelling but seemed to have missed the revival's whole aesthetic point. As it grew in the spotlight of popular culture, the National Storytelling Festival developed its own set of technical requirements, and sometimes these requirements subtly undercut the values of community, relatedness, tradition, and service that funded the revival in the first place. Because the festival was the movement's highest profile platform, it tended to shape people's idea of what a storyteller should be. As the eighties wore on, it began to gel the clear light of the storyteller archetype with the pinks and purples of virtuoso stage business.

Simms reflected:

> The painful part of being on the board for me was that most people believed that I was choosing and rejecting. I think it was really always a board decision; and I think, in looking back to it, we made very good decisions, for certain people, by not inviting them in certain years. Because, I think that over the years, their performance did get better, and they were ready for it. It [the NAPPS festival] is not an easy situation.
>
> We had standards and profound questions about what was or was not storytelling. There were some people who were coming up in the storytelling world who were dynamic and provocative, and someone on the board really felt it was strong, or it was a necessary strand that had to be included. And some of them—I don't want to talk too much about that—but I felt very sad about certain decisions we made. Because I felt that it was necessary first and foremost to really develop storytelling for what was uniquely storytelling, so that it existed as an art form on its own. And that not everybody who uses story is a storyteller. There were many people who really didn't have the relationship to the audience or any understanding of story. . . . So I was just afraid storytelling would get watered down. And I think, to some degree that is happening. I think the interesting part is the tremendous amount of very, very talented performers who are coming forward. And some of them are able to transmit stories. And others are just able to transmit their tremendous talent. And rouse audiences to a kind of emotional orgasm. Without any content, without any real value, or interest in story. (telephone interview, December 23, 1991)

At the same time that the new breed of young urban professional storyteller was crowding the scene, the older breed of librarian-storyteller, who had traditionally displayed a mixture of welcome and territorial scruples toward the growth of the storytelling revival, was feeling increasingly left out. Ellin Greene, the distinguished teacher of the New York Public Library lineage, ran for the board in 1979 and won. Yet she did not feel that her style of storytelling was well-served by NAPPS: "I thought at that time that the performer-storyteller was very much dominant. And I used to really be—I don't think I expressed it openly—but upset by Jimmy Neil Smith—whom I liked very much—but that he seemed to listen so closely to those performer-storytellers. . . . I think it was a gradual thing with him, to learn that there were a lot of librarians and a lot of teachers out there who were very interested in storytelling. . . . I think that in the beginning it was the performer types who captured his imagination." Horner, who had been Greene's student in library school, agreed:

> I think that George [Shannon] and Ellin are excellent examples of how the organization has changed. Because their type of storytelling—Ellin's primary focus in her storytelling was to get children to read books, and George's came out of getting children to read books, and . . . motivating children to learn to create—and there was a time when there got to be no place for that at NAPPS. Because the festival, which was the primary focus of the organization, had become big-time, large-group type storytellers. And there just wasn't staff or time to do everything, and so the organization leaned toward that. I know when I came on the board, people like Ellin were feeling very frustrated.

These were some of the artistic and political issues that the National Storytelling Congress was intended to air. In the process, particularly at the first two congresses, the community had to do more gazing into the shadows of the storytelling revival.

St. Louis: The Congress on Ethics

The first National Storytelling Congress was held in St. Louis in June 1987. It was the first large-scale NAPPS event to be produced outside of East Tennessee. There were several topics on the agenda: regional caucuses were convened for the first time in NAPPS history, and plans were explored for regional development; in addition, seminars were held relating storytelling and ministry, theater, and the oral tradition, to name a few. But the St. Louis event is still most widely remembered as the congress on storytelling ethics.

The particular ethical issue that shook the community in St. Louis was that of the rightful "ownership" of stories and the etiquette of requesting permission and giving credit for use of other storytellers' material. This was an issue that had been simmering in the community for many years. As early as June 1978, a note in the *Yarnspinner* newsletter entitled "Acknowledge Story Sources" admonished storytellers: "Most stories appearing in printed form are copyrighted by the author or publisher, and storytellers using such material have a legal—and moral—obligation to identify the source of each story, especially those in books or publications. . . . As a NAPPS member, you can help folks involved with storytelling become more aware of the legal obligation and ethical courtesy of correctly acknowledging story sources."

However, in the summer of 1986, a formal code of storytelling ethics proposed by Doug Lipman and Lee-Ellen Marvin in NAPPS's *National Storytelling Journal* and circulated among storytelling organizations nationwide brought the issue to a much sharper pitch. The crucial difference in Lipman and Marvin's code was their extension of intellectual property rights to oral variants of tales. Lipman had had several disturbing experiences of showing up for performances, only to find that another storyteller in his New England community had been to the same venue before him and told the same folktale that he had planned for the centerpiece of his own program. Furthermore, the other storyteller's version had been taken directly from Lipman's own carefully researched adaptation, without requesting his permission. He felt this was not only a discourtesy but also an immediate threat to his livelihood that needed to be confronted. Lipman and Marvin crafted a five-point statement of ethical principles, which they hoped to have discussed, amended, and if possible ratified by the nationwide storytelling community.

The subject was debated in heated and sometimes divisive forums at storytelling festivals, conferences, and guilds around the country, culminating in a long, hard day of discussion at the St. Louis congress. Transcripts of a series of the forums, including the one at the congress, were printed in the fall 1987 issue of the *National Storytelling Journal,* along with exchanges of letters on the subject (see Stewart, ed., "Ethics and Storytelling"; Bausman; Twillmann; and Sobol, "Storytelling Ethics").

This is not a place to enter into the intricacies of the proposals and counterproposals advanced. What is significant is the degree to which the entire debate sparked feelings of violation in the community. The very notion of a legalistic "code" of ethics struck at the heart of the spontaneous communitas on which many had come to depend. To even suggest such a code seemed to certify that the cherished communitas itself, built on the blissfully boundless sharing of oral tradition, was insufficient to prevent thievery, mistrust, and betrayal. May recalled the journey from innocence to experience that the ethics controversy forced him to take:

[The Washington College Conference] gave the false impression, actually—I think it was a false impression—that it was a much tighter and
sharing community among professional storytellers than in fact I think
it really was. I think being there, and then actually starting to tell stories;
and then, when I started to get to know people better and getting to
know them at festivals, and hearing how *scared* everybody was of having
their stories stolen; and all those disputes and stuff—I found that I had
romanticized the community. Which is probably typical of me.

After the first congress, another storyteller wrote to the *National Storytelling Journal:*

Following our morning session on ethics, I left feeling the way I did the
day I found out Santa Claus was not a real being. There were feelings of
disappointment, guilt, shock, worry. . . . All of a sudden the basic draw of
storytelling for me—that "grass roots" feeling so hard to verbalize, the
naturalness of it, the smooth flow of the words as they tumble from my
mouth—that appeal of storytelling was getting tossed around and torn
apart as words such as *copyright, infringement, mine, yours, compensation*
came out with such force from some fellow storytellers' statements. I
honestly felt by 1:00 this afternoon that I was going to probably get out
of storytelling entirely. . . . (Twillmann 2)

The storyteller did manage to fight off her despair; her letter proceed-
ed in true storytelling style to enumerate her magical helpers ("the en-
raptured audiences, the smiles my storytelling would bring, the questions and input from both old and young after they had listened to one
of my sessions, the flow of creative and imaginative minds" [2]), each a
reimmersion in the affect-world of spontaneous, right-brained "flow."
But the threat posed by this imposition of normative structure on revival
communitas had clearly shaken her deeply, as it must have shaken the
teller who wrote, "Unlike other storytelling events I have attended, I
didn't leave the National Storytelling Congress with new energy: I left
feeling very drained. I didn't leave with lots of answers, in fact, I left with
more questions than I had come with. But what I did leave with was a
very strong sense of belonging to the greater 'community' of storytelling. And inherent in that concept is the feeling of having a responsibility to that community, to other storytellers, and to the stories I pass
along" (Bausman 27).

There was a consensus in the storytelling world that ethical concerns
needed to be addressed and scruples strengthened. The legislative action
befitting a "congress," however, left many cold. No single ethical code was

ever formally adopted, though the debate spurred both individuals and local groups to reconsider and reformulate their own (a particularly thoughtful and balanced example is the statement compiled by the West Coast tellers Barbara Griffen, Olga Loya, Sandra MacLees, Nancy Schimmel, Harlynne Geisler, and Kathleen Zundell, which was reprinted in David Holt and William Mooney's *Storyteller's Guide*, 97).

For Horner, "The first congress was a victory. . . . There was a conscious effort to make a break from the idea that the board will not look at what was happening around the country. That to me was the most exciting one, and was the true congress. . . . It was totally a political event." For Wellner, it was a victory, too, in retrospect:

> There were some very serious issues that came up, and some very serious, gut-level disagreements. But it was a forum for it. People could leave still being friends. And of course the test of that is, could you tease people about their position, and have them laugh. And that happened. So even though there were people who were frightened by the first couple of congresses, and left thinking, I don't know, this is pretty serious stuff—maybe I'd better not do this—still people were left with a sense of responsibility, but also the knowledge that we were in it as a group.

Santa Fe: The Congress on Cultural Diversity

The ethical crisis in the storytelling world that surfaced so powerfully at St. Louis only deepened during the second congress, held in Santa Fe, New Mexico, in June 1988. Where the conflict at the first congress remained within the tribe of storytellers and focused on their too facile borrowing from one another, the challenge at Santa Fe came from some of the actual tribes and ethnic groups from which revivalist storytellers were borrowing folktales to form the scenery of their utopia. Storyteller-activists from African American, Hispanic, Jewish, and particularly Native American backgrounds made a point of telling the storytellers from other groups that they were not gratified to hear their cultural property so blithely appropriated.

As with the infamous "Blood on the Porch" story-swap, the first two congresses revealed the extent to which the zeitgeist of the eighties had overtaken the innocent seventies in the storytelling movement. The real storytelling nightmare was not just the specter of blood on the sharing porch. There suddenly arose a vision of the ancient, archetypal storytelling tribe invaded and colonized by a new strain of young urban profes-

sionals—tense, driven, middle-class wannabees acquiring homely folk-tales from marginalized culture-groups (or copying them from one another) and retailing them for personal gain like exotic decorative objects for the performing ego.
Wellner recalled:

> There was the sense at that Santa Fe congress that we white kids were there being told by the *real* ethnics that what we were doing was bad, and we should cut it out. But we needed to hear that, too. There was a lot of bad storytelling going on in the name of multiculturalism. And we were forced to face some of that, as a community. So it was really good. But I remember, ooh, what a downer it was. I remember at the end of the congress, people coming up to me and saying, "I think I'll quit storytelling." Or "I'm never going to come to another NAPPS event—this is too heavy." Or, "I've lost my entire repertoire—I've got to start over again!"
>
> I'll tell you what characterized it for me and said that it was an important event. That Saturday night, the storytelling was done by a regional group. There were people from all around a very large region. And during the course of the evening, some of the stories that were told were perfect examples of the kinds of things that we had been hearing, all Friday night and all day Saturday, that we should never do.
>
> There was a lot of discomfort in the audience. 'Cause people were thinking, "Uh-oh! That's what this is about!" We were hearing white guys get up there and tell stories, with all good intentions, and told very competently—but now we were asking ourselves very serious cultural questions. About, is this really cultural imperialism? Are we raping these cultures by the ways we're using these stories? A lot of people's storytelling lives were changed irrevocably. But probably for the better. Because I don't think a lot of us in the storytelling community had asked ourselves the questions we needed to ask.

Armed only with a sword of spiritual optimism and the works of Joseph Campbell for an intellectual shield, revival storytellers had ventured into the oral traditions of the world, taking freely from whatever versions caught their fancies. This attitude had been wonderfully liberating, for a while. It seemed as if the cultural treasures of all times and places were at our command, simply by virtue of membership in the universal brother/sisterhood of storytellers. It was an intoxicating draught, in relief of the cultural desert that plagues the American spirit. Yet after the first two congresses, storytelling seemed much more serious and perilous a business. It now seemed more akin to a descent into Aladdin's cave: there were treasures that glinted on every hand, but revivalist tellers were warned against touching any but the ones that would form their own particular lamp.

One outcome of the first two congresses was a dramatic shift in the repertoires of many professional storytellers away from traditional folk-tales and toward original, personal experience stories. In part, this can be traced to the influence of such tellers as Spalding Gray, Garrison Keillor, or Donald Davis, who demonstrated that these kinds of stories are accessible and powerful to adult audiences. But it can also be seen as a reaction to the ethics controversies—personal stories are both easier to claim ownership of and harder to steal. They belong to the teller personally in ways that folktales rarely can. As such, they demonstrate respect for the injunctions of the ethnic activists at Santa Fe, who told the community, "Find your own stories; don't rely on ours."

In a developmental sense, the turn toward personal stories was also a kind of individuation process for the community. Wonder tales, fool tales, trickster tales, and legends all come from the communal dreamworld of the preliterate mind. They are packed with unconscious, transferential metaphors that help an innocent sensibility adjust to the dilemmas of the world without confronting it too directly with operations it cannot accept. The revival's fascination with folklore had that kind of childlike, remedial, even fetishistic quality. It helped people of a wide range of ages assimilate new spiritual teachings, psychological understandings, life-style changes, and gender-role questionings. But at a certain point in the assimilation process, a different kind reality testing set in. Storytellers began to notice that teen-agers and adults would tend to listen more intently to "true" stories—or stories that could be told or accepted as actual. It seems that the shadow forces of maturity demand to be faced directly, with our mundane selves as the last accessible metaphoric buffers. As W. B. Yeats wrote in "The Circus Animals' Desertion," near the end of a lifetime spent creating metaphoric "ladders" out of ancient Irish myths and legends:

. . . Now that my ladder's gone
I must lie down where all the ladders start,
In the foul rag-and-bone shop of the heart.

"The Storytelling Ethos Blues"

In 1989, the National Storytelling Congress moved back east, to Raleigh, North Carolina, where the theme was "Storytelling and the Performing

Arts." Workshops and symposia at Raleigh covered the integration of storytelling with music, theater, mime, and dance. The theme and the event might have taken the ascendancy of the performer-storyteller head-on, but it never developed the heavy negative charge of the two previous congresses—partly because teachers and librarians are less volatile than either free-lance professionals or ethnic activists, partly because everyone was exhausted, and partly because the closet of shadow issues had begun to empty. The wars of the Reformation were winding down.

Wellner, who was still a NAPPS board member, contributed a song called "The Storytelling Ethos Blues," which was sung at the beginning and the end of the Raleigh congress. In typical community fashion, it served as a ritual outlet for the gathering to release tensions of the past few years:

Oh, it started out in St. Louis, MO,
When they told me stealing stories had to go.
I saw my whole repertoire wink out like a star,
And for months I was feeling so low.

Chorus:
I've got the storytelling ethos blues,
And I'm trying to pay my dues.
I stay up late at night feeling very uptight,
I've got the storytelling ethos blues.

Well then I travelled down to Santa Fe
To keep them storytelling demons at bay.
I was telling tales from China, Iran, and North Carolina,
Till they said I had to mend my ways.

Chorus

Now I'm sitting here in Raleigh, NC
Just as blue as I can be.
I don't sing, I don't dance, I don't do perform*ance*
I just tell tales my daddy told me.

Chorus

But a new day is dawning for me,
'Cause since I met you I can see
We're all in the same boat, and we can keep it afloat
With friendship and integrity.

Chorus. . . .

The tune was a rolling, minor-key lament, akin to the Great Depression classic "Buddy Can You Spare a Dime?" or Pete Seeger's Vietnam-era "Waist Deep in the Big Muddy." It stylized the tribulations of the movement's confrontation with its shadow, while maintaining its penchant for happy endings. For the next two congresses—the Congress on Storytelling and the Electronic Media, held in St. Paul in 1990, and the Congress on Storytelling and Education, held in Connecticut in 1991—"The Storytelling Ethos Blues" was hollered out with modest musicality but exemplary vigor to open and close the gatherings, with hastily contrived verses added to set up each year's theme. It was an invented tradition that fulfilled its purpose relatively quickly and expired unmourned with the reabsorption of the National Storytelling Congress into the reformed National Storytelling Conference in 1992.

Although the event gradually shifted into the mode of an ordinary professional conference, its format was still less hierarchical and far less mythic than the earlier NAPPS conferences. A wider variety of workshops was offered, on themes and at sites that would change yearly, by leaders who were now framed as peers instead of masters. Regional caucuses were continued, and there was a movement toward affinity caucuses of the various kinds of story-users in the association—teachers, librarians, therapists, ministers, and free-lance performers. Caucuses and the expansion of the board to a nationally representative body, which was accomplished by 1991, put all regions and affinities on a more equal footing within NAPPS.

This came as something of a shock to some free-lance performers, who discovered that casual story-boosters now heavily outnumbered them in the membership. The NAPPS publications shifted to accommodate this new one-member-one-vote policy. The elegantly appointed *National Storytelling Journal,* once so strongly an organ of the *revival movement* and its most passionate and serious devotees, metamorphosed in 1989 into the smiley-faced *Storytelling Magazine,* which hired professional, free-lance writers, not storytellers, to fill its pages. The tone changed to a chatty buffet of subject surveys, personality pieces, and reprints from popular books and articles—what some dissidents have called a "Storytelling U.S.A. Today" approach. The magazine, for better or worse, strove to represent storytelling revived, as an art and a profession like many others, with its own bright space on the rack of popular culture.

The process for being selected to perform at the festival or to lead workshops at the congress or conference also was rationalized. Applications and proposals would now be submitted to the NAPPS staff—not the board—which was substantially enlarged to handle the increased workload. When the board let go of the reins of festival programming, it marked a conclusive shift in the way the charisma-generating cycle operated for the festival and, by reflection, for the entire storytelling world. Gay Ducey, a board member from Berkeley, California, recalled the decision:

> We took a whole year to study it and think about it and fuss over it, kind of anguish over it; and also get excited. When we finally met, the executive committee met, which of course was almost half the board—we met at Donald's church. And we sat and hammered the proposal which I had submitted to the board for that meeting, and the proposal which Jimmy Neil had submitted. And when we got to the part about the festival, I—short-sighted, looking back—said, "This is going to be the hardest thing for the board to give up. They will not—no one will wish to give up both the power and the responsibility that comes with making the choices. And this is what I propose. . . ." And I can't remember now precisely what it was, except I think I proposed that Jimmy Neil be assisted by a third of the board each year, in making the decision, so that the board would have input and he would have input, but that at no time would any particular quarter of the board be able to garner the power to make or break the festival. A fairly wise political maneuver, but as it turned out, an infinitely unwise take on what was really happening.
>
> Because, inevitably, what the board did was, the board said, "You know what? We're telling ourselves that program belongs to staff. And if they do a good job, then we've done a good job by hiring them. And if they don't do a good job, then we need to think about how we can help them do a better job. Because, you know, we employ them. So let's give it to them."

Though all the board members participated in the changes, Gay Ducey is given much credit for the grace with which they were accomplished. Ducey had been the director of a social work agency before she became a storyteller. She came on the board in 1987 to fill the unexpired term of Laura Simms. Horner said, "When Gay came on the board, things started changing. But nobody could deny that she had organizational experience that they didn't have." Clare Cuddy said that Ducey "put a lot of shape and structure to the opening up that had been going on; and I think really pulled it up into a professional arena. Simple things, like redoing bylaws, and Robert's rules of order. Committee work." Milbre Burch recalled, "The boards that I have sat on for the organization have been remarkable. And the most remarkable person has been Gay, in her leadership. Because she really is able to combine a sense of the rules and fair play, with this tremendous sense of justice. And an ability to listen."

When Davis's term as chair of the board expired in 1989, Ducey was elected to succeed him. She was the first NAPPS board chair, apart from Smith, who had not established herself as a teller through performing at the national festival. She was also the first, in a sense, who was not a member of the Jonesborough support group. There was thus a distinct separation between the work she did for the organization and the art and for her own performing career. The charisma loop between the board, the festival, and the site was finally broken.

No account of the difficult path to the preservation and perpetuation of NAPPS can fail to consider the role of Jimmy Neil Smith, its founder, namer, and executive director throughout most of its history. He is certainly the single most constant, unifying influence on the association. Yet he has consistently remained in the background, guiding, directing, organizing, promoting, but always pushing others forward into the national spotlight.

There is no doubt that if Smith had not developed the high level of commitment that he has shown to contemporary storytelling, to NAPPS, and to promoting its synergistic relationship with his hometown, the movement would have followed a very different course. Just what sparked Smith's passionate relationship with the art form is something of a mystery. He still earnestly proclaims that he is "not a storyteller, but a businessman." Yet he was also a teacher, a writer, a publicist, and a regional activist before he conceived the storytelling festival. The movement seems to have given him, like many other storytelling revivalists, a way to incarnate all of his gifts and drives.

Smith can be likened to the early founders of Nashville's Grand Ole Opry (see Hurst 64–92, 126–41; and Wolfe) or to Bascom Lamar Lunceford, who founded Asheville's Mountain Dance and Folk Festival (Whisnant, "Finding the Way" 135–54). He is a university-educated, restlessly ambitious southerner who combines professional-class status with strong emotional ties to his folk roots. Like Lunceford or Edward Craig, the Nashville insurance executive who had a passion for bringing folk music to the brand new medium of radio, Smith has developed a frame that identifies his town with a characteristic folk performance and magnifies it through modern public relations and technological skills. In so doing, he has contrived to elevate both—folk art and hometown—to a national platform. NSA and the national revival of storytelling form the signature story that Smith has shaped and told the world for years. It is a story that has literally cast as powerful a spell over the crowd as the folktale repertoire itself.

As a leader, Smith has shown an extraordinary ability to hear and adapt to the needs of the national membership while still maintaining his own local and regional agenda. It has often been a struggle for him, as it has been for the members of the board. He has had to deal with political opponents' charges that he has run the town for the benefit of NAPPS—even as he has faced NAPPS members' rumblings that he has run NAPPS for the benefit of the town. Even Smith's close friends have had to wonder where the balance lies. Carolyn Moore commented:

> The town has a bad habit—we find that it is very difficult to make a distinction between what Jimmy is doing and what NAPPS is doing. And one of the problems of economics that exists in the town now—I think we are, most of us, aware that any time a board of directors wants to move something, they can. Because we've had plants close all over the area, or the Japanese come up and buy it. So that NAPPS has become . . . it's become an industry, and it's not necessarily so local. If there is an Appalachian fear, it is that you all will go away and we will still be left.
>
> But the thing of it is, if you get us going paranoid as Appalachians: if Jonesborough loses its charm, then Jonesborough in essence loses $196,000 in the media tent in three days. And that is staggeringly impressive.

When I recalled her comment to Smith, he was incredulous that anyone could imagine NAPPS's leaving Jonesborough. In fact, storytelling has become intertwined with both the public face and revenue base of the town. In 1993, according to the *Yarnspinner,* the organization took a lease on the Chester Inn, the largest historic property in the downtown district, and most of the lease's value was donated by the town and the state of Tennessee. It has also purchased two adjacent properties, to develop and expand its local center with a projected performance space and storytelling museum. Smith's wife, Jean, commented:

> I think it's interesting that a nonprofit organization, if things happen the way Jimmy wants them to, can at one point own an entire block of a town that only has four thousand people in it. Tourism is their mode of survival. And they've got that whole city block tied up in a nonprofit or-

ganization—which could be a tax revenue-generating business for the town of Jonesborough. I just think it's interesting. Because I daresay there wouldn't be another town that would have that large a proportion of its space taken up by an arts organization. And *if* they get the buildings that they want, and *if* they build the theater where they want it to be built, it will be really interesting. Especially to all those students in city planning. They're gonna say, "Well, that can't work! You can't take your prime property, downtown, and give it to an *arts organization!*" And yet. . . .

And yet, for all the diversification of the movement over the past decade, the National Storytelling Festival and its symbolic site in Jonesborough remain intertwined with the public face and the internal prestige patterns of the storytelling world. Jonesborough has made itself indispensable to that world, as Jimmy Neil Smith has made himself indispensable to the association. Until the very late stages of this project, I had heard not so much as a murmur of a move to separate the festival from its home in Tennessee. In 1997, this began to change, because of NSA's absorption with its building projects to the neglect of its membership's immediate needs. There is growing talk of splitting the organization into a membership branch and a separate "foundation," dedicated to fund-raising for the building and maintenance of the Jonesborough "Center." In the latter stages of a revival movement, real estate develops an agency of its own. But the thought of moving the festival still seems heretic to many, comparable to moving the Grand Ole Opry out of Nashville or the Roman Catholic church out of Rome.

Beth Horner recalled her six-year tenure on the board, ending in 1992, with an image that encapsulated the transition from the intimacy of a tribe to the complexity of a nation: "By the time I finished on the board, we were getting these massive, organized books from Jimmy, before we attend the board meeting. And everything is done in committee *outside* the board meeting. My first board meeting, we were just around this little table. And by my last board meeting, we were around this *hu-u-u-mongous table*—all of these little tables put together."

"Things Grow and Expand"

As for the National Storytelling Festival, a certain leveling off of interest, passion, and growth could be detected as the festival reached this stage. Some enthusiasts who had come to the movement for its intimacy and

sense of family began to drift away. Simply by virtue of scale, the cathar-
tic ritual of the event began to be overshadowed by production and entertainment. The liminal form of the festival, too, even as it was crystal-
lizing, began to be obscured by the alterations necessary to accommodate
the masses. In 1986, the ghost storytelling in the cemetery was replaced
by a mammoth "Storytelling Showcase" at Freedom Hall, the civic auditorium in Johnson City. The intimate figure of the homespun storyteller
was reduced to a tiny swatch on a giant stage framed by massive stacks of
P.A. equipment. The festival had circled back to where it began, with Jerry Clower at the Davy Crockett High School, and, as Regan-Blake said of
that night, it was "like TV. . . . it was gone when it was gone" (telephone
interview, January 21, 1992).

After that experiment, the Saturday evening performances were returned
to Jonesborough in 1987, with ghost stories in all of the tents, to safely contain the crowds. But that was the year that the sacred telling on Sunday
morning was scuttled, in a board of directors' battle over whether it was
possible to have a "sacred" storytelling at all without reference to any particular religious tradition. After a popular outcry, the "tradition" of the sacred telling was restored the following year, but it was in two tents instead
of one, at which point the sacred telling took on a bit more of the sense of
an ordinary storytelling olio. The choice of tents diluted the sense of communal obligation that had been a part of the rite—made it less liminal, more
typically liminoid. The single tent was restored in 1989 and 1990; in 1991,
there were two again. In 1992, the twentieth anniversary of the festival, all
the featured tellers from previous years were invited back—more than ninety came. The Saturday night ghost telling was held in the Mill Stream Park,
with olios concurrently going on in each of the seven separate tents. The
sacred telling was scheduled in four large tents on Sunday morning. Attendance was projected at over ten thousand people.

But the economic contractions of the nineties, along with a rain-
dampened attendance on Sunday, left the organization and the festival
seriously in debt. After severe staff cuts and other belt-tightening measures, the festival returned in 1993 to its earlier form. Registration leveled off at 7,500, down from 1992 but up from 1991, and according to
NAPPS staffers, their "economic recovery plan" seemed to be holding.
By 1997, the staff had rebounded considerably. The organization had
plunged ahead with plans to tear down the old hardware store and gro-
cery adjacent to the Chester Inn, as well as the Dinner Bell restaurant in
the rear, and to build a national headquarters complex that would in-

clude permanent performance spaces, a storytelling museum, restaurants, and a wall of fame.

Kathryn Windham told me:

> I still stand in awe and amazement, each time I go to Jonesborough, at the variety, and, well, just the sheer numbers of people who are attracted there. But I keep wanting them to feel some warmth, and even some love. And I think that's what's missing in some of our storytelling. That there are so many people in the audience, that you can't let each one of 'em know how much you care about 'em. It's become so professional. And so slick, and so much audio, and so much, "Let's go off and meditate before we tell stories." And all that kind of—that's not what storytelling is! Storytelling is natural and simple and fun. And we're spoiling it. And it grieves me. I don't think what we do up there at Jonesborough now is real storytelling—that's performing. And I think there's a vast difference. I might as well sit at home and watch television as to be in the back of a tent with two thousand people.

Simms spoke of it in a more detached tone:

> It was really interesting for me to be at the NAPPS festival this year [1991]. It was really different, because there were very few people I recognized in the audience. And I had changed a great deal as well.
> There are thousands and thousands of people coming. And you still meet lots of people. But there are a lot of tourists, fascinated and curious about storytelling. It was a very personal festival for all of us, don't you think, in the years past, where it mostly was people really who wanted to be storytellers, who told stories in schools and such. It had a kind of secret intimacy to it, and depth. [Now] there's corporate sponsorship, and bigger and bigger tents. I would say that the core of one or two thousand people at the festival are really story devotees, and the other four thousand people are coming for a good time. And they get a good time. It's great that they have a chance to listen. (telephone interview, December 23, 1991)

The telephone line went silent for a moment, her thoughts drifting to the ideal village that her own youth's passionate longing had once helped conjure into being. "But it's inevitable," she concluded, shaking it off. "Things grow and expand."

O Brave New World

Sitting in on a NAPPS board meeting in April of 1992, I witnessed one of those moments when a brave new world comes into view. A member of the expanded, fifteen-member board raised a hand to ask about the name: "When I call the office, you answer the phone, 'National Storytelling Resource Center.' Why? What is our name, anyway?"

A staff person tried to explain: to answer the phone, "NAPPS," would be too mysterious; "National Association for the Preservation and Perpetuation of Storytelling," too time-consuming for a cold caller.

"Then why don't we call ourselves the "National Storytelling Association," or something?" she demanded. "If we can't answer our own phone with our own name, what's the point?"

Before my eyes a wave of rationality swept the table. Voice after voice chimed in, "Yeah, yeah, what's the point? Why not 'National Storytelling Association?'" Finally Gay Ducey, judicious soul that she is, stepped in. "A name," she said, "is a powerful thing. Perhaps it *is* time to let go of NAPPS and to go to something simpler, like 'National Storytelling Association.'" "But for now," she said, "I'm going to take it upon myself to table this motion."

Two years later, the following announcement reached my desk:

After almost two decades of being known as the National Association for the Preservation and Perpetuation of Storytelling, the association's board voted unanimously to change the organization's name.

NAPPS is now the National Storytelling Association. . . .

"NAPPS's name, once considered catchy and cute, is no longer as useful to the association as it once was," said Jimmy Neil Smith, the association's executive director who gave the organization its name in 1975. "Today, the full name often hinders us from gaining true credibility as an important national organization."

In the 1992 membership survey, only 18 percent of NSA's members were opposed to the name change. The remaining 82 percent agreed with changing the name or didn't care.

"I think the name change reflects the maturing of America's storytelling revival and the association which supports and nurtures the movement," added Smith. "Our agenda is changing, and to be effective in national, even international advocacy programs, we must present the most positive, professional image possible." ("The Name Is Changed" 1)

The Storytelling Revival is dead. Long live the Storytelling Revival.

7

Stories and Morals: Reflections on an American Revival

What, now, is the result of the miraculous passage
and return?
—Joseph Campbell, *The Hero with
a Thousand Faces*

In 1991, Lee Pennington reflected on his first experiences at Jonesborough, back in 1974 and 1975:

It was so new at that moment, one wondered, will it last a year, or five years, or what. Somewhere shortly after that, I think, I predicted, I made the association that storytelling was doing approximately the same thing that folk music had done in America. Starting in the forties, probably most apparently with the Weavers, and then culminating at Woodstock. And I suggested that somewhere along the way, probably two or three years along, that storytelling would have a similar sort of renaissance. In fact I predicted that somewhere about fifteen years we would have our Woodstock. It doesn't seem to be. The renaissance seems to be developing as several of us saw it developing, but I think the staying power of it is at least apparently much stronger than I guessed it would be.

Perhaps, though, the rainy Sunday of the twentieth National Storytelling Festival in 1992, coming on the heels of the "Blood on the Porch" conference and the first contentious congresses, served as a subtle analogue to events at Newport, Woodstock, and Altamont that revealed the exploded seams of the folk music movement. This was an annunciation as quiet as the rain, for the nature of the storytelling medium gave this folk revival a far gentler public profile than its predecessor had. As always, it was less confrontational, less volatile, less amenable to the melodramatic projections of mass media. Early on, Lee Pennington had a clue as to why it would be so:

[In 1975 or 1976] I was standing out in front of the log house right before the festival started; and Jimmy Neil came runnin' out and said, "Here, come here and take this telephone call." Said, "It's CBS Evening News and they want a story."
And I said, "Okay." So I ran in there, and—
I don't remember who the reporter was, but he said, "This is CBS Evening News," and said, "we want to do a story on the news."
And I said, "Well, alright," I said, "We'll try that." And I said, "What do you have in mind?"
And he said, "Well, I'd like a Jack tale."
And I said, "How much time have I got?"
And he said, "Twenty-six seconds."
And I said, "The shortest Jack tale I know, I could probably pull it off in ten minutes."
And he said, "Well, could you just give me an outline?"
And I said, "No, I don't think a Jack tale's going to work."

The crucial works at the core of the storytelling revival have simply been too expansive, too demanding of imaginative over sensual apprehension—the medium itself too inward, quiescent, and thus stubbornly esoteric—to be fully metabolized by electronic media. Consider that the biggest "crossover stars" the movement has produced are a former *New Yorker* parodist and public radio voice (Garrison Keillor), a veteran of the New York avant-garde theater scene of the sixties (Spalding Gray), a poet turned performing polemicist (Robert Bly), an elderly retired college professor (the late Joseph Campbell), and a fast-talking former fertilizer salesman (Jerry Clower)—all of whom operated independently of the Jonesborough storytelling world but nourished and were fed by the same hunger for fresh cultural root matter. It clarifies for us the resistance of the entire enterprise to the kind of runaway iconization that seized and transfigured folk music popularizers, from Jimmy Rodgers to Elvis, Dylan to the Grateful Dead.

When the storytelling movement finally reached a public plateau and its chief institution began to wobble, to struggle for survival, and to grasp at institutional camouflage and self-commemoration to sustain itself, the precipitating event was no riot or bachanalia—only a quieter-than-expected Sunday morning with too many featured storytellers to go around. But the movement's very failure to precipitate either mass catharsis or catastrophe is also perhaps its best hope for a graceful aging.

"Structure and Anti-Structure"

Victor Turner's reflections in *The Ritual Process,* published in 1969 when the turbulent zeitgeist was still very much directed toward overthrowing social structural constraints, still hold valuable perspectives to students of the storytelling movement. As a seasoned anthropologist, he wrote about the difference between a revivalist ideal of preindustrial communitas and the actual phenomena he had observed in the field:

> The often made etymological homology between the nouns "existence" and "ecstasy" is pertinent here; to exist is to "stand outside"—i.e., to stand outside the totality of structural positions one normally occupies in a social system. To exist is to be in ecstasy. But, for the hippies—as indeed for many millenarian and "enthusiastic" movements—the ecstasy of spontaneous communitas is seen as *the* end of human endeavor. In the religion of preindustrial societies, this state is regarded rather as a means to the end of becoming more fully involved in the rich manifold of structural role-playing. (138–39)

In an argument clearly directed to the contemporary needs of his students and colleagues, Turner conceives of the impulse toward unstructured communitas as a complementary and dialectical phase of the impulse toward perduring social structure—or, as the subtitle of his book would have it, "structure and anti-structure." Both impulses must be accommodated, he suggests, in any functioning community or any functioning theory or account of community. His warnings about the inevitable human drive for structure in communal relations and the perils of ignoring that drive in the romantic search for ecstatic union ring true to the experiences of storytelling revivalists in the eighties:

> Once more we come back to the necessity of seeing man's social life as a process, or rather as a multiplicity of processes, in which the character of one type of phase—where communitas is paramount—differs deeply, even abyssally, from that of all others. The great human temptation, found most prominently among utopians, is to resist giving up the good and pleasurable qualities of that one phase to make way for what may be the necessary hardships and dangers of the next. Spontaneous communitas is richly charged with affects, mainly pleasurable ones. Life in

"structure" is filled with objective difficulties: decisions have to be made, inclinations sacrificed to the wishes and needs of the group, and physical and social obstacles overcome at some personal cost. (139)

Turner's comments vividly evoke the tensile opposition between the serendipitous joy of a revival movement in its days of discovery and the organizational struggles and practical sacrifices necessary for it to grow and establish itself in the culture:

> Spontaneous communitas has something "magic" about it. Subjectively there is in it the feeling of endless power. But this power untransformed cannot readily be applied to the organizational details of social existence. It is no substitute for lucid thought and sustained will. On the other hand, structural action swiftly becomes arid and mechanical if those involved in it are not periodically immersed in the regenerative abyss of communitas. Wisdom is always to find the appropriate relationship between structure and communitas under the *given* circumstances of time and place, to accept each modality when it is paramount without rejecting the other, and not to cling to one when its present impulse is spent. (139)

It is an abiding ideological temptation for critics of folk revivalism to overemphasize the extent to which the consumer capitalist matrix of the storytelling movement determined its descent into structure. Without that matrix, we might think, there would be no need to create hierarchies of professional performers or to submit to the inflationary clutches of booking agents or those fancied cliques of storytelling Svengalis at NSA headquarters, whose priorities keep returning to the bottom line. These forces certainly influenced the movement, by providing molds into which it grew. Turner reminds us, however, from his own experience among the Tallensi, the Ashanti, the Nuer, the Ndembu, and others, that status hierarchies are not the invention of the modern festival promoter—preindustrial societies, too, function largely on the basis of differentiated and rigidly enforced hierarchies of status and prestige, with ritual interludes of festival, carnival, passage, and healing to restore (and contain) protean communitas. The storytelling revival community, in its rapid development, echoed some of these earlier, tribal, and "magical" forms of charismatic hierarchy, even as it swiftly outgrew them to pass into a modern organizational structure, in which charisma is decentralized and diffused.

Turner rebukes his romantic predecessors and colleagues for succumbing to "the error made by such thinkers as Rousseau and Marx: the confusion between communitas, which is a dimension of all societies, past and present, and archaic or primitive societies." He continues:

> Yet as most anthropologists would now confirm, customary norms and differences of status and prestige in preliterate societies allow of little scope for individual liberty and choice—the individualist is often regarded as a witch. . . . Membership of rivalrous segments in such societies as the Tallensi, Nuer, and Tiv does not allow even of tribal brotherhood: such membership commits the individual to structure and to the conflicts that are inseparable from structural differentiation. However, even in the simplest societies, the distinction between structure and communitas exists and obtains symbolic expression. . . . In different societies and in different periods, one or the other of these "immortal antagonists" (to borrow terms that Freud used in a different sense) comes uppermost. But together they constitute the "human condition," as regards man's relations with his fellow man. (130)

Such are lessons that the flying boys and girls of the storytelling revival—who cast away constraints that they might spend their lives at a festival—are now confronting, or avoiding at peril.

"Stolen Language"

Roland Barthes claims that myth is an inherent pathology of language and, through language, thought. If this is so, it may be equally true that the cure is inherent in the disease. Mythic speech is a traditional way of knowing at every level, from those of the journalists, advertisers, and imperialists that are Barthes's bugbears to those of the scholastics, contemplatives, mystics and bards. It has always been the province of storytellers. To concentrate meanings in an image is precisely to contemplate the archetypal realm, where images unfold themselves into stories—pattern themselves like smoke from a lamp into beginnings, middles, and endings—only to vanish back into the void from which their meanings have been drawn.

The liberating outcome of a myth, as of a piece of music or a storytelling, is in the moment of completion. But how is it completed? In the days of its power over a cultural group, myth is completed in *performance,* whether through the medium of narrative or ritual. Completion of a myth is not the same as finishing, any more than a completed act of love finishes a marriage. But there has to be—the myth demands—performance, descent into form, with an energetic trajectory and resolution of the drama or the story that fulfills the mythic appetite of the group and renews it for another cycle. Properly performed, the myth achieves a wholeness and intensity according to its own formal laws, without exhausting its symbolic resonance. At the climax, the performer stands aside. In the vacuum so created, the form clings tightly to the silence of the mind for one bright instant, before dissolving into light. It may seem a great deal of work to expend on that small reward, but that small reward contains the universe. As Laura Simms told me, "We endlessly are creating stories, which are lies. And that's the work of the mind. And it is only through story that you can explode that. So the deeper level of story is definitely in the telling: in the mind-to-mind transmission of the story, which undoes conceptual thinking and creates timelessness, in the moment" (December 22, 1991).

In *The Tourist,* Dean MacCannell constructs his "dialectics of authenticity"—in which the socially constructed opposition of authentic and inauthentic experience becomes the motivating ground of the modern search for self, as revealed by MacCannell through the rituals of tourism. These dialectics of authenticity provide a ground for my revival dialectic of the idealized (authentic) past and future and the wounded (inauthentic) present. At the same time, his discussion illuminates the ways that institutionalized representations of authenticity become implicated in the reproduction of inauthentic experience—which starts the dialectical process pumping all over again. This course description from NAPPS's 1984 *National School of Storytelling* brochure could have come directly from MacCannell's own catalogue of illustrations:

> LIVING THE STORYTELLING TRADITION. . . . What could be more fascinating than to travel into the hotbed of storytelling tradition, to experience first-hand the lives and stories of some of our most revered traditional storytellers? Nothing, of course, especially when your guide is the personable Doc McConnell. . . . Doc will board a van with participants and journey into the tree-covered mountains of North Carolina to visit the likes of Ray Hicks, Stanley Hicks, and Bobby MacMillan, right in their own homes. . . . If you value tradition and authenticity in storytelling, you won't want to miss this special weekend.

The "authenticity" of the longing this excursion was meant to satisfy only sharpens our need to question the stereotypical process by which it was commodified. John D. Dorst carries MacCannell's analysis into the labyrinth of representations around a particular touristic site but weaves into it the subsequent threads of postmodernist critical discourse. His theoretical contributions force us to assess the degree of self-consciousness involved in Jonesborough's postindustrial transformation of a community-centered folk art into a medium of import-export trade. Dorst's critique of Chadds Ford, Pennsylvania, which promotes itself as the home of the Wyeth family and fountainhead of the Brandywine River School of visual arts, could apply equally well to Jonesborough:

> I have made much of Chadds Ford's self-referentiality and auto-ethnographic self-inscription. But this is not to say that these controlling processes of reproduction and self-citation are "aware" of themselves as processes. One might go so far as to suggest that the ideological efficacy of Chadds Ford depends upon a misrecognition of itself. The obvious changes that have occurred there over the last twenty-five years can be couched in the familiar "machine in the garden" terms of the encroachment of the modern world on rural, village life, or be perceived as the depredations of industry and suburbanization, and so on. But it simply would not do for Chadds Ford cultural production to theorize its own postmodernity, that is, become fully conscious of its own textuality. Were it to do so, Chadds Ford would have to be categorized as a different kind of postmodern Site than the one I am attempting to depict in this study. The closest approximation we have to this other kind of Site, one that is not only infinitely self-referential but also capable of textualizing (and commodifying) even this very awareness, is the theme park. . . . Chadds Ford is a species of postmodern Site for which we have no good name but that might be described as like a theme park minus the self-consciousness. One symptom of this lack of detachment is the seeming absence of a self-directed sense of humor in Chadds Ford's cultural production. For the most part Chadds Ford takes itself quite seriously. (115)

Jonesborough can be seen as part of a continuum of regional responses to socioeconomic transformation, specifically those responses that use local cultural resources as their economic fuel. A couple hours' drive down the Blue Ridge from Jonesborough, on the edge of the Great Smoky Mountains National Park, are the theme park communities of Gatlinburg and Pigeon Forge, home of "Dollywood." And a couple of hours north along the Cumberland Plateau, straddling the Kentucky-Virginia border, is the town of Whitesburg, home of Roadside Theater and the Appalachian nationalist media arts cooperative Appalshop. The political ideologies of these enterprises, the degree of their embrace of venture capital, and their mode of intervention in the physical environment may diverge, yet they share some fundamental impulses in common. All three communities are involved in retailing the traditions, the histories, and the folklife of their land and people, and all three are implicated in an ongoing struggle for control of the rights to those histories: who will be the tellers and the audiences, what will be the media in which the stories are set, what versions will endure and which be buried, and who will reap the royalties from the tellings? As a longtime core member of Roadside Theater told me:

> What you have to do today, though—and that's what Roadside Theater started doing—was creating the social environment that allowed the telling of the stories. But now you have to create the event. The deliberate construction comes primarily because of the changing social environment. The intention and the style and the material and the connection to the environment, because of our own personal identities and our connection to that living environment, and our intention to try to continue to live in this place and be a part of that [remains the same]. I don't see what I'm doing as that drastically different from what my grandfather did. Except I'm not a coal miner. I'm not a farmer. And the reason is that those elements of economics have also changed, to where I can't be a farmer no more. Because the land, the social and economic environment has changed so that it won't allow for that. And I'm not going to be a coal miner. Because my father learned very quickly and taught me that that led to no end but the destruction of your own self and the land that you live in. So I had to find some way to maintain that sense of identity, and also find a livelihood.

Where Pigeon Forge and Gatlinburg illustrate extremes of popularizing and even caricaturing Appalachian culture for mass tourist consumption, and Appalshop and Roadside represent a rigorous cultural activism in restoring regional complexity both for locals and informed outsiders, Jonesborough has taken a middle path. By concentrating on a neglected art form—an art with regional associations yet international connections—the town has created a restored identity for itself in a diversified regional economy. The political thrust of Roadside's work does not fit smoothly into the sandblasted surfaces of Jonesborough; neither have the gargantuan hucksterisms of Gatlinburg penetrated the pristine downtown. Jonesborough has chosen its own story.

It is simple enough, from this distance, to criticize Jonesborough's elegiac revision of itself. What Dorst, for one, does not accommodate in his postmodernist critique are the trajectories of fervor that impel a revitalization movement and the modes of cultural production that flow from that charged state. There are higher modes of sensibility than irony, as Rainer Maria Rilke once wrote in a letter to a young poet (24). Irony is a means for coping with multiple motives and oblique planes of reference; but as one approaches the sacred, these multiple references demand to be focused to a point. Mythic codes of thought, such as storytelling, allow for that affective focus. Yet in the marketing of myth, the vocabulary of multiple motives is restored, and ironic frameworks of response reassert themselves.

Confronting the critiques of MacCannell and Dorst, both strongly indebted to Barthian contramythology, inevitably forces the historian of the storytelling revival to face an ambivalence about Jonesborough's place in the storytelling revival mythos. Jonesborough has truly exerted a spell over the national storytelling community. As Lee Pennington's remembrance of schemes to declare Jonesborough "the storytelling center of America" show, it was a spell that was woven with a kind of naive deliberation from the first, even as the cosmetic reconstruction of Jonesborough was just getting underway. The historic renovation of the town acted in conjunction with the efforts of its citizens and storyteller-allies to concentrate there the power of desire embodied in the mythic construct "the storytelling revival." It is a classic example of mythic speech, in Barthes's semiotic sense: the transformation of meaning into form. The image of the "little town that time forgot" is an exquisite concretion of an idealized past—which has been literally remembered and reappointed in every tuck and cobble according the latest notions of reconstituted authenticity. The town is a virtual prosthesis for the revivalist imagination. As an aid to contemplation, it focuses the mind wonderfully as we approach the sacred aspects of story. All refractory details (almost), all ironizing references, all oblique angles of poverty and doubt have been buffed out of the picture to better concentrate on the meanings that we have poured into the form.

Yet we remember the ancient mage's precept—nothing is created out of nothing. For meaning to pool here, it must have flowed from elsewhere, or everywhere. Barthes, myth-keeper of the secular world, called the process "stolen language." Campbell, keeper of the sacred, called it "sacrifice." From out of the hills, up from Florida and Alabama, down from the cities of the Northeast, in vanloads and busloads from the Midwest, and in planeloads from New Mexico, Colorado, and California, the desire for myth flows into Jonesborough. On the journey, something of the particularity, the grit, the resistance of our stories is rubbed out, sacrificed, tithed to Jonesborough in order to power the revival. Our stories, our speech, our lives will become art, something transferable, exchangeable, even, as we saw at the congresses, thievable. The capitol always takes its wagonloads of tribute from the provinces and gives back, when the empire is sound, ritual structure, a place for pilgrimage (the original form of spiritual tourism), *pax Romanum,* and blessed assurance that, once there, we will have touched the marble heart of the world.

I recall another image: on Main Street in Jonesborough, wedged between the neatly sandblasted brick and freshly painted frame houses was a single site of resistance. It was a wooden house, just as old and full of "architectural character" as those on either side that proudly wore their numbered plaques. But this one was unnumbered, unrestored, unregenerate. It was gray and grimy, shedding its coats of old paint like leprous scales. The porch was sagging; weeds twined between the broken rails. There were rusty tools, pieces of crumbling machinery, and randomly assorted junk in the yard, which was deliberately, outrageously unkempt. Instead of a numbered plaque, there was an old, peeling, hand-lettered signboard nailed above the porch, advertising a family auctioneering business. The motto read, "We Sold Your Neighbor."

The house was owned, or so I heard, by an old Jonesborough family, bitter political enemies of Jimmy Neil Smith and the Civic Trust clique. The family refused to sell the place, even though none of them lived there anymore; and they refused to clean it up, angered perhaps that they were restrained by historic preservation ordinances from tearing it down and turning it into whatever they pleased. So there it sat, in the middle of the historic district, a living historical stalemate. It was an ideological affront, a blistering patch on the smooth temporal sleight-of-mind that is downtown Jonesborough. It insisted on its obnoxious prerogative to sell its neighbor in its own, unvarnished manner. This house, too, wore its past on its porch, but its past refused to be colonized.

It is important to note here that I have loved the town of Jonesborough since the day I first set foot in it, and I have great respect and affection for its projects and its people. I love the Victorian decency of its tidy old buildings, welcoming without garishness, and I love the way the streets are lit without the tangled shadows of power lines and telephone poles. I love the care and the scrupulousness with which the people of the town have defied or finessed the pervasive American ethos of abandoning its material past to the vultures of exploitation or the dogs of decay. Above all, I have loved the festival they have birthed and nurtured into a magnificent, many-hued giant that opens its arms to enfold an ideal nation.

And yet, each time I passed the peeling house with the sign that read "We Sold Your Neighbor," I felt a twinge of secret gratitude. The plainness of its critique restored irony to the debate over representational practice. Like some of the storytellers we might have seen at the festival in the seventies, it was a cranky old character, not a polished performer. The house was what Gamble Rogers would have called "a feed-store philosopher," making its points with the ornamental equivalent of a well-aimed rope of spit.

Jo Carson, a poet and playwright from nearby Johnson City, wrote about her storytelling neighbors in a letter to some friends in Rome:

> I see this resurgence of storytelling, in part, as a claiming of cultural diversity and real history, but there is another story here too. A week of stories? Jack Tales scheduled for an afternoon? . . . The festival itself is the making of storytelling, in an effort to keep it, into something so precious and removed that people don't do it anymore, just storytellers. Like happened to poetry. Like happened to theater. It is the transformation of stories into artifacts, a stone hatchet, a Jack Tale, and removing them from things that happen to people. (8)

To create a class of specialists out of an art form that is avowedly everyone's is, on some unavoidable level, an imperial act. Specialists exact tribute from those for whom they tell their stories. Out of that tribute, that language-robbery, they build a mythic journey, a career, and a profession. I do not believe that this expropriation was a conscious act on anyone's part in the storytelling movement—on the contrary, the language on our lips was all "empowerment": *Everyone is a teller.* But gradually, the sunlight faded, and the shadows came out. It was back to the nights of the folk music boom, when everyone became a folksinger, as Michael Smith said in a recent storytelling show, "for about ten minutes." After that, he continues, "Five folksingers became millionaires. And three of them were Bob Dylan."

What the professionalization of storytelling did for the everyoneness of the art, the capitolization of Jonesborough did for its everywhereness. "Why are you going to Tennessee?" ask George Shannon's interlocutors in his brilliant tribute to Jonesborough in the *Yarnspinner.* "To hear stories," he answers. "Can't you hear stories closer to home?" they resist, until he finally silences them with the irresistible answer, "Ritual"—to which we might add its corollary term, *Myth*—though it may be as freighted as the word *Love* with levels of blessing and treachery.

Where would the storytelling revival be without Jonesborough as its ritual center and mythic embodiment? The near-financial ruin of NAPPS in 1993 almost forced the community to find out. Many would have answered, in their loss and grief, "Nowhere." But the loss might have forced us to search again until we had recovered the answer, "Everywhere."

The Breaking of Vessels

In the end, there are contradictions that cannot be resolved, ambiguities that will not be reconciled, sacred wounds that refuse to be neatly healed. When Don Quixote, a prototypical cultural revivalist, tilted at the windmill and was defeated, he explained his defeat by deciding that his enemy, the Great Enchanter, had at the last moment turned the giant into a windmill. If Don Quixote had succeeded in his joust and had wound up, say, indenturing the giant to the production of wind-generated electric power, his victory might have exposed him to a different kind of defeat: partnership with the Great Enchanter. Whether we call the Enchanter postindustrial capitalism, the social field of structural role-playing, the tree of the knowledge of Good and Evil, or time itself, the enchantment reasserts itself after every victory and recollects itself after each defeat. The wound in the Fisher King's thigh reopens for each generation to ask, with aching heart, "What ails thee, Uncle?"

According to an ancient Jewish legend called "The Breaking of the Vessels," the primordial unity of Godhead was shattered at the very dawn of creation, when spirit poured its divine light through the eyes of the first created image, the spirit-man Adam Kadmon. The light poured from the source in Adam Kadmon's forehead into his lower limbs, the vessels that were to hold the lower worlds in unbroken communion. But the lower vessels were not strong enough to contain the flow of divine light. They shattered, sending a shower of brilliant sparks into the void formed when spirit withdrew from its own perfection to make way for creation. In falling, the shards of the shattered vessels became the *kelippot*—the husks of illusion that enshroud the holy sparks in this finite world. The sparks themselves became what the Kabbalists called the roots of our souls.

Yet, as the sages relate, bits of those same holy sparks also dwell in all things: in other animal, vegetable, or mineral beings, in such tangible artifacts as tools and craft objects, even in such intangible forms as songs, dances, or stories. The living longing and the destiny of all these scattered sparks is restoration, or reunification (in Hebrew *tikkun*), which can only be effected by human beings, acting in remembrance of their sacred nature. In this way alone can the holy sparks be freed from the husks of darkness and the primordial unity of Adam Kadmon be restored (Goldberg 1–2, 592–93).

Such a mythological imagining creates a profound warrant for the storyteller. As Martin Buber (*Hasidism and Modern Man*) and Robin Goldberg each show, it became the essential framework for the Hasidic religious revival in eighteenth-century Judaism. The founder of Hasidism was both an actual historical figure, Israel ben Eliezar of Miedzyboz in Podolia, and a legendary culture hero, known to his followers as the Baal Shem Tov, the incarnation of a people's dreams and longings. The Baal Shem Tov taught that storytelling, performed with the proper intention, could bring about *tikkun.* As with other communal performances, such as devotional song or dance, it could open bridges from heart to heart, dissolving the husks of darkness that separate beings from one another, allowing the sparks within to unite and flame upward together, and restoring them, at least for a moment, to their proper place in the body of God. In a phrase that has gained currency among storytelling revivalists, it could *restory the world.*

The myth of the breaking of the vessels is an origin tale of *hitlahavut,* the fervor that flares around a revival movement in its day of discovery. Sparks of sacred longing are awakened within us through contact with the sparks that lie dormant in folk artifacts and in the vision of primal cultural wholeness symbolized by the cultures from which the objects come. Folktales, folk songs, folk dances, and folk crafts become vehicles through which we experience a sense of reunion with our common humanity. Scattered sparks of the primal being flame together in the heat of performance, and our sense of community and of our individual destiny is raised into life anew.

But the *kelippot,* the shells of darkness, ever gather around the forms created by the revival process. Some of those shells reside in the very institutions that form to ensure the revival's continuity, as they publicize, canonize, standardize, and, in many subtle and not-so-subtle ways, seek to commodify the utopian impulse. Other shells form in the processes of imitation and exploitation that succeed the processes of self-actualization and service in the movement's followers. Charisma becomes routine, profit motives vie with the joy of discovery, careerists jostle pilgrims off the path. Shells of darkness are attracted to the flaring of sacred energy as inevitably as are other sparks of light, and it is fit that the *kelippot* should flock to sources of new life in the world, for they, too, seek life, even as they work to smother it. Eventually the smothering of the light will bring us to despair, out of which we will winnow the sparks of our longing, and those sparks will flame together in the light of another revival.

The only release is Armageddon, the final battle between darkness and light, and many are the revitalization movements that have waited on or sought to hasten this end. Anthony F. C. Wallace calls them "millenarian movements"; popular wisdom calls them "cults." At Waco the sparks flared upward with desolating finality; Heaven's Gate members smothered their earthly shells to free the sparks of light. Three generations into the Hasidic movement, according to Buber (*For the Sake of Heaven*), a group of the Baal Shem Tov's most prominent successors gathered in a room above an inn and attempted by means of Kabbalistic signs and magical incantations to turn the Napoleonic wars into the herald of the Messiah. The effort failed, and each of those leaders died shortly thereafter. God the storyteller will not be rushed, and each time "happily ever after" seems assured, another transgression sends us off on yet another quest.

Meanwhile, the ripples of passion and industry set off by the storytelling revival continue to eddy through the culture. As it began in scattered outposts of experience, which only afterward fused together into a world, so the basic human impulses that powered the movement continue to flow in the life-streams of individuals and to radiate into their daily lives.

Every Friday night in Chicago, New York, San Francisco, or Seattle, performers who would have once been satisfied to call themselves actors, comedians, musicians, or vaudevillians now sit in darkened rooms telling stories from their lives to groups of strangers. The word *storytelling* may be nowhere on their conscious agenda, yet formal gestures, attitudes, and assumptions about performance and the performer-audience relationship have soaked across the subcultural membrane separating the storytelling movement from these "performance artists." Even when the folk music boom suffered its commercial collapse at the end of the seventies, it left endless echoes in the sound and look of American popular music. So with the storytelling revival—it need not be claimed as a source in order to be marked as part of the cultural context that continues to breed theatrical métis like Spalding Gray, Lynn Redgrave's *Shakespeare for My Father,* or a holy host of autobiographical "one-person shows."

On a typical Thursday morning in September, a converted high school gymnasium in Chicago's northwest suburbia is lined with display tables, each heaped with offerings from eager school performers. PTO representatives dutifully file by for forty minutes around lunchtime, collecting brochures and doing as much business as their overloaded senses will permit, before being herded back into the auditorium for another parade of ten-minute showcases. Storytellers vie for gigs here, side by side with theater troupes, musicians, magicians, jugglers, puppeteers, laser artists, illuminated jump-rope dancers, antidrug deejays, and performing zoologists with monkeys and mynah birds for partners. Of the 150 arts enterprises listed in the program book, 21 group themselves under the heading of "Storytelling"—more than in any other category except music and theater. The storytelling banner here gathers in everything from well-traveled veterans of the National Storytelling Festival, such as Syd Lieberman or Jim May, to retired librarians in Mother Goose regalia, to fledgling freelancers sounding their first fanfares to the marketplace. Commerce is the great equalizer, and the revived god is passed around on glossy flyers along with all the rest of the latter-day descendants.

Syd looks grim as he mans his booth. "I hate these things worse than anything I do," he tells me through clenched teeth, and he rushes for his car the moment the afternoon showcases begin. Jim May is onstage first this afternoon. I walk over to the auditorium just in time to hear him give a low-key, ten-minute reprise of the storytelling revival myth to a roomful of PTO matrons: "In our grandparents' generation these stories were told to pass on values of kindness, courage, and faith that no matter how tough things got, you could still get through it," he says, after squeezing in a single episode of a twenty-minute Jack tale. Then he adds, "I used to think television was the great villain of our culture in murdering the oral tradition. But now I've totally made my peace with television; I've decided that the blame should really go to central heating."

On a weekend morning in Austin, Raleigh, or Santa Cruz, groups of men or women sit in a circle listening raptly to a workshop leader declaim from "Iron John," "The Water of Life," or "Woman Who Runs with the Wolves." Then they may pass around a ritual talking stick, taking turns using the folktales as tools for excavating their own relationships with fathers, brothers, mothers, lovers, sons, selves. Inchoate memories from participants' lives suddenly emerge with new structure, definition, and metaphoric richness borrowed from the traditional tales and are reinterpreted and reexperienced through the language of Jungian analysis and the emerging group mythos. As Marie-Louise von Franz in the early sixties told a group of her students at the Jung Institute (including James Hillman, and through Hillman, Robert Bly, Michael Meade, Claudia Pinkola Estes, Gioia Timpanelli, and a broad, essential flank of the eventual storytelling revival), "We interpret for the same reason as that for which fairy tales and myths were told: because it has a vivifying effect . . . and brings one into peace with one's unconscious instinctive substratum, just as the telling of fairy tales always did. Psychological interpretation is our way of telling stories; we still have the same need and we still crave the renewal that comes with understanding archetypal images. We know quite well that it is just our myth" (32).

And in Jonesborough each October—but also in Spring Grove, Illinois; Austin, Minnesota; Nevada City, California; Charlotte, North Carolina; St. Louis, Missouri; Louisville, Kentucky; and dozens of other towns and cities at some (for them) special season of the year—a stage and a tent will go up, and an ancient, idealized relationship of artist and community will be rehearsed for another weekend, until the bells of Sunday have rung, the tents have been struck, and the whole carnival of dreams has departed for another year into the murk of the coming millennium.

Cathryn Wellner told me of the unexpected paths her storytelling has led her on since her fledgling efforts at Rafe Martin's Oxcart Bookshop in Rochester, New York, way back in the early eighties. She moved to Seattle, worked for years as a free-lance teller, divorced and remarried, and then moved from Seattle to a farm in British Columbia. There she reflected on the links between storytelling and the work of living softly on the earth:

> We bought this small farm, and suddenly had eleven acres, and looked out at these fields and thought, We have a responsibility here. There's some stewardship involved here. What do we do? So we got a few chickens and some little lambs. And thought, well, we'll raise them over the summer, and have a small organic garden, and that will be our thing. Come winter we'll have sold off the produce or eaten it. The lambs will have cleared some pasture for us, and we'll sell those and sell off the chickens. And then for our *real* thing, we'll be writers and storytellers in the winter, and have no farm responsibilities.
>
> But by winter we had a flock of sheep, and turkeys, and lots of hens. And realized that we did not want a lot of the livestock we had because they were modern hybrids. But we began to look at them and realize some of the problems they had because they'd been manipulated genetically. And so [we] began to do a lot of reading and have become quite politicized. In fact, the local farmers figure that we're the ones that have the weird sheep and the strange chickens. Because we're really looking for old breeds and breeding them. And we really feel lucky, because everything's tied in beautifully with our interest in storytelling and writing.

If I were stepping back and looking at my own life, I'd be fascinated by the turn of events. Because that very concern for there being a broad gene pool in storytelling, has been part of my evolution toward becoming concerned that the gene pool remain broad and viable in flora and fauna. To protect the diversity, rather than some narrow band. Because there are a lot of stories involved with the loss of genetic diversity. And with the tremendous impact on nature that we humans have had in a very short period of time. And with the uncertain future because of what we've done to the earth. We've become very politicized by the whole thing. And it's a perfect opportunity for us; because we can talk about it, we can write about it, we can tell stories about it . . . our being in this place at this time, we're like a link between past and future, and we're trying to figure out how do you live for the seventh generation? How do we stop being divided by the various stories we live by? How do we find common stories?

Doug Lipman told me the following story to illustrate his sense of the ongoing storytelling revival in his life:

Last weekend I was in New York City. And on Saturday I did a private coaching workshop. And then Sunday was the Jewish Storytelling Celebration. And I drove back Sunday night. And usually when I'm in the car, I have a pile of storytelling tapes, and I want to listen to the radio or listen to the tapes. But for the first two hours of the drive, I just wanted to be alone, savoring the feeling I had. And the feeling was *"I have found my life's work. I am doing it, and I am doing it well."*

And that theme wouldn't be there if it weren't for the storytelling revival. And it's an ongoing thing. At the workshop I did on Saturday, there were people who were just discovering it, with just as much hope and apprehension and naïveté as I had when it was my turn. When I do weekend workshops, I always have people end with their vision, and out of their vision then goals, and out of that next steps to do. And my vision at this point is of this grassroots, underground, and therefore totally incorruptible movement of people *just being human to each other.* And meeting with stories.

And Diane Wolkstein told me of her sustained and sustaining effort to create "sacred ground" (January 13, 1992): a spot where humanizing narratives could take root in people's psyches, whether at the late conference in Jonesborough or around the statue of Hans Christian Andersen in New York's Central Park. In accord, at last, with the will to happy endings borrowed from a movement that called me to the adventure of my early manhood, I let it stand as an emblem of the frail seed of hope at the beginning of the storytellers' journey that may grow, despite every withering weather, into a flowering tree:

I guess the most exciting thing for me about having told for twenty-five years in Central Park is that people who were ten years old when I began are now bringing their own children. They're now thirty-five, and their children are ten. But they've grown up and returned. Incredible continuity. And there's a particular story that I've told almost from the beginning, called "Elsie Piddock Skips in Her Sleep," written by Eleanor Farjeon. It used to be, every time I would tell it I would cry. It had to do with sacred ground. Which is what I think a lot about in terms of storytelling—that storytellers create sacred ground. Whether it's visible or invisible.

And the fact that Elsie saves it, and that she dedicates her life to it, and that she never stops skipping. Her tenacity and her devotion and her loyalty—*for* the community—is for me the symbol of the storyteller. Who is weaving this circle. And the rope goes around and around, creating a magical circle, for everybody. The storyteller keeps the tradition; and Elsie Piddock keeps skipping, she never stops skipping—she's *still* skipping . . . and that's how the story ends.

Works Consulted

Interviews

Arguello-Sheehan, Ruthmarie. Telephone. Scottsdale, Ariz., January 22, 1992.

Baker, Augusta. Telephone. Columbia, S.C., March 31, 1992.

Birch, Carol. Telephone. Southbury, Conn., April 10, 1992.

Blaustein, Richard. Personal. Johnson City, Tenn., November 24, 1991.

Bledsoe, Toby. Personal. Jonesborough, Tenn., November 18, 1991.

Brown, Margie. Telephone. Berkeley, Calif., May 14, 1992.

Burch, Milbre. Telephone. Pasadena, Calif., February 24, 1992.

Cabral, Len. Telephone. Providence, R.I., April 7, 1992.

Cannarozzi, Sam Yada. Telephone. Paris, France, March 28, 1992.

Chase, Richard. Recorded at Berea College, Berea, Ky., April 10, 1975.

Cotter, Michael. Telephone. Austin, Minn., May 11, 1992.

Cuddy, Clare. Telephone. Washington, D.C., January 8, 1992.

Davis, Donald. Personal. Office, Christ United Methodist Church, High Point, N.C., January 30, 1985.

———. Personal. Office, Christ United Methodist Church, High Point, N.C., May 29, 1985.

———. Personal. Office, Christ United Methodist Church, High Point, N.C., July 15, 1985.

———. Telephone. Ocracoke, N.C., April 9, 1992.

DeSpain, Pleasant. Telephone. Seattle, Wash., January 4, 1992.

Ducey, Gay. Telephone. Berkeley, Calif., January 14, 1992.

Elliott, Doug. Telephone. Union, N.C., December 16, 1991.

Ellis, Elizabeth. Telephone. Dallas, Tex., January 11, 1992.

Forest, Heather. Telephone. Huntington, N.Y., February 23, 1992.

Freeman, Barbara. Telephone. Asheville, N.C., January 18, 1992.

Gillman, Jackson. Telephone. Portland, Maine, April 3, 1992.
Gray, Spalding. Telephone. New York, N.Y., April 8, 1992.
Greene, Ellin. Telephone. Point Pleasant, N.J., December 14, 1991.
Harley, Bill. Telephone. Seekonk, Mass., January 15, 1992.
Hedberg, Greta (Talton). Telephone. Charlottesville, Va., April 23, 1992.
Hicks, Ray. Personal. Beech Mountain, N.C., November 23, 1991.
Hill, Hugh Morgan (Brother Blue). Telephone. Cambridge, Mass., January 4, 1992.
Holt, David. Telephone. Fairview, N.C., December 17, 1991.
Horner, Beth. Telephone. Evanston, Ill., December 20, 1992.
Insignares, Harriette Allen. Personal. Nashville, Tenn., February 1, 1992.
Johnson, Larry, and Elaine Wynne. Telephone. Minneapolis, Minn., April 11, 1992.
Jolly, Brad. Telephone. Johnson City, Tenn., April 14, 1992.
Kennedy, William. Personal. Jonesborough, Tenn., November 25, 1991.
Kessel, Louise. Telephone. Bynum, N.C., December 18, 1991.
Lane, Marcia. Telephone. New York, N.Y., December 4, 1991.
Lawrence, Ardi St. Clair. Telephone. Nashville, Tenn., February 4, 1992.
Ledbetter, Gwenda. Telephone. Asheville, N.C., March 30, 1992.
———. Telephone. Asheville, N.C., May 14, 1992.
Lewis, John. Interview. *ABC Nightline,* WLS, Chicago, March 3, 1994.
Lipman, Doug. Telephone. West Somerville, Mass., April 2, 1992.
Livo, Norma. Telephone. Lakewood, Colo., April 21, 1992.
Martin, Rafe. Telephone. Rochester, N.Y., January 21, 1992.
Marvin, Lee-Ellen. Telephone. Santa Cruz, Calif., January 26, 1992.
May, Jim. Telephone. Woodstock, Ill., April 16, 1992.
McConnell, Ernest "Doc." Taped reminiscences. November 1991.
———. Telephone. Rogersville, Tenn., January 17, 1992.
Miller, Reid. Telephone. Madison, Wis., January 6, 1992.
Moore, Carolyn. Personal. Jonesborough, Tenn., February 8, 1992.
Moore, Robin. Telephone. Springhouse, Pa., December 11, 1991.
Moroney, Lynn. Telephone. Oklahoma City, Okla., December 21, 1991.
Niemi, Loren. Telephone. Minneapolis, Minn., April 3, 1992.
O'Callahan, Jay. Telephone. Marshfield, Mass., December 23, 1991.
Parent, Michael. Telephone. Charlottesville, Va., December 26, 1991.
Park, Fred. Telephone. Swannanoa, N.C., January 4, 1992.
Pellowski, Anne. Telephone. New York, N.Y., April 4, 1992.
Pennington, Lee. Telephone. Middleton, Ky., December 15, 1991.
Peyer, Hollis. Telephone. Philadelphia, Pa., May 11, 1992.
Regan-Blake, Connie. Personal. Asheville, N.C., April 29, 1992.
———. Telephone. Asheville, N.C., January 21, 1992.
———. Telephone. Asheville, N.C., April 9, 1992.

Ross, Gayle. Telephone. Fredricksburg, Tex., April 22, 1992.
Rubenstein, Robert. Telephone. Eugene, Oreg., January 5, 1992.
Rubright, Lynn. Telephone. Kirkwood, Mo., December 11, 1991.
Ryan, Patrick. Telephone. London, England, March 28, 1992.
Sanfield, Steve. Telephone. Nevada City, Calif., December 15, 1991.
Schimmel, Nancy. Telephone. Berkeley, Calif., January 4, 1992.
Schram, Peninnah. Telephone. New York, N.Y., March 31, 1992.
Short, Ron. Telephone. Whitesburg, Ky., April 24, 1992.
Simms, Laura. Telephone. New York, N.Y., December 22, 1991.
———. Telephone. New York, N.Y., December 23, 1991.
Smith, Jean. Personal. Jonesborough, Tenn., April 29, 1992.
Smith, Jimmy Neil. Telephone. Jonesborough, Tenn., March 30, 1992.
Smith, Mary Carter. Telephone. Baltimore, Md., January 19, 1992.
Spelman, Jon. Telephone. Washington, D.C., April 13, 1992.
Stallings, Fran. Telephone. Bartlesville, Okla., December 21, 1991.
Stivender, Ed. Telephone. Philadelphia, Pa., January 7, 1992.
———. Telephone. Philadelphia, Pa., May 19, 1992.
Stone, Kay. Telephone. Winnepeg, Manitoba, January 26, 1992.
Timpanelli, Gioia. Telephone. Bearsfield, N.Y., December 22, 1991.
Toelken, Barre. Telephone. Logan, Utah, April 14, 1992.
Torrence, Jackie. Telephone. Salisbury, N.C., January 23, 1992.
Turner, Ron. Telephone. St. Louis, Mo., December 18, 1991.
Wellner, Cathryn. Telephone. Duncan, British Columbia, April 4, 1992.
Wilhelm, Robert Bela. Telephone. Washington, D.C., April 17, 1992.
Williamson, Robin. Telephone. Los Angeles, Calif., May 1, 1992.
Windham, Kathryn Tucker. Telephone. Selma, Ala., December 20, 1991.
Wolkstein, Diane. Telephone. New York, N.Y., January 13, 1992.
———. Telephone. New York, N.Y., April 18, 1992.

Books, Articles, Papers, Audio Materials Cited in Text, and Dissertations

Aarne, Antti. *The Types of the Folk-tale: A Classification and Bibliography.* Translated by Stith Thompson. New York: Lenox, 1928.
Abernethy, Rose L. "A Study of Existing Practices and Principles of Storytelling for Children in the United States." Ph.D. diss., Northwestern University, 1964.
"Acknowledge Story Sources." *Yarnspinner* 3, no. 2 (1978): 1–2.
Alvey, Richard G. "The Historical Development of Organized Storytelling for Children in the United States." Ph.D. diss., University of Pennsylvania, 1974.
Baker, Augusta, and Ellin Greene. *Storytelling: Art and Technique.* New York: Bowker, 1977.

Works Consulted

Bakhtin, Mikhail. *The Dialogic Imagination.* Translated by Caryl Emerson and Michael Holmquist. Austin: University of Texas Press, 1981.
———. *Rabelais and His World.* Translated by Helene Iswolsky. Bloomington: Indiana University Press, 1984.
Barthes, Roland. *Mythologies.* New York: Noonday, 1972.
Bauer, Caroline Feller. *Handbook for Storytellers.* Chicago: ALA, 1977.
Bauman, Richard. "Differential Identity and the Social Base of Folklore." In *Toward New Perspectives in Folklore,* edited by Americo Paredes and Richard Bauman. Austin: University of Texas Press, 1972.
———. *Story, Performance, and Event.* Cambridge: Cambridge University Press, 1986.
———. *Verbal Art as Performance.* Rowley, Mass.: Newbury, 1977.
Bausman, Jennifer Jones. "The National Storytelling Congress." Letter. *National Storytelling Journal* 4, no. 4 (1987): 25–27.
Becker, Howard S. *Art Worlds.* Berkeley: University of California Press, 1982.
Ben-Amos, Dan. "Toward a Definition of Folklore in Context." In *Toward New Perspectives in Folklore,* edited by Americo Paredes and Richard Bauman. Austin: University of Texas Press, 1972.
Ben-Amos, Dan, and Kenneth Goldstein, eds. *Folklore: Performance and Communication.* Hague: Mouton, 1975.
Benjamin, Walter. "The Storyteller." In *Illuminations.* New York: Schocken, 1968.
Bettelheim, Bruno. *The Uses of Enchantment.* New York: Alfred A. Knopf, 1976.
Birch, Carol, and Melissa Heckler, eds. *Across the Great Divide: Aesthetic and Ethical Issues in Storytelling.* Little Rock, Ark.: August House, 1996.
Bly, Robert. *Iron John: A Book about Men.* Reading, Pa.: Addison, 1990.
Bly, Robert, James Hillman, and Michael Meade. *Men and the Life of Desire.* Audiocassette. 1991. Oral Traditions Archive, Pacific Grove, Calif.
Bruchac, Joseph. *Keepers of the Earth: Native-American Stories and Environmental Activities for Children.* Golden, Colo.: Fulcrum, 1989.
Bruner, Jerome. *Actual Minds, Possible Worlds.* Cambridge, Mass.: Harvard University Press, 1986.
Buber, Martin. *For the Sake of Heaven.* Philadelphia: Jewish Publications Society, 1953.
———. *Hasidism and Modern Man.* New York: Harper, 1958.
Burroughs, Lea. "An Ethnographic Sketch of the San Francisco Bay Area Storytelling Community." Paper presented at the annual meeting of the American Folklore Society, Oakland, Calif., October 20, 1990.
Calame-Griaule, Genevieve. *Le renouveau du conte* (The Revival of Storytelling). Paris: Centre National de la Recherche Scientifique, 1991.

Campbell, Joseph. "Folkloristic Commentary." In *The Complete Grimm's Fairy Tales,* translated by Margaret Hunt and James Stern. New York: Pantheon, 1944.

———. *The Hero with a Thousand Faces.* Princeton, N.J.: Princeton University Press, 1972.

———. *The Power of Myth.* New York: Doubleday, 1988.

Cantwell, Robert. "Conjuring Culture: Ideology and Magic in the Festival of American Folklife." *Journal of American Folklore* 104, no. 412 (1991): 148–63.

———. *Ethnomimesis.* Chapel Hill: University of North Carolina Press, 1993.

———. "Response to Peter Seitel." *Journal of American Folklore* 104, no. 414 (1991): 496–99.

———. *When We Were Good: The Folk Revival.* Cambridge, Mass.: Harvard University Press, 1996.

Carson, Jo. "From the Mud on Polk Avenue: An Essay in the Form of a Letter." Unpublished essay, 1989.

Chase, Richard, ed. *American Folk Tales and Songs.* New York: NAL, 1956.

———. *Grandfather Tales.* Boston: Houghton, 1948.

———. *The Jack Tales.* Boston: Houghton, 1943.

Clifford, James. *The Predicament of Culture.* Cambridge, Mass.: Harvard University Press, 1988.

———. *Writing Culture.* Berkeley: University of California Press, 1986.

Clower, Jerry. *Clower Power.* LP/Cassette. Los Angeles: MCA, 1972.

———. *Storytelling Has Been Very Good to Me. . . .* Audiotape of live performance recorded at Davy Crockett High School Auditorium, Jonesborough, Tenn., October 4, 1973. NSA Archives, National Storytelling Resource Center, Jonesborough, Tenn.

Coles, Robert. *The Call of Stories.* Boston: Houghton, 1989.

Collins, Rives, and Pamela Cooper. *Look What Happened to Frog: Storytelling in Education.* Scottsdale, Ariz.: Gorsuch, 1993.

Colwell, Eileen. *Storytelling.* London: Bodley Head, 1980.

Cox, Harvey. *The Feast of Fools.* Cambridge, Mass.: Harvard University Press, 1969.

Crowell, Marnie Reed. "Beginnings." *Yarnspinner* 8, no. 11 (1983): 2.

Davis, Donald D. "Inside the Oral Medium." *National Storytelling Journal* 1, no. 3 (1984): 7.

Davis, Donald D., and Kay Stone. "'To Ease the Heart': Traditional Storytelling." *National Storytelling Journal* 1, no. 1 (1984): 3–6.

Degh, Linda. "Folk Narrative." In *Folklore and Folklife,* edited by Richard Dorson. Chicago: University of Chicago Press, 1972.

———. *Folktales and Society.* Bloomington: Indiana University Press, 1969.

Denisoff, R. Serge. *Great Day Coming: Folk Music and the American Left.* Urbana: University of Illinois Press, 1971.

Dorst, John D. *The Written Suburb: An American Site, an Ethnographic Dilemma.* Philadelphia: University of Pennsylvania Press, 1989.

Dundes, Alan, ed. *Sacred Narrative: Readings in the Theory of Myth.* Berkeley: University of California Press, 1984.

Estes, Claudia Pinkola. *Women Who Run with the Wolves.* New York: Ballentine, 1992.

Evans, Ron. "The Storyteller Knows Me." Presented at the National Storytelling Festival, Jonesborough, Tenn., October 3, 1982. In *Storytelling: The National Festival.* Cassette. Jonesborough, Tenn.: NAPPS, 1983.

Ferguson, Marilyn. *The Aquarian Conspiracy.* Los Angeles: Tarcher, 1980.

Fine, Elizabeth C. *The Folklore Text: From Performance to Print.* Bloomington: Indiana University Press, 1984.

Fink, Paul M. *Jonesborough: The First Century of Tennessee's First Town.* Johnson City, Tenn.: Overmountain, 1989.

———. "The Rebirth of Jonesboro." *Tennessee Historical Quarterly* 31, no. 3 (1973): 223–39.

Fox, Matthew. *Creation Spirituality.* San Francisco: Harper, 1991.

Franz, Marie-Louise von. *Introduction to the Interpretation of Fairy Tales.* New York: Spring, 1970.

Freud, Sigmund. "The Occurrence in Dreams of Material from Fairy Tales." In *Collected Works,* vol. 12, translated by James Strachey. London: Hogarth, 1958.

Geertz, Clifford. *The Interpretation of Cultures.* New York: Basic Books, 1973.

———. *Local Knowledge.* New York: Basic Books, 1983.

Georges, Robert. "Toward an Understanding of Storytelling Events." *Journal of American Folklore* 82, no. 326 (1969): 313–28.

Glass, Renecia. "The Story Lady." In *Bronze Reminiscence.* Atlanta, Ga.: Lakeshore High School, 1987.

Glassie, Henry. *All Silver and No Brass.* Bloomington: Indiana University Press, 1975.

———. *Passing the Time in Ballymenone: Culture and History of an Ulster Community.* Philadelphia: University of Pennsylvania Press, 1982.

Goffman, Irving. *Frame Analysis.* New York: Harper, 1974.

Goldberg, Robin. "Imagining the Feminine: Storying and Restorying Womanhood among Lubavitch Hasidic Women." Ph.D. diss., Northwestern University, 1991.

Gorog, Veronika. "Qui conte en France aujourd'hui? Les nouveaux conteurs." *Cahiers de littáture orale* 11 (1982): 95–116.

Goss, Linda, and Marian E. Barnes, eds. *Talk That Talk: An Anthology of African-American Storytelling.* New York: Touchstone, 1989.

Gray, Spalding. *Sex and Death to the Age of Fourteen.* New York: Vintage, 1986.

———. *Swimming to Cambodia.* New York: Theatre Communications, 1985.

Greene, Ellin, and George Shannon. *Storytelling: An Annotated Bibliography.* New York: Garland, 1986.

Griego, Jose. "A Closer Look at Stories from Hispanic, Jewish, African-American, and American Indian Cultures." Panel discussion with Mary Carter Smith, Lynn Gottlieb, and Larry Littlebird at the NAPPS Congress, Santa Fe, N.M., June 17, 1988.

Grimm, Jacob, and Wilhelm Grimm. *Complete Fairy Tales.* New York: Pantheon, 1944.

Haley, Alex. *Roots.* Garden City, N.Y.: Doubleday, 1976.

Halper, Jon, ed. *Gary Snyder: Dimensions of a Life.* San Francisco: Sierra Club, 1991.

Harley, Bill. "The Kid Who Had No Story." Performance at the National Storytelling Festival, Jonesborough, Tenn., October 1992.

Harris, Joel Chandler. *Uncle Remus: His Songs and His Sayings.* New York: Hawthorn, 1921.

Harvey, Margaret Clodagh. "A Contemporary Perspective on Irish Traditional Storytelling in the English Language." Ph.D. diss., University of California at Los Angeles, 1987.

———. "Contemporary 'Traditional' Storytelling: Creating and Mediating Realities." Paper presented at the annual meeting of the American Folklore Society, Oakland, Calif., October 20, 1990.

Hillman, James. *A Blue Fire.* New York: Harper, 1989.

———. "A Note on Story." In *Loose Ends: Primary Papers on Archetypal Psychology.* Dallas: Spring, 1983.

Hobsbawm, Eric. "Introduction: Inventing Traditions," in *The Invention of Tradition,* edited by Eric Hobsbawm and Terence Ranger, 1–14. Cambridge: Cambridge University Press, 1883.

Hobsbawm, Eric, and Terence Ranger, eds. *The Invention of Tradition.* Cambridge: Cambridge University Press, 1983.

Holt, David, and William Mooney, eds. *The Storyteller's Guide.* Little Rock, Ark.: August House, 1996.

Houston, Jean. *The Hero and the Goddess: The Odyssey as Mystery and Initiation.* New York: Ballentine, 1992.

Hurst, Jack. *The Grand Ole Opry.* New York: Abrams, 1975.

Hymes, Dell. "Breakthrough into Performance." In *Toward New Perspectives in Folklore,* edited by Américo Paredes and Richard Bauman. Austin: University of Texas Press, 1972.

———. *In Vain I Tried to Tell You: Essays in Native American Ethnopoetics.* Philadelphia: University of Pennsylvania Press, 1981.

Jordan, Neil. *The Crying Game.* Orion Films, Los Angeles, 1991.

Jung, Carl G. *Memories, Dreams, Reflections.* Translated by Richard and Clara Winston. New York: Random House, 1961.

———. "The Phenomenology of the Spirit in Fairy Tales." In *Collected Works,* vol. 9, translated by R. F. C. Hull. Princeton, N.J.: Princeton University Press, 1969.

Jung, Carl G., and C. Kerenyi. *Essays on a Science of Mythology.* New York: Harper, 1963.

Kamenetsky, Christa. *The Brothers Grimm and Their Critics: Folktales and the Quest for Meaning.* Athens: Ohio University Press, 1992.

Keen, Sam. *Fire in the Belly: On Being a Man.* New York: Bantam, 1991.

———. *To a Dancing God.* 1970. Reprint. San Francisco: Harper, 1990.

Keen, Sam, and Anne Valley-Fox. *Your Mythic Journey.* Los Angeles: Tarcher, 1989.

Kennedy, William. *Historic Jonesborough Presentation.* Audiotape. 1975. NSA Archives, National Storytelling Resource Center, Jonesborough, Tenn.

Kinkead, Gwen. "An Overgrown Jack." *New Yorker,* July 18, 1988, 33–41.

Lehrer, Warren. *Brother Blue.* Seattle: Bay, 1995.

Leiboff, Michael D. "Northern Appalachian Storytelling Festival: Ten Years and Growing." Paper presented at the meeting of the Speech Communications Association, Chicago, November 1, 1990.

Lieberman, Robbie. *"My Song Is My Weapon": People's Songs, American Communism, and the Politics of Culture.* Urbana: University of Illinois Press, 1989.

Livo, Norma J., and Sandra A. Rietz. *Storytelling: Process and Practice.* Littleton, Colo.: Libraries Unlimited, 1986.

Lord, Albert. *The Singer of Tales.* Cambridge, Mass.: Harvard University Press, 1960.

MacCannell, Dean. *The Tourist.* New York: Schocken, 1989.

Martin, Joseph F., ed. *Foolish Wisdom: Stories, Activities, and Reflections from Ken Feit.* San Jose, Calif.: Resource, 1990.

Marvin, Lee-Ellen, and Doug Lipman. "Ethics among Professional Storytellers." *National Storytelling Journal* 3, no. 3 (1986): 13–15.

McAdams, Dan P. *Stories We Live By.* New York: Morrow, 1993.

McCarthy, William Bernard, Cheryl Oxford, and Joseph D. Sobol, eds. *Jack in Two Worlds: Contemporary North American Tales and Their Tellers.* Chapel Hill: University of North Carolina Press, 1994.

McConnell, Ernest "Doc." "Tucker's Knob." In *Storytelling: The National Festival.* Cassette. Jonesborough, Tenn.: NAPPS, 1983.

McDermitt, Barbara. "Comparison of a Scottish and American Storyteller." Ph.D. diss., School of Scottish Studies, Edinburgh, Scotland, 1986.

———. "Duncan Williamson." *Tocher,* no. 34 (1979): 141–48.

———. "Storytelling and a Boy Named Jack." *North Carolina Folklore Journal* 31, no. 1 (1983): 3–22.

McLuhan, Marshall. *The Gutenberg Galaxy.* Toronto: University of Toronto Press, 1962.

———. *The Mechanical Bride: Folklore of Industrial Man.* New York: Vanguard, 1951.

———. *Understanding Media: The Extensions of Man.* New York: McGraw, 1965.

Meade, Michael J. *Men and the Water of Life.* San Francisco: Harper, 1993.

Medicine Eagle, Brooke. *Buffalo Woman Comes Singing.* New York: Ballentine, 1992.

Melton, J. Gordon, with Aidan A. Kelly and Jerome Clark. *New Age Encyclopedia.* Detroit: Gale, 1990.

Moore, Robin. *Awakening the Hidden Storyteller: How to Build a Storytelling Tradition in Your Family.* Berkeley, Calif.: Shambhala, 1991.

Moore, Sally F., and Barbara G. Myerhoff, eds. *Secular Ritual.* Amsterdam: Van Gorcum, 1977.

"The Name Is Changed, the Purpose Remains the Same." In *Inside Story.* Jonesborough, Tenn.: NSA, 1994.

NAPPS. Correspondence with the Board of Directors, 1974–91. NSA Archives, National Storytelling Resource Center, Jonesborough, Tenn.

"NAPPS Inching toward a Permanent Home." *Yarnspinner* 17, no. 6 (1993): 7.

National Catalog of Storytelling Resources. Jonesborough, Tenn.: NAPPS, 1993.

National Directory of Storytelling. Series. Jonesborough, Tenn.: NAPPS, 1983–94.

National School of Storytelling. Brochure. Jonesborough, Tenn.: NAPPS, 1984.

Oberle, Marcella, Gordon R. Owen, and Isabel W. Crouch, eds. *The Renaissance of Storytelling: Proceedings of Seminar/Conference on Oral Tradition.* Las Cruces: New Mexico State University, 1983.

Ong, Walter J. *Interfaces of the Word.* Ithaca, N.Y.: Cornell University Press, 1977.

———. *Orality and Literacy.* London: Routledge, 1982.

———. *The Presence of the Word.* New Haven, Conn.: Yale University Press, 1967.

O'Sullivan, Sean. *Folktales of Ireland.* Chicago: University of Chicago Press, 1966.

Oxford, Cheryl. "'They Call Him Lucky Jack': Three Performance-Centered Case Studies of Storytelling in Watauga County, North Carolina." Ph.D. diss., Northwestern University, 1987.

Parry, Milman. *The Making of Homeric Verse: The Collected Papers of Milman Parry.* Edited by Adam Parry. Oxford: Clarendon, 1971.

Pellowski, Anne. *The World of Storytelling.* 2d ed. New York: Bowker, 1990.

Pennington, Lee, and Joy Pennington. "Folktales of Harlan County." Unpublished ms., 1965.

Plimpton, George. "Can't Anyone Here Tell a Great Ghost Story?" *Quest/79* 3, no. 8 (1979): 48–53.

Powers, Ron. *Far from Home.* New York: Random House, 1991.

Propp, Vladimir. *The Morphology of Folktales.* Austin: University of Texas Press, 1968.

Reich, Charles. *The Greening of America.* New York: Random House, 1970.

Ricoeur, Paul. *Time and Narrative.* Vol. 1. Translated by Kathleen McLaughlin and David Pellaur. Chicago: University of Chicago Press, 1984.

Rilke, Rainer Maria. *Letters to a Young Poet.* Translated by M. D. Herder Norton. New York: W. W. Norton, 1954.

Roberts, Leonard W. *Sang Branch Settlers: Folksongs and Tales of an Eastern Kentucky Family.* Pikeville, Ky.: Pikeville College Press, 1980.

Rogers, Gamble. *The Warm Way Home.* Phonodisc. Plainfield: JEM Records, 1980.

Rosenberg, Neil, ed. *Transforming Tradition.* Urbana: University of Illinois Press, 1993.

Ross, Ramon Royal. *Storyteller.* 2d ed. Columbus, Ohio: Merrill, 1972.

Rydell, Kathryn T. "A Community of Storytellers." Paper presented at the annual meeting of the American Folklore Society, Oakland, Calif., October 20, 1990.

Sawyer, Ruth. *The Way of the Storyteller.* New York: Viking, 1942.

Sayre, Henry M. *The Object of Performance.* Chicago: University of Chicago Press, 1989.

Schechner, Richard. *Between Theater and Anthropology.* Philadelphia: University of Pennsylvania Press, 1985.

———. *The Future of Ritual.* London: Routledge, 1993.

———. "Victor Turner's Last Adventure." Introduction to Victor Turner, *The Anthropology of Performance.* New York: PAJ, 1988.

Schimmel, Nancy. *Just Enough to Make a Story.* Rev. ed. Berkeley, Calif.: Choice, 1991.

Schram, Peninnah. *Jewish Stories One Generation Tells Another.* Northvale, N.J.: Aronson, 1987.

Seeger, Pete, and Bob Reiser. *Everybody Says Freedom.* New York: W. W. Norton, 1989.

Shah, Idries. *Tales of the Sufis.* London: Cape, 1967.

———. *The Way of the Sufi.* London: Cape, 1968.

Shannon, George. "Dear *Yarnspinner.*" *Yarnspinner* 6, no. 12 (1982): 3.

——. *Folk Literature and Children: An Annotated Bibliography of Secondary Materials.* Westport, Conn.: Greenwood, 1981.

——. "Shared Treasures: Folktales, Joy, and the Listening Child as Artist." *National Storytelling Journal* 1, no. 3 (1984): 3–7.

Shedlock, Marie. *The Art of the Storyteller.* New York: Dover, 1951.

Shelton, Robert, and David Gahr. *The Faces of Folk Music.* New York: Citadel, 1968.

Simms, Laura. "The Lamplighter: The Storyteller in the Modern World." *National Storytelling Journal* 1, no. 1 (1984): 8–11.

——. *Welcome to the National Storytelling Festival.* Festival brochure. Jonesborough, Tenn.: NAPPS, 1985.

Smith, Jimmy Neil, ed. *Homespun: Tales from America's Favorite Storytellers.* New York: Crown, 1988.

Smith, Mary Carter. *A Brief History of the National Association of Black Storytellers, Inc.* Baltimore: NABS, 1991.

Smith, Michael. *Michael, Margaret, Pat, and Kate: A Musical Reminiscence.* Performance at Victory Gardens Theatre, March 19, 1994, Chicago, Ill.

Sobol, Joseph D. "Everyman and Jack: The Storytelling of Donald Davis." M.A. thesis, University of North Carolina at Chapel Hill, 1987.

——. "Innervision and Innertext: Oral Traditional and Oral Interpretive Modes of Storytelling Performance." *Oral Tradition* 7, no. 1 (1992): 66–86.

——. "Jack in the Raw." In *Jack in Two Worlds: Contemporary North American Tales and Their Tellers,* edited by William Bernard McCarthy, Cheryl Oxford, and Joseph D. Sobol. Chapel Hill: University of North Carolina Press, 1994.

——. "Storytelling Ethics." Letter. *National Storytelling Journal* 3, no. 3 (1986): 2–3.

Spelman, Jon. "The Man Who Had No Story." Performance at the National Storytelling Festival, Jonesborough, Tenn., October 1992.

Stallings, Fran. "Journey into Darkness: The Story-Listening Trance." Unpublished paper, 1993.

——. "The Web of Silence: Storytelling's Power to Hypnotize." *National Storytelling Journal* 5, no. 2 (1988): 6–21.

Stekert, Ellen. "Cents and Nonsense in the Urban Folksong Movement 1930–1966." In *Folklore and Society: Essays in Honor of Benj. A. Botkin,* edited by Bruce Jackson. Hatboro, Pa.: Folklore Associates, 1966.

Stephens, James. *The Crock of Gold.* New York: Macmillan, 1912.

Stewart, Finley. "A Response to the Ethics Question." *National Storytelling Journal* 4, no. 3 (1987): 5–11.

——, ed. "Ethics and Storytelling." *National Storytelling Journal* 4, no. 4 (1987): 4–12.

Stipe, Robert E., and Antoinette J. Lee, eds. *The American Mosaic: Preserving a Nation's Heritage*. Washington, D.C.: US/ICOMOS, 1987.

Stone, Kay. *Burning Brightly: New Light on Old Tales Told Today*. Peterborough, Ontario: Broadview, 1998.

———. "Jack's Adventures in Toronto." In *Jack in Two Worlds: Contemporary North American Tales and Their Tellers,* edited by William B. McCarthy, Cheryl Oxford, and Joseph D. Sobol. Chapel Hill: University of North Carolina Press, 1994.

———. "Old Stories, New Contexts." Paper presented at the annual meeting of the American Folklore Society, Oakland, Calif., October 20, 1990.

———. "Oral Narration in Contemporary North America." In *Fairy Tales and Society: Illusion, Allusion and Paradigm,* edited by Ruth B. Bottigheimer. Philadelphia: University of Pennsylvania Press, 1986.

Stone, Merlin. *Ancient Mirrors of Womanhood: Our Goddess and Heroine Heritage*. New York: New Sibyllene, 1979.

———. *When God Was a Woman*. New York: Harcourt, 1976.

Storm, Hyemyosts. *Seven Arrows*. New York: Harper, 1972.

Tannen, Deborah. *Talking Voices: Repetition, Dialogue and Imagery in Conversational Discourse*. Cambridge: Cambridge University Press, 1989.

———, ed. *Spoken and Written Language*. Norwood: Ablex, 1982.

Tedlock, Dennis. *Finding the Center: Narrative Poetry of the Zuni Indians*. Translated from performances in the Zuni by Andrew Peynetsa and Walter Sanchez. New York: Dial, 1972.

———. *The Spoken Word and the Work of Interpretation*. Philadelphia: University of Pennsylvania Press, 1983.

Thompson, David W., ed. *The Performance of Literature in Historical Perspective*. Lanham, Md.: University Press of America, 1983.

Thompson, Stith. *The Folktale*. New York: Dryden, 1946.

Toelken, Barre. *The Dynamics of Folklore*. Boston: Houghton, 1979.

Trinh, T. Minh-ha. *Woman, Native, Other*. Bloomington: Indiana University Press, 1989.

Turner, Victor. *The Anthropology of Performance*. New York: PAJ, 1988.

———. *From Ritual to Theatre*. New York: PAJ, 1982.

———. *The Ritual Process*. Ithaca, N.Y.: Cornell University Press, 1969.

Twillmann, Bev. "Sharing Not Regulating." Letter. *National Storytelling Journal* 4, no. 4 (1987): 2.

Von Schmidt, Eric, and Jim Rooney. *Baby Let Me Follow You Down*. Garden City, N.Y.: Anchor, 1979.

Wallace, Anthony F. C. "Revitalization Movements." *American Anthropologist* 58 (1956): 264–81.

Weinberg, Nathan. *Preservation in American Towns and Cities*. Boulder, Colo.: Westview, 1979.

Weyler, Rex. "On the Road with the Folktellers." *New Age* 6, no. 1 (1980): 26–33, 62–63.

Whisnant, David. *All That Is Native and Fine.* Chapel Hill: University of North Carolina Press, 1983.

——. "Finding the Way between the Old and the New: The Mountain Dance and Folk Festival and Bascom Lamar Lunsford's Work as a Citizen." *Appalachian Journal* 7, no. 1–2 (1979–80): 135–54.

Wiesel, Elie. *The Gates of the Forest.* New York: Holt, 1966.

Windham, Kathryn, and Margaret Gillis Figh. *Thirteen Alabama Ghosts and Jeffrey.* Huntsville: Strode, 1967.

Wolfe, Charles K. *The Grand Ole Opry.* London: Old Time Music, 1973.

Yeats, William Butler. *Collected Poems.* New York: Macmillan, 1952.

——. *Essays and Introductions.* New York: Collier, 1961.

——. *Mythologies.* New York: Collier, 1959.

Other Works by Storytellers in This Study

Compilations

American Storytelling Series. Video. 8 vols. New York: H. W. Wilson, 1982–84.

Best Loved Stories from the National Storytelling Festival. Audiocassette. 2 vols. Jonesborough, Tenn.: National Storytelling Press, 1990–92.

Best Loved Stories Told at the National Storytelling Festival. Jonesborough, Tenn.: National Storytelling Press, 1989.

Family Circle Storyland Videos. 4 vols., with Rafe Martin, Jay O'Callahan, Laura Simms. New York: Paperback Videos, 1988.

Graveyard Tales. Audiocassette. Jonesborough, Tenn: National Storytelling Press, 1987.

Homespun: Tales from America's Favorite Storytellers. New York: Crown, 1988.

Homespun Tales. Audiocassette. Jonesborough, Tenn.: National Storytelling Press, 1989.

A Medley of Tellers and Tales. Cassette. Cambridge, Mass.: Yellow Moon, 1983.

More Best-Loved Stories Told at the National Storytelling Festival. Jonesborough, Tenn.: National Storytelling Press, 1992.

Storytelling: The National Festival. Cassette. Jonesborough, Tenn.: NAPPS, 1983.

A Storytelling Treasury: Tales Told at the Twentieth Anniversary National Storytelling Festival. Cassette. Jonesborough, Tenn.: National Storytelling Press, 1993.

Tales of Fools and Wise Folk. Audiocassette. Jonesborough, Tenn.: National Storytelling Press, 1990.

Tales of Humor and Wit. Audiocassette. Jonesborough, Tenn.: National Storytelling Press, 1990.

Individual Productions

(Most of these materials are self-produced [s.p.] and are available directly from the storytellers.)

Birch, Carol. *Happily Ever After: Love Stories, More or Less.* Cassette. Southbury, Conn.: s.p., n.d.

———. *Nightmares Rising.* Cassette. Southbury, Conn.: s.p., n.d.

Brown, Margie. *Jesus' Friends.* Cassette. San Jose, Calif.: Resource, 1986.

———. *Once upon. . . the End.* Cassette. San Jose, Calif.: Resource, 1989.

———. *Stick Stories.* Cassette. San Jose, Calif.: Resource, 1983.

Burch, Milbre. *In the Family Way.* Cassette. Pasadena, Calif.: Kind Crone [s.p.], 1993.

———. *The Mary Stories.* Cassette. Pasadena, Calif.: Kind Crone [s.p.], 1991.

———. *Metamorphosis and Dragonfield.* Cassette. Pasadena, Calif.: Kind Crone [s.p.], 1988.

———. *Saints and Other Sinners.* Cassette. Pasadena, Calif.: Kind Crone [s.p.], 1991.

———. *Touch Magic, Pass It On.* Cassette. Weston, Conn.: Weston Woods, 1987.

Davis, Donald. *Barking at a Fox-Fur Coat.* Little Rock, Ark.: August House, 1990.

———. *Jack Always Seeks His Fortune.* Little Rock, Ark.: August House, 1992.

———. *Listening for the Crack of Dawn.* Little Rock, Ark.: August House, 1989.

———. *More Than a Beanstalk.* LP/cassette. Weston, Conn.: Weston Woods, 1985.

———. *Storytelling Series.* 11 vols. Cassette tapes. Okracoke, N.C.: s.p., 1981–94.

DeSpain, Pleasant. *Thirty-three Multicultural Tales to Tell.* Little Rock, Ark.: August House, 1993.

Ellis, Elizabeth. *Like Meat Loves Salt and Other Tales.* Cassette. Dallas: s.p., n.d.

———. *Stories: Imagine That.* Cassette. Dallas: s.p., n.d.

Forest, Heather. *The Animals Could Talk.* Book/cassette. Little Rock, Ark.: August House, 1994.

———. *The Baker's Dozen. . .: A Colonial American Tale.* New York: Harcourt, 1988.

———. *The Eye of the Beholder.* Cassette. Cambridge, Mass.: Yellow Moon, 1991.

———. *Sing Me a Story.* Cassette. Albany, N.Y.: Gentle Wind, 1986.

———. *Songspinner.* Cassette and LP. Weston, Conn.: Weston Woods, 1982.

———. *Tales around the Hearth.* Cassette. Albany, N.Y.: Gentle Wind, 1989.

———. *Tales of Womenfolk.* Cassette and LP. Weston, Conn.: Weston Woods, 1985.

———. *The Woman Who Flummoxed the Fairies.* New York: Harcourt, 1990.

Freeman, Barbara, and Connie Regan-Blake (The Folktellers). *Chillers.* Cassette/LP. Asheville, N.C.: Mama-T [s.p.], 1983.

———. *Christmas at the Homeplace.* Cassette. Asheville, N.C.: Mama-T [s.p.], 1992.

———. *Pennies, Pets, and Peanut Butter.* Video. Asheville, N.C.: Mama-T [s.p.], 1994.

———. *Stories for the Road.* Cassette. Asheville, N.C.: Mama-T [s.p.], 1992.

———. *Storytelling: Tales and Techniques.* Video. Asheville, N.C.: Mama-T [s.p.], 1994.

———. *Tales to Grow On.* Cassette. Asheville, N.C.: Mama-T [s.p.], 1981.

———. *White Horses and Whipporwills.* Cassette. Asheville, N.C.: Mama-T [s.p.], 1983.

Gillman, Jackson. *Downstate Ballads by Ruth Moore and Others.* Cassette. Mt. Desert, Maine: s.p., 1987.

Gold, Reuven. *Tales of the Hasidic Rebbes.* Cassette. Chicago: s.p., 1977.

Harley, Bill. *Come on out and Play.* Cassette. Seekonk, Mass.: Round River [s.p.], 1990.

———. *Cool in School.* Cassette. Seekonk, Mass.: Round River [s.p.], 1987.

———. *Coyote.* Cassette/LP. Seekonk, Mass.: Round River [s.p.], 1988.

———. *Dinosaurs Never Say Please.* Cassette. Seekonk, Mass.: Round River [s.p.], 1987.

———. *Fifty Ways to Fool Your Mother.* Cassette. Seekonk, Mass.: Round River [s.p.], 1986.

———. *Grownups Are Strange.* Cassette. Seekonk, Mass.: Round River [s.p.], 1990.

———. *Monsters in the Bathroom.* Cassette/LP. Seekonk, Mass.: Round River [s.p.], 1984.

Hicks, Ray. *Jack Alive!* Whitesburg, Ky.: June Appal, 1989.

———. *Ray Hicks of Beech Mountain, North Carolina Jack Tales Telling Four Traditional "Jack Tales."* LP. Sharon, Conn.: Folk Legacy, 1963.

Hill, Hugh Morgan (Brother Blue). *Street Cat.* Cassette. Brookline, Mass.: Out of the Blue [s.p.], 1992.

Holt, David. *The Hairy Man.* Cassette. Fairview, N.C.: High Windy [s.p.], 1981.

———. *The Hogaphone and Other Stories.* Video. Fairview, N.C.: High Windy [s.p.], 1991.

———. *Tailybone.* Cassette and LP. Fairview, N.C.: High Windy [s.p.], 1985.

Horner, Beth. *Encounter with a Romance Novel: Heroines in Everyday Life.* Cassette. Wilmette, Ill.: s.p., 1994.

———. *An Evening at Cedar Creek.* Cassette. Wilmette, Ill.: s.p., 1991.

Johnson, Larry, and Elaine Wynne (Key of See Storytellers). *Running Scared and Flying High*. Cassette. Minneapolis, Minn.: Heritage, 1988.

Ledbetter, Gwenda. *The Bee, the Harp, the Mouse, and the Bumclock*. Cassette. Asheville, N.C.: s.p., 1985.

———. *In Sound and Sight of the Sea: Stories of Growing up on the Eastern Shore*. Cassette. Asheville: s.p., 1992.

Lipman, Doug. *The Amazing Teddy Bear*. Cassette. West Somerville, Mass.: Enchanter's Press [s.p.], n.d.

———. *Coaching Storytellers: A How-To Videotape for Tellers and Teachers*. Video. West Somerville, Mass.: Enchanter's Press [s.p.], n.d.

———. *Folktales of Strong Women*. Cassette. Cambridge, Mass.: Yellow Moon, n.d.

———. *The Forgotten Story: Tales of Wise Jewish Men*. Cassette. Cambridge, Mass.: Yellow Moon, n.d.

———. *Grass Roots and Mountain Peaks: Visions for the Storytelling Movement*. Cassette. West Somerville, Mass.: Enchanter's Press [s.p.], n.d.

———. *Hopping Freights: A Wild Sixties Adventure*. Cassette. Cambridge, Mass.: Yellow Moon, n.d.

———. *Keep on Shaking: Participation Stories and Songs*. Cassette. Albany, N.Y.: Gentle Wind, n.d.

———. *Milk from the Bull's Horn: Tales and Songs of Nurturing Men*. Cassette. Cambridge, Mass.: Yellow Moon, n.d.

———. *Now We Are Free: Stories and Songs for Passover*. Cassette. West Somerville, Mass.: Enchanter's Press [s.p.], n.d.

———. *One Little Candle: Participation Stories and Songs for Hanukkah*. Cassette. West Somerville, Mass.: Enchanter's Press [s.p.], n.d.

———. *The Storytelling Coach: How to Listen, Praise, and Bring out People's Best*. Little Rock, Ark.: August House, 1995.

———. *Tell It with Me: Participation Stories and Songs*. Cassette. Albany, N.Y.: Gentle Wind, n.d.

———. *We All Go Together: Music Activities*. Book/cassette. Phoenix, Ariz.: Oryx, 1994.

Livo, Norma, and Dia Cha. *Folk Stories of the Hmong*. Englewood, Colo.: Libraries Unlimited, 1992.

Martin, Rafe. *Animal Dreaming: Encounters in the Natural World*. Cassette. Cambridge, Mass.: Yellow Moon, 1993.

———. *The Boy Who Lived with the Seals*. New York: Putnam, 1993.

———. *The Boy Who Loved Mammoths and Other Tales*. Cassette. Weston, Conn.: Weston Woods, 1987.

———. *Foolish Rabbit's Big Mistake*. Cassette/Filmstrip. New York: Random House, 1987.

———. *Ghostly Tales of Japan*. Cassette. Cambridge, Mass.: Yellow Moon, 1989.

———. *The Hungry Tigress, and Other Traditional Asian Tales*. Berkeley, Calif.: Shambhala, 1984. Revised ed., Berkeley, Calif.: Parallax, 1992.

———. *The Rough-Faced Girl*. New York: Putnam, 1992.

———. *A Storyteller's Story*. N.p.: Richard C. Owen, 1992.

———. *Will's Mammoth*. New York: Putnam, 1989.

Marvin, Lee-Ellen. *Animal Tails*. Cassette. Cambridge, Mass.: Yellow Moon, 1989.

May, Jim. *The Farm on Nippersink Creek: Stories from a Midwestern Childhood*. Little Rock, Ark.: August House, 1994.

———. *Grandpa's Farm*. Cassette. Woodstock, Ill.: s.p., n.d.

———. *Horse Sense*. Cassette. Woodstock, Ill.: s.p., n.d.

———. *Purple Bogies and Other Ghost Tales*. Cassette. Woodstock, Ill.: s.p., n.d.

Miller, Reid. *Hey! Hey! Hey! (Folk Songs and Tales for Youngsters)*. Cassette. Madison, Wis.: s.p., 1984.

Moore, Robin. *Awakening the Hidden Storyteller*. Berkeley, Calif.: Shambhala, 1990.

———. *The Bread Sister of Sinking Creek*. Book/Cassette. Springhouse, Pa.: Groundhog [s.p.], 1986.

———. *Five Tales from Early America*. Cassette. Springhouse, Pa.: Groundhog [s.p.], n.d.

———. *Maggie among the Seneca*. San Francisco: Harper Collins, 1988.

Niemi, Loren. *Grim Moderne*. Cassette. St. Paul, Minn.: Eclectic, n.d.

———. *Plot and Detail*. Minneapolis, Minn.: Hometown, n.d.

O'Callahan, Jay. *The Dance*. Cassette. Marshfield, Mass.: Artana [s.p.], 1992.

———. *Earth Stories*. Cassette. Marshfield, Mass.: Artana [s.p.], 1984.

———. *The Golden Drum*. Cassette. Marshfield, Mass.: Artana [s.p.], 1984.

———. *The Gouda*. Cassette. Marshfield, Mass.: Artana [s.p.], 1989.

———. *Herman and Marguerite*. Video. Marshfield, Mass.: Artana-Vinyard [s.p.], n.d.

———. *The Herring Shed*. Cassette. Marshfield, Mass.: Artana [s.p.], 1983.

———. *The Island*. Cassette. Marshfield, Mass.: Artana [s.p.], 1988.

———. *Jeremy: A Christmas Story*. Cassette. Marshfield, Mass.: Artana [s.p.], 1991.

———. *The Little Dragon/Orange Cheeks*. Cassette. Marshfield, Mass.: Artana [s.p.], 1982.

———. *A Master Class in Storytelling*. West Tisbury, Mass.: Vineyard Video, 1983.

———. *The Minister of Others' Affairs*. Cassette. Marshfield, Mass.: Artana [s.p.], 1984.

———. *Mostly Scary.* Cassette. Marshfield, Mass.: Artana [s.p.], 1987.
———. *Petrukian.* Cassette. Marshfield, Mass.: Artana [s.p.], 1986.
———. *Pill Hill Stories: Coming Home to Someplace New.* Cassette. Marshfield, Mass.: Artana [s.p.], 1990.
———. *Rasberries.* Cassette. Marshfield, Mass.: Artana [s.p.], 1983.
———. *The Silver Stream.* Cassette. Marshfield, Mass.: Artana [s.p.], 1990.
———. *Six Stories About Little Heroes.* Video. Marshfield, Mass.: Artana-Vinyard [s.p.], n.d.
———. *The Strait of Magellan.* Cassette. Marshfield, Mass.: Artana [s.p.], 1985.
———. *Village Heroes.* Cassette. Marshfield, Mass.: Artana [s.p.], 1986.
Roadside Theater. *Mountain Tales.* Cassette/Phonodisc. Whitesburg, Ky.: June Appal, 1977.
Ross, Gayle. *How Rabbit Tricked Otter.* Book/Cassette. New York: HarperCollins/Parabola, 1994.
———. *To This Day: Native American Stories.* Cassette. Fredricksburg, Tex.: s.p., 1982.
Rubright, Lynn. *Lynn Rubright Tells Tall Tales.* Cassette. Kirkwood, Mo.: s.p., n.d.
———. *Storytelling Teaching Tape.* Kirkwood, Mo.: s.p., n.d.
Sanfield, Steve. *The Adventures of High John the Conqueror.* New York: Orchard, 1989.
———. *The Confounding: A Paiute Tale to Be Told Aloud.* Monterey, Ky.: Larkspur, 1980.
———. *Could This Be Paradise?* Cassette. Nevada City: 1988.
———. *The Feather Merchants, and Other Tales of the Fools of Chelm.* New York: Orchard, 1991.
———. *A Natural Man: The True Story of John Henry.* Boston: Godine, 1986.
———. *Singing up the Mountains.* Cassette. Columbia, Mo.: Nita [s.p.], 1981.
———. *Steve Sanfield Live at the Sierra Storytelling Festival.* Cassette. San Juan, Calif.: s.p., 1992.
Schram, Peninnah. *Elijah's Violin and Other Jewish Fairy Tales.* Cassette. New York: s.p., n.d.
———. *The Golden Watch and Other Jewish Fairy Tales.* Cassette. New York: POM, n.d.
———. *Jewish Tales One Generation Tells Another.* Northvale, N.J.: Aronson, 1987.
———. *The Rooster Who Would Be King.* Video. Chicago: Telling Tale, n.d.
———. *A Storyteller's Journey.* 2 vols. Cassette. New York: POM, n.d.
———. *Tales of Elijah the Prophet.* Northvale, N.J.: Aronson, 1991.
Schram, Peninnah, and Steven M. Rosman. *Eight Tales for Eight Nights: Stories for Chanukah.* Northvale, N.J.: Aronson, 1990.

Simms, Laura. *Incredible Journey.* Cassette. Albany, N.Y.: Gentle Wind, n.d.
———. *Making Peace: Heart Uprising.* CD and Cassette. Chicago: Earwig, 1993.
———. *Moon on Fire: Calling Forth the Power of the Feminine.* Cassette. Cambridge, Mass.: Yellow Moon, n.d.
———. *Nightwalkers: Tales of the Visible and Invisible Worlds.* Cassette. N.p: Northword, n.d.
———. *Stories Just Right for Kids.* Cassette and LP. N.p.: Whitman, n.d.
———. *Stories Old as the World, Fresh as the Rain.* Cassette and LP. Weston, Conn.: Weston Woods, n.d.
———. *There's a Horse in My Pocket.* Cassette and LP. N.p.: Whitman, n.d.
———. *Women and Wild Animals.* Cassette. N.p.: Northword, 1991.
Stivender, Ed. *An Evening with Ed Stivender at Friends General Conference.* Video. Philadelphia: s.p., 1986.
———. *Once. . .: Stories for Kids.* Cassette. Philadelphia: s.p., 1992.
———. *Raised Catholic, Can You Tell?* Book/cassette. Little Rock, Ark.: August House, 1992.
———. *Yankee Come Home.* Cassette. Jonesborough, Tenn.: s.p., 1992.
Timpanelli, Gioia. *Tales from the Roof of the World: Folktales of Tibet.* New York: Viking, 1984.
Torrence, Jackie. *Brer Rabbit Stories.* Cassette/LP. Weston, Conn.: Weston Woods, n.d.
———. *Country Characters.* Cassette. Chicago: Earwig, n.d.
———. *The Importance of Pot Liquor.* Little Rock, Ark.: August House, 1996.
———. *Jackie Tales.* New York: Avon, 1998.
———. *Legends from the Black Tradition.* Cassette/LP. Weston, Conn.: Weston Woods, 1982.
———. *Mountain Magic: Jack Tales.* 2 vols. Cassette/LP. Chicago: Earwig, n.d.
———. *My Grandmother's Treasure.* Little Rock, Ark.: August House, 1992.
———. *Tales for Scary Times.* Cassette. Chicago: Earwig, n.d.
Wellner, Cathryn. *Slow-Time People in a Fast-Time World.* Cassette. Mill Valley, Calif.: InsightOut, 1989.
Williamson, Robin. *Celtic Classics.* 5 vols. Cassette. Los Angeles: Pigs Whisker, 1983–87.
Windham, Kathryn. *Alabama: One Big Front Porch.* Tuscaloosa: University of Alabama Press, 1988.
———. *Alabama Folk Tales.* Cassette. Selma, Ala.: s.p., n.d.
———. *Ghost Stories.* 5 vols. Cassette. Selma, Ala.: s.p., 1979–84.
———. *The Jeffrey Series of True Southern Ghost Stories.* 6 vols. Tuscaloosa: University of Alabama Press, 1988–89.
———. *Odd Egg Editor.* Jackson: University of Mississippi Press, 1989.
———. *Recollections.* 4 vols. Cassette. Selma, Ala.: s.p., 1987–90.

———. *A Serigamy of Stories.* Jackson: University of Mississippi Press, 1987.

Wolkstein, Diane. *The Banza: A Haitian Story.* Book/Cassette. New York: Listening Library, 1988.

———. *California Fairy Tales.* Cassette. New York: Spoken Arts, 1976.

———. *Eight Thousand Stones: A Chinese Folktale.* Garden City, N.Y.: Doubleday, 1972.

———. *Eskimo Stories: Tales of Magic.* New York: Spoken Arts, 1975.

———. *Fairy Tales from Estonia.* Cassette. New York: Cloudstone [s.p.], 1989.

———. *The First Love Stories.* New York: HarperCollins, 1992.

———. *Hans Christian Andersen in Central Park.* LP/Cassette. Weston, Conn.: Weston Woods, 1983.

———. *Innana: A Sumerian Epic.* Cassette/Video. New York: Cloudstone [s.p.], 1988.

———. *Joseph.* Cassette. New York: Cloudstone [s.p.], 1986.

———. *Little Mouse's Painting.* New York: Morrow, 1992.

———. *The Magic Orange Tree.* New York: Harper, 1978.

———. *The Magic Orange Tree and Other Haitian Tales.* Cassette/CD. New York: Cloudstone [s.p.], 1994.

———. *Oom Razoom: Go I Know Not Where, Bring Back I Know Not What, a Russian Fairy Tale.* New York: Morrow, 1991.

———. *Psyche and Eros.* Cassette. New York: Cloudstone [s.p.], 1988.

———. *The Red Lion: A Persian Tale.* New York: Crowell, 1977.

———. *Romping (Seven Whimsical Stories).* New York: Cloudstone [s.p.], 1985.

———. *Squirrel's Song: A Hopi Tale.* New York: Alfred A. Knopf, 1974.

———. *Step by Step.* New York: Morrow, 1994.

———. *Tales of the Hopi Indians.* Cassette. New York: Spoken Arts, 1974.

———. *White Wave: A Chinese Tale.* New York: Crowell, 1979.

Wolkstein, Diane, and Samuel Noah Kramer. *Inanna.* New York: Harper, 1983.

Index

Index

Joseph Daniel Sobol has worked since 1981 as a professional storyteller, musician, and folklorist. He has an M.A. in folklore from the University of North Carolina and a Ph.D. in performance studies from Northwestern University. He has written extensively on traditional and contemporary storytelling. From 1994 to 1998 he toured the United States with *In the Deep Heart's Core,* an original musical theater piece he created on the life of the Irish poet and pioneering folk revivalist William Butler Yeats. He currently teaches storytelling and folklore at DePaul University's School for New Learning.